Wu Wenying and the Art of
Southern Song Ci *Poetry*

 Wu Wenying and the Art of Southern Song Ci Poetry

GRACE S. FONG

Princeton University Press · Princeton, New Jersey

Published by Princeton University Press, 41 William
Street, Princeton, New Jersey 08540
In the United Kingdom: Princeton University Press,
Guildford, Surrey

Library of Congress Cataloging in Publication Data will
be found on the last printed page of this book

ISBN 0-691-06703-1

Publication of this book has been aided by: a grant from the
Publications Program of the National Endowment for the
Humanities, an independent Federal agency, and a grant
from The Andrew W. Mellon Foundation.

This book has been composed in Monotype Lasercomp
Plantin Light by Asco Trade Typesetting Ltd., Hong Kong

Clothbound editions of Princeton University Press books
are printed on acid-free paper, and binding materials
are chosen for strength and durability.

Printed in the United States of America by Princeton
University Press, Princeton, New Jersey

TO CHIA-YING CHAO-YEH

CONTENTS

 *PREFACE*

During the last decade, scholars of Chinese poetry in the West have come to recognize the literary and cultural importance of the *ci* genre. Major critical studies have now treated representative *ci* poets from the late Tang (ninth century) to the Northern Song (960–1126). Those periods span the history of the *ci* from its origin as popular song through its evolution into an established literary genre. By the late Song, *ci* poetry had evolved into a self-conscious and sophisticated art form. Late Song *ci* poets and critics were much concerned with normative aesthetics of *ci* composition, and this preoccupation brought about an unprecedented degree of both sensitivity and complexity in the diction of *ci*. The refinement and sophistication they brought to the genre significantly consolidated its aesthetics and provided impetus for its further development in the Qing period (1644–1911). An adequate representation of the genre therefore requires that developments in the Southern Song be analyzed and accounted for. The present study is offered as a first step toward a comprehensive investigation of Southern Song *ci* poetry and poetics. It takes as its focus the work of Wu Wenying (ca. 1200–ca. 1260), a key figure in the development of *ci* poetry and poetics.

Wu Wenying stands among the vanguard of late Song stylistic trends. His *ci* poetry has been characterized by critics as "elegant," "dense," and "difficult." This stylistic complexity and elegance, however, has given rise to widely divergent, even flatly contradictory, assessments, elegantly epitomized in the epithet that the late Song poet and critic Zhang Yan (1248–1320?) applied to Wu Wenying's poetry: "a many-jewelled edifice which dazzles the eye." While acclaimed by some critics for his brilliance of style and profundity of emotion, Wu Wenying has also been categorically dismissed as a decadent aesthete whose *ci* amount to no more than empty artifice. A poetry which provokes such disparate opinions calls for investigation, and the conflicting views must themselves be examined and reassessed from a literary-historical perspective. It is my contention that the controversy surrounding Wu Wenying's poetic style reflects critical attitudes toward the Southern Song period style, in particular toward certain tendencies in the Southern Song style exemplified by Wu Wenying's poetry. Thus, by elucidating Wu Wenying's theory and practice of poetry in a synchronic as well as a diachronic critical context, I aim not only to throw light on the controversy and situate Wu Wenying's significance, but at the same time to demonstrate the importance of Southern Song developments in *ci* criticism.

To define the art of Southern Song *ci* and locate Wu Wenying's praxis, I examine critical formulations in two important late Song treatises on *ci* composition, the *Yuefu zhimi* and *Ciyuan*. The *Yuefu zhimi*'s critical canons embody Wu Wenying's poetics of indirection, which favors allusive and connotative language and produces imagistic and semantic density in the poetic structure. In opposition to Wu's poetics of density, an aspect of indirection, the *Ciyuan* proposes a poetics of transparency. However, the antinomy is only apparent: it represents two linguistic modes of expression that are both, in spite of their difference, subsumed in the *ci*'s complex movement towards metaphor and symbolism. For the poetics of transparency advocated in the *Ciyuan* is reducible to a formalistic lucidity located primarily in the linguistic structure of the poem, which, nevertheless, in late Song views of *ci* aesthetics, should ideally support an indirect, allusive, and figural language.

In the chapter devoted to the exegesis of individual poems, I work with the three categories that best represent Wu Wenying's achievements as a *ci* poet. These are his *yongwu ci* (poems on objects), his love poems, and his occasional poetry. Study of the dichotomy between verbal artifice and poetic metaphor in his *yongwu* poems and between self and other in his occasional poems show them to rest on a fundamental distinction between poetry as social art and poetry as self-expression. Significantly, the metaphoric dimension of his *yongwu* poems illustrates the evolutionary possibilities of this subgenre in *ci*. Wu's love poetry originates in an *idée fixe*, a persistent longing for the beloved, which is translated into recurrent images and motifs embedded in his most elegant diction, resulting in a superb union.

Any overview of criticism on Wu Wenying must take into account both the *ci* hermeneutics developed during the Qing, a period when poets and critics successfully revived the art of *ci*, and twentieth-century perspectives. While Qing period *ci* practitioners, with their dominant concern for style and stylistic models, found the sophistication and artistry of the Southern Song style highly appealing, many modern Chinese critics with new critical or ideological commitments have reacted adversely to the mannerism of Southern Song *ci*, of which Wu Wenying has always been taken as representative. The verbal density and surface elegance of his *ci* have thus won both critical acclaim and disapprobation. An objective integral appreciation of his poetry is possible all the same, as I hope this study demonstrates.

ACKNOWLEDGMENTS

This book owes its existence to the guidance and support given to my writing by a number of friends and teachers. I wish to thank first of all my teacher Chia-ying Chao-Yeh, who taught me how to read and appreciate *ci* poetry, and whose profound knowledge and insight into Chinese poetry continue to be a source of inspiration. Her guidance and tireless patience in reading through with me the entire collection of Wu Wenying's poems helped me to penetrate the allusive language and often obscure syntax of these texts. I also wish to thank Professor E. G. Pulleyblank for his guidance in my study of Song history and for clarifying some grammatical and linguistic points when I was writing the section on "The Poetics of Density." But most of all, I am grateful to him for his generous encouragement and support throughout the writing of my dissertation, of which the present book is a minor metamorphosis. My manuscript was fortunate enough to have gone through a reading by Professor James R. Hightower, whose austere style of classical elegance helped to pare some of my baroque convolutions. To Stephen Owen and Kang-i Sun Chang, who read the manuscript, and to Ronald Egan, Wayne Schlepp, and Terry Russell, who read the section on "*Yongwu ci*," I express my sincere thanks for their invaluable comments and suggestions. Some of my translations of Wu Wenying's poems are indebted to helpful comments by Michael Bullock, Stephen C. Soong, and Jerry Schmidt. Lastly I wish to thank a very special reader, Daniel Bryant. With his boundless energy and altruistic sacrifice of precious time, he combed through the entire manuscript, pointing out even the slightest infelicities, inaccuracies, and ambiguities, and suggesting alternatives for me

ACKNOWLEDGMENTS

to consider. It was his painstaking and meticulous reading that imparted a final polish to the manuscript. But imperfection persists, if only because I have sometimes stubbornly resisted change despite the well-intentioned suggestions of my readers. For the errors that remain, I am therefore solely responsible.

Wu Wenying and the Art of
Southern Song Ci *Poetry*

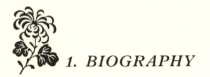

1. BIOGRAPHY

I. Early Life

Wu Wenying (*zi* Junte, *hao* Mengchuang) was born circa A.D. 1200 in the Siming district of Zhedong circuit (present day Yin County in Zhejiang province).[1] During the Song, the Southeast circuits were steadily becoming the leading economic and cultural nexus in the empire. When the north was captured by the Jurchens in 1126, subsequent political turmoil eventually forced the new Southern Song court to relocate its capital to Hangzhou in 1138. Ironically, the shameful loss of half an empire and the resultant geographical dislocation only consolidated an on-going fundamental southward shift that had begun several centuries

[1] The lack of official documentation of Wu Wenying's life necessitates the reliance on various contemporary thirteenth-century sources such as the works of other poets and scholar-officials, informal essay-type records of people and events, anthologies of *ci* poetry, and local gazetteers for information significant in shedding light both on the life and personality of the principal and the society in which he was active. Information concerning the people he associated with, whether found in the official history or in informal writings, has proven helpful in reconstructing certain periods in his life. But Wu Wenying's own prefaces (subtitles) to his poems are no less important as a source of information, for they often include circumstantial details—date, place, and occasion of composition, and the person to whom the poem is addressed. In fact, they provide the starting point of any research on his life. The biographical sketch given here follows in general the chronology established by Xia Chengtao in "Wu Mengchuang xinian," in *Tang Song ciren nianpu* (Shanghai: Shanghai guji chubanshe, 1979), pp. 455–91. Yang Tiefu's "Mengchuang shiji kao," in *Mengchuang ci quanji jianshi* (Taipei: Haixue chubanshe, 1974), pp. 359–78, has also been consulted. Where these differ, I have generally favored Xia's more solid scholarship. A recent article by Chen Bangyan proposes 1212 to post-1272 for Wu Wenying's dates. I find his evidence insufficient and his argument unconvincing. See Chen Bangyan, "Wu Mengchuang shengzu nian guanjian," *Wenxue yichan*, 1 (1983): 64–67.

3

before.[2] In the triennial civil service examinations which furnished the state bureaucracy with potential new recruits, the Southeast, in particular the two most populous and urbanized circuits, Zhedong and Fujian, came to supply most of the candidates for the competition.[3] In Wu Wenying's own time, a significant share of successful *jinshi* graduates came from his native district Yin County,[4] and his elder brother was on the list of graduates for the year 1217.[5] Although Wu Wenying himself never attained this distinction, due to lack of participation or to failure in the examinations, the very locale in which he grew up bespeaks a cultured and sophisticated milieu.

Of Wu Wenying's relations, only two brothers bearing the different surname Weng are known. No recorded source accounts for the disparity in the surnames, the most plausible explanation being that Wu Wenying, né Weng, was adopted into a Wu family.[6] Wu's elder brother Weng Fenglong (*z.* Jike, *h.* Shigui)

[2] For a summary of the southward shift of the demographic, economic, and cultural centers of gravity in Song times, see Ho Ping-ti, *Ladder of Success in Imperial China* (New York: Science Editions, 1964), pp. 226–30. The fundamental shift took place after the An Lushan Rebellion when the Tang court began to rely chiefly on the south for financial support. See Denis Twitchett, ed., *The Cambridge History of China*, vol. 3:1 (New York: Cambridge University Press, 1979), pp. 22–24.

[3] See E. A. Kracke, Jr., "Region, Family, and Individual in the Examination System," in *Chinese Thought and Institutions*, ed. John K. Fairbank (Chicago: University of Chicago Press, 1957), pp. 255–57.

[4] During the years 1214–1232 approximately 15 percent of the successful candidates from Zhejiang province hailed from Yin County. This information is based on figures in *juan* 127 of *Zhejiang tongzhi*, comp. Shen Yiji et al. (1736; rpt. Shanghai: Commercial Press, 1934).

[5] *Baoqing Siming zhi*, comp. Luo Jun and Fang Wanli, in *Song Yuan difangzhi congshu* (Taipei: Zhongguo dizhi yanjiuhui, 1978), 8:*j*.10/13b.

[6] Both Xia Chengtao and Yang Tiefu agree on this as the most common and natural explanation for the discrepancy. See *Tang Song ciren nianpu*, p. 456 and *Mengchuang ci quanji jianshi*, p. 361. An alternative suggested by Liu Yusong (quoted by Xia Chengtao in *Tang Song ciren nianpu*, p. 456), that Wu Wenying's mother may have had a lowly position in the Weng household, i.e., as a maid or concubine, and that after giving birth to Wu Wenying may have remarried into a Wu household, is discredited by Xia and Yang on the basis that since Wu Wenying was the second-born of the three brothers, his mother could not have returned to the Wengs to have the third son. My position is that, without further evidence, no conclusive statement can be made on this issue. However, Liu's theory is tenable if we do not exclude the possibility of Wu Wenying and the two Wengs being half brothers, in other words, Weng Fenglong and Weng Yuanlong's mother would be the principal wife or concubine, and Wu's mother, a secondary concubine who took him along when she remarried.

obtained his *jinshi* ("doctorate") degree in 1217, and is known to have held the position of Vice-administrator of Pingjiang (present day Suzhou) for a period between 1237 and 1240.[7] Not only did Weng Fenglong distinguish himself by passing the civil service examination and thereby entering a career in officialdom, he also acquired some recognition as a *shi* poet.[8] He was mentioned by Dai Fugu (1167–after 1246), an important poet of the "Rivers and Lakes" School of the Southern Song,[9] in a poem entitled "On reading the manuscripts of the four poets Weng Jike, Xue Yishu, Sun Jifan and Gao Jiuwan."[10] There are two extant poems addressed to Weng Fenglong in Wu Wenying's collection. Judging from their tone and content, it appears that the brothers had a rather congenial relationship with some contact maintained throughout their lives. One poem, to the tune pattern *Liushao qing* (*Quan Song ci* 2928/5),[11] dated post-1243 from the preface, was composed on the occasion of viewing snow with Weng Fenglong from a tower named Yanyi.[12] The other poem (*QSC* 2928/4), written at a later date and subtitled, "Ascending Yanyi after Guiweng (Weng Fenglong) had passed away," reminisces with sadness about the irretrievable times when they had been together, revealing through the imagery and allusions a measure of the brotherly intimacy that had existed between them. The younger brother, Weng Yuanlong (*z.* Shike, *h.* Chu-

<hr />

[7] Li E, *Songshi jishi* (Shanghai: Commercial Press, 1937), 10:1671. For Song official titles I follow E. A. Kracke, Jr., *Translation of Sung Civil Service Titles* (Paris: Mouton & Co., 1957).

[8] Weng Fenglong's collected poetry is not extant. The *Songshi jishi* records two poems by him, 10:1671.

[9] This school was composed of poets who did not take official service and lived in retirement; its members were active toward the end of the twelfth century and the first quarter of the thirteenth century. On Dai Fugu and this school, cf. Yoshikawa Kōjirō, *An Introduction to Sung Poetry* (Cambridge: Harvard University Press, 1967), pp. 175–79.

[10] *Shiping shiji* (*Sibu congkan xubian* ed.), *j.*6/46b.

[11] The edition of Wu Wenying's *ci* used is in *Quan Song ci* (hereafter *QSC*), comp. Tang Guizhang (Beijing: Zhonghua shuju, 1965), 4:2873–942, References are to the page number, and after the virgule to the numerical order on the page of the poem cited. In subsequent chapters, only volume and page reference will be cited.

[12] The preface reads, "I ascended Yanyi with Guiweng to view the snow, and reminisced about our excursion on horse to Broken Bridge one morning in the twelfth month of the year *guimao* (1243)." Thus it dates the present poem post-1243.

jing), seems to have followed in Wu Wenying's footsteps. Not having passed the examination and entered officialdom, he also made a name among his contemporaries as a *ci* poet, though one whose reputation, to judge by the late Song poet and writer Zhou Mi's (1232–1308) observation, may have been somewhat eclipsed by Wu's own.[13] Nevertheless to all appearances he lived by his talent as a *ci* poet and enjoyed the patronage of certain high officials. A metaphorically phrased, highly complimentary post-script to his *ci* poetry is preserved in the collected writings of the chief councillor Du Fan (d. 1245), who is known to have been Weng Yuanlong's patron.[14] There are also two extant poems by Wu to his younger brother (*QSC* 2881/3, 2931/6).

In spite of the paucity of information, the few details we have concerning the brothers suggest a family of literati background and an education that perhaps cultivated in them a love of literature and helped shape their shared poetic talent.

Very little is known about Wu Wenying's early life. When Weng Fenglong became a *jinshi* in 1217, Wu was in his late adolescence. It is possible that Wu was brought into contact with a broader literary society that had connections with the government bureaucracy around this time as a consequence of his brother's success and subsequent debut in official life.

From references made in some late poems, it can be inferred that as a youth Wu Wenying had traveled away from his native district and had also sojourned at intervals during a period of ten years in the capital Hangzhou, where he had his first love affair with a singing girl.[15]

---

[13] Zhou Mi, *Haoranzhai yatan* (*Cihua congbian* ed., vol. 1), 170. There are twenty *ci* poems by Weng Yuanlong extant; see *QSC*, 4:2942–46.

[14] The postscript is in *Du Qingxian ji*, *Siku quanshu zhenben erji* (Taipei: Commercial Press, 1971), *j*.17/13a–14b.

[15] The preface to an undated poem (*QSC* 2903/1) reads, "It has already been thirty-five years since I went with Jiang Shizhou to travel along the rivers Tiao and Xia. Returning now I am grieved by the present and memories of the past, so I have written this poem to sing my feelings." The Tiao and Xia are two rivers in Zhejiang; the Tiao passes through Hangzhou and Deqing, and when it reaches Wuxing it becomes the Xia River. The time indicated in this preface may coincide with Wu's first or second trip to Deqing (see text following). In any case, it shows that Wu had traveled in his youth. For visits to Hangzhou, see *QSC* 2930/5 (lines 10–14), 2891/1, 2935/1 (lines 23–28); Chang'an in these poems stands for Hangzhou. On the love affair, see sec. 3.

BIOGRAPHY

Wu's earliest poem is dated 1224.[16] It was composed in Deqing County in Zhexi circuit (northern Zhejiang), which, according to lines 11–15, he evidently had already visited sometime prior to this date. To the tune *He xinlang* and prefaced "A lyric on Small Rainbow Bridge written for Magistrate Zhao of Deqing," this youthful and rather artful attempt reads:

1   Ripple reflections wrinkle in tortoise shell patterns.
     Dipped in mist, half moistened are the red and green
     Of windows pillowed on the stream.
     A thousand feet of roseate cloud recline languidly on
              the water.
5   Myriad arrays of silk screens embrace embroidery.
     Again and again, the boats to Wu turn their bows,
     And wild geese returning north would not reach Lake
              Tai:
     I ask the man fishing through snow in the vastness if he
              knows—
     A woodman's song, remote,
10   Traverses the deep verdure.

     Coming here again I arrived in time for the blossoms.
     I recall lingering among these empty hills in the night
              rain,
     Then spring wine at the pavilion of parting.
     Under newly planted peach and plum trees where a
              footpath forms,
15   All this after the wanderer left.
     Still the mandarin prunus at the East Lodge is
              delicately thin.
     A single splash of oars—in the green of hills and
              stream.
     During the day the swallows are silent, the wind stills,
              curtains hang motionless.
     In the hushed chill,
20   With sleeves dangling I chant.

                                              (*QSC* 2898/4)

---

[16] See Xia Chengtao, *Tang Song ciren nianpu*, pp. 459–60.

7

浪影龜紋皺。
蘸平煙、青紅半溼,
枕溪窗牖。
千尺晴霞慵臥水,
萬疊羅屏擁繡。
漫幾度、吳船回首。
歸雁五湖應不到,
問蒼茫、釣雪人知否。
樵唱杳,
度深秀。

重來趂得花時候。
記留連、空山夜雨,
短亭春酒。
桃李新栽成蹊處,
盡是行人去後。
但東閣、官梅清瘦。
欸乃一聲山水綠,
燕無言、風定垂簾畫。
寒正悄,
舞吟袖。

This poem serves to illuminate several aspects of Wu Wenying's life. First, it demonstrates the minimal extent of Wu's travels to that date, involving a route that could easily have taken him through the metropolis Shaoxing and the capital Hangzhou.[17] Secondly, since this poem was written for a magistrate (upon his request?), Wu Wenying may already have enjoyed some fame as a young poet, and Magistrate Zhao only inaugurates a long list of government officials and high dignitaries with whom he associated and for whom he composed many poems throughout his life. Stylistically, this poem already exhibits certain salient characteristics of Wu's verse as a whole: the penchant for unusual words and novel images (line 1), metonymic language (lines 2–3), an implied rather than explicit logic in the structure, and frequent use of allusions.

[17] As Deqing lies north of Hangzhou, in order to travel from the coastal district Siming, which lies southeast of it, the normal course would be to go west through Shaoxing fu, the provincial capital of Zhedong circuit, then north through Hangzhou.

Thus far we can picture Wu Wenying as a young man, not terribly ambitious, in all likelihood devoting much of his time and energy to learning the art of writing *ci* poetry and growing proficient in it. He ranks among the few Southern Song *ci* poets with an expert knowledge of music; there are a number of much admired tune patterns created by him.[18] Wu's sole fame as a *ci* poet and his apparent lack of success in public life have occasioned one writer's remark that, though no doubt intelligent, Wu might have been of the type that was "addicted to poetry and dull in the Classics."[19] Instead of treading the traditional time-honored path to worldly success, Wu traveled, cultivated the friendship of officials—those who had already made their mark, and perhaps tried to find in their employ or patronage some means of support. In fact, the next known period in Wu's life, the early 1230s, finds him in the staff of the Grain Transport Office in Suzhou.

II. The Suzhou Period (ca. 1232–ca. 1244)

The exact dates of Wu Wenying's move to Suzhou and of his entry into the Grain Transport Office remain obscure.[20] The preface to a poem dated 1232 (*QSC* 2920/3) provides some basis for assuming that Wu had already been working at the Grain Transport Office for a time: "In the company of colleagues from the Granary I attended a farewell banquet held for Sun Wuhuai

---

[18] As *ci* became a literary genre in the hands of scholar-officials not so well-versed in music, "filling in words" came to be the standard practice. On this practice, see Glen Baxter, "Metrical Origins of the *Tz'u*," in *Studies in Chinese Literature*, ed. John L. Bishop (Cambridge: Harvard University Press, 1966), pp. 187–88. Although it was the vogue among late Southern Song *ci* poets to pay much attention to the musical aspect of *ci*, Wu Wenying was among the few *ci* poets who actually composed some of their own tunes.

[19] Yang Tiefu, *Mengchuang ci quanji jianshi*, p. 361.

[20] Suzhou (i.e., Pingjiang fu) was one of the three main centers of grain transport and storage in the Southern Song. Rice, as regular tax grain and special requisitions, was transported by canal to Suzhou. See *Caoyun* (Grain Transport) section in *Song shi*, comp. Tuo Tuo (Beijing: Zhonghua shuju, 1977), 175/4250–61. During the Song, the circuit fiscal intendant had charge of grain transport and storage. To be employed at the granary or Grain Transport Office probably meant being on the clerical staff under the fiscal intendant. See Zheng Qian, *Cixuan* (Taipei: Huagang chubanshe, 1972), p. 131. Also cf. entry on *zhuanyunshi* in *Song shi*, 167/3964–65.

at the garden residence of Guo Xidao on the day before the leap Double Ninth."[21] He was then in his thirties. Beginning around this time and lasting until about 1244, his sojourn in Suzhou continued for roughly twelve years. For a number of these years, Wu was employed on the clerical staff of the Grain Transport Office.[22] With the exception of some possible official assignments, which took him to a few locales within the general confines of Zhexi circuit (Jiangsu and Zhejiang), and some trips to Hangzhou, Wu's activities, for the most part, were centered in the vicinity of Suzhou.[23]

Prefaces that can be dated to this period provide the only substantive and specific record of Wu Wenying's activities. From them it can be gathered that he circulated among the staff of the Grain Transport Office, officials in the district, career poets,[24] and a group of friends of apparently wealthy gentry background.[25] Together these members of the educated elite

[21] For the dating of this poem, see Xia Chengtao, *Tang Song ciren nianpu*, pp. 460–61.

[22] That Wu Wenying was with the Grain Transport Office for some time is suggested by the following: (a) There are four poems with prefaces that make direct mention of the Grain Transport Office and of the names of certain colleagues (*QSC* 2899/4, 2916/3, 2920/2, 2926/2). It is reasonable to assume that these were written over an extended period. The only dated poem, as stated in the text, is from 1232; (b) The preface to *Mulanhua man*, "An excursion to Tiger Hill with colleagues from the Grain Transport. At this time Wei Yizhai has already been selected for transfer, and Chen Fenku and Li Fang'an will soon finish their terms" (*QSC* 2916/3), implies that he had seen the arrival and departure of colleagues at the Grain Transport Office in relation to their terms of service.

[23] Poems that suggest travel on assignment are: *Jinzhanzi* (*QSC* 2909/4), *Yan qingdu* (*QSC* 2883/3), *Xi qian ying* (*QSC* 2918/3). Some poems with references to Hangzhou during this period are *Tan fangxin* (*QSC* 2919/1) and *Liushao qing* (*QSC* 2928/5).

[24] This is a class of wandering poets, including some of the poets of the "Lakes and Rivers" School such as Dai Fugu, who did not study for the civil service examination but tried to live on their poetic talents by seeking out prominent officials as patrons. Two poems from this period were written to Sun Weixin (1179–1243), one of the well-known eccentrics of this group (*QSC* 2904/2, 2923/2). On Sun Weixin, see Shuen-fu Lin, *The Transformation of the Chinese Lyrical Tradition* (Princeton: Princeton University Press, 1978), pp. 34, 56–57, and 197.

[25] Ding Yu (*QSC* 2888/2 and 4, 2899/3, 2901/1, 2918/1, 2921/1), Mao Hetang (2892/2, 2896/5, 2904/3, 2905/3, 2914/3, 2922/4, 2924/2, 2934/1), Guo Xidao (2893/2, 2899/2, 2911/1, 2912/1, 2918/1, 2920/3, 2925/4) and Li Fang'an (2904/2, 2916/3, 2919/1, 2927/2) all appear to have belonged to the same coterie. Moreover, they all seem to have owned rather extensive properties with gardens and villas where

cultivated a style of living imbued with the elegance and refine-
ment afforded by the material prosperity of the Southern Song.[26]
The more affluent among them had estates on which were con-
structed villas and luxuriously landscaped gardens where fre-
quent social gatherings were conducted. The ways and manner of
entertainment and literary diversion were considerable and often
lavish; we come across occasions such as the banquet aboard a
large decorated boat where potted peonies provided the theme of
attraction (QSC 2890/1), or the morning garden party at which
the guests engaged in lute playing and games of chess—the polite
arts of a scholar-gentleman (QSC 2919/4)—or the simple cele-
bration of the completion of a new house (QSC 2925/4). The
occasions for social affairs seemed endless and all called for verse
making. Wu Wenying consequently left a large volume of occa-
sional and commemorative ci poems, written at birthday and
farewell banquets, flower-viewing and other parties, and during
excursions to scenic and historic sites. Given the popularity of ci
poems for such occasions in the Southern Song and Wu's fame as
a ci poet, we may infer that Wu was commissioned to write some
of these poems, and in fact it is quite likely that many of these
were impromptu lyrics, each written within a time limit and
performed on the very occasion that the lyric celebrates.[27] Much
is jotted down that is merely technically skillful, floating, or
suggested by the exigencies of rhyme or the demand for appro-
priate allusions. As poetry, many in this category lack intrinsic
literary merit but are valuable for the vignettes of literary society

incessant banquets and gatherings were held. Though Suzhou was a prosperous
textile and trading center in the Song, I hesitate to suggest that any of these
people could have been wealthy merchants. First of all, the traditional scorn held
toward the mercantile class would have discouraged interaction. If, however,
some of these people were indeed nouveaux riches of merchant background, the
information would have been discreetly suppressed in a literary record such as a
preface to a poem.

[26] For a concise account of the relationship between the economic prosperity of
the Southern Song and the upper classes' style of living, see Shuen-fu Lin, *The
Transformation of the Chinese Lyrical Tradition*, pp. 13–16.

[27] On such occasions Wu would not be alone as the versifier. Often there would
be other poets and participants, making a kind of poetry contest. One common
custom referred to involved carving a notch in the side of a candle. The duration
of the contest would be the time it took for the candle to burn down to the notch.
See *Yan qingdu*, line 14 (QSC 2883/3) and *Jiangdu chun*, line 4 (QSC 2911/2).

they offer. Wu Wenying seems to have delighted in the company of high society and, with his poetic talent, must have fulfilled his role with consummate ease. The preface to the poem dated 1236, which he wrote on the night of the Lantern Festival (the fifteenth day of the first month) reveals a youthful exuberance soon to be clouded by age and personal tragedies:

> This year the Lantern Festival in Suzhou was more spectacular than usual. While lodging in a quiet and secluded ward, I met many eminent people of the time. A banquet with wine was held, followed by the joys of polite company. It was indeed a grand affair. I received the rhyme word *jing*. (*QSC* 2919/2)

During this relatively long and stable period in Suzhou, Wu Wenying established lasting associations with certain high functionaries, which may have permitted him to later adopt a mode of life whose economic basis rested on an artist-patron affiliation. Most notable among these associations were those with Wu Qian (1196–1262), the top candidate among the *jinshi* graduates of 1217, and Shi Zhaizhi (1205–1249), from both of whom Wu enjoyed some form of patronage during certain periods after he left Suzhou. Although there is no direct evidence, a third figure could also be included in this category. This is Yin Huan, who together with Shi Zhaizhi is addressed more frequently than anyone else in Wu Wenying's extant works. Not much is known about Yin Huan other than that he also obtained his *jinshi* in 1217, the same year as Weng Fenglong and Wu Qian; was promoted to the position of Left Division Chief in the Department of Ministries in 1247; and is known to have composed *ci* poetry.[28] Most important in relation to Wu Wenying, Yin Huan wrote a preface, still extant, to a now lost collection of Wu's *ci* poetry. One may recall the Councillor Du Fan's postscript to Weng Yuanlong's *ci*

---

[28] It is recorded in the *Xianchun Lin'an zhi*, a Song Hangzhou gazetteer, that Yin Huan was a supervisory official in 1246, and in 1247 he was promoted to the Left Division. See *j*.50/11b, in *Song Yuan difangzhi congshu*, vol. 7. Wu Wenying, however, refers to Yin being promoted to the position of *Right* Division Chief in the preface to *Fengchi yin* (*QSC* 2902/2). This discrepancy may be an instance of textual corruption in the transmission of Wu's collection of poetry. Yin Huan's collection of poetry, entitled *Meijin ji*, is not extant. *QSC* records three *ci* poems by him; see vol. 4, p. 2708.

poetry; it was not an uncommon practice for patrons to write a preface or postscript to their protégés' work.

One may well ask at this point how Wu Wenying managed to cultivate these relationships, and if there is no more reliable evidence for such patronage than inferences and inductions. In considering the first question, two things need to be kept in mind. First is Wu Wenying's growing renown as a *ci* poet, and second is that his personal connections through his elder brother Weng Fenglong enabled him to meet and be noticed by the official class in Suzhou. One cannot, for example, overlook the possibility that his friendship with Yin Huan and Wu Qian grew out of initial introductions to them that came about because they had passed the *jinshi* in the same year as Weng Fenglong.

Toward the end of this period in Suzhou, Wu Wenying was demonstrably an accomplished, mature poet of substantial reputation. His poems were being included in contemporary anthologies of *ci* poetry.[29] His "canon" of *ci* composition was recorded in the *Yuefu zhimi* by the poet and critic Shen Yifu (?–after 1297), who first met Wu in 1243 toward the end of the Suzhou period.[30] Although no dates can be associated with their appearances, sources indicate that Wu Wenying's poems were printed during the Song in an edition of poetry entitled *Liushi jia ci* [Ci by sixty poets],[31] and that a manuscript of his poetry in his own handwriting entitled *Shuanghua yu* was in circulation.[32] The no longer extant collection to which Yin Huan had com-

---

[29] Thirteen selections are found scattered in the *Yangchun baixue*, compiled by Zhao Wenli circa 1244, *Yueyatang congshu* ed. Huang Sheng included nine in *juan* 10 of the *Zhongxing yilai juemiao cixuan*, in his anthology *Hua'an cixuan* (Preface 1249; rpt. Hong Kong: Zhonghua shuju, 1962), pp. 354–57.

[30] *Yuefu zhimi* (*Cihua congbian* ed., vol. 1), 229.

[31] See Zhang Yan (1248–1320?), *Ciyuan* (*Cihua congbian* ed., vol. 1), 201. From Zhang Yan's phrasing, it seems that this work was already lost or hard to come by even in his day.

[32] Zhou Mi and Zhang Yan, two of Wu's younger contemporaries, both wrote *ci* poems as colophons to this manuscript. Zhou Mi's poem *Yulou chi* (*QSC* 3288/3) is subtitled "Inscribed on Wu Mengchuang's *Shuanghua yu Ci Collection.*" Zhang Yan's collection contains two poems on this subject. *Shengsheng man* (*QSC* 3481/4) has two subtitle versions: "On a remaining calligraphy by Wu Mengchuang," and "Inscribed at the end of Mengchuang's manuscript with his own tune composition *Shuanghua yu*;" *Zui luopo* (*QSC* 3496/4) is subtitled "Inscribed on the *ci* manuscript in Wu Mengchuang's own handwriting in the collection of Zhao Xiagu."

posed a preface must have been compiled at the end of this period or shortly afterwards, since this preface was partly quoted, along with a selection of Wu Wenying's poems, in the anthology of *ci* poetry compiled by Huang Sheng (fl.1240–49) in 1249. In this preface, Yin accords Wu highest honors among his contemporaries: "If one were to seek models of *ci* poetry in our age of the Song, there was Zhou Bangyan in the past and now there is Wu Wenying. These are not only my words, but the unanimous opinion within the four seas." [33]

While Weng Fenglong was Vice-administrator of Suzhou from 1237 to 1240, the record of Administrators in the Suzhou gazetteer *Wuxian zhi* shows three names for this period which, significantly, are also found in Wu Wenying's collection of poetry.[34] From 1237 to 1238 the post was held by Wu Qian, to whom we shall return at a later stage in Wu's life, and from 1239–1241, by Zhao Yuchou (fl.1240s), whose relevance to Wu's life is uncertain, since Wu only addressed one extant poem to him (*QSC* 2907/3). The administrator of Suzhou in these years whose relationship with Wu Wenying offers tangible areas for speculation is Shi Zhaizhi.

Also a native of Siming, and son of the notorious chief councillor Shi Miyuan (1164–1233),[35] Shi Zhaizhi began his official career with the emperor's bestowal of a *jinshi* degree in 1233.[36]

---

[33] *Zhongxing yilai juemiao cixuan*, in *Hua'an cixuan*, p. 354. It is difficult to say absolutely whether this collection is the same as the handwritten manuscript *Shuanghua yu*, since the latter's date of compilation has not been established. Since the poem to the tune *Shuanghua yu* (*QSC* 2901/2) is about an excursion to Stone Lake in the environs of Suzhou, Xia Chengtao speculates that *Shuanghua yu* could either be the manuscript collection of his poetry made in the Suzhou period, or it could be a collection that was made in his old age. See Xia Chengtao, *Tang Song ciren nianpu*, p. 482. Judging from internal evidence (lines 6 and 8), this poem seems to be a work dating from after his sojourn in Suzhou. This being the case, the handwritten manuscript that bears the same title would necessarily be form a later period.

[34] In *Wuxian zhi*, comp. Wu Xiuzhi et al. (1933; rpt. Taipei: Chengwen chubanshe, 1970),1 : 100, *juan* 7.

[35] Shi Miyuan's biography is in *Song shi*, 35 : 12415–19. A powerful chief councillor during Ningzong's reign (1195–1224), Shi engineered the murder of his predecessor, the infamous Han Tuozhou. His other notorious act was the arbitrary deposition of the designated heir apparent and the installation of Lizong as the next emperor after Ningzong's death. Indebted to Shi Miyuan, Lizong showered favors on his descendants, among them Shi Zhaizhi.

[36] Basic Annals of Lizong, *Song shi*, 1 : 799.

14

Shi had two terms of office in Suzhou; succeeding Wu Qian in 1238, he left for the capital in 1239 when Zhao Yuchou assumed the post and returned in 1241 for a second term, which lasted till the beginning of 1243. During his first term as Administrator of Suzhou, Shi renovated the historical public building Qiyun Tower.[37] There is a poem by Wu Wenying with this building as subject (*QSC* 2884/2). Both the poem and Wu's acquaintance with Shi are thought to date from about this time.[38] As mentioned, there are more extant poems addressed to Shi Zhaizhi and Yin Huan by Wu than to anyone else. Though Shi was a few years Wu's junior, the deferential titles *xiansheng* and *weng* by which Wu invariably addresses him suggest more respect than might be warranted simply by Shi's seniority in rank. Furthermore, all the poems in question were either congratulatory or written at banquet gatherings—on just those occasions when a readily available talent was called for. The above factors would tend to support the possibility of a patron-artist relationship. Of the six poems whose place of composition can be determined, one was written at a banquet on a boat in Suzhou (*QSC* 2801/1), three were congratulatory lyrics written in Hangzhou (*QSC* 2875/5, 2919/5, 2935/4), another was from a night banquet held at Shi's garden residence, probably located in his native district Siming (*QSC* 2914/1), and the last one was composed during an excursion to view snow at Feiyi Tower in Shaoxing (*QSC* 2916/1). Of the remaining five poems, three were written at Shi's residence, though at which one of his residences is not clear. Considering the varied locales of Wu's poems for Shi, it seems fairly safe to say that Wu had formed part of Shi's entourage at times. It is likely that, with his purported interest in poetry,[39] Shi Zhaizhi may have invited Wu Wenying to act as a kind of poet-in-residence at times during the period from 1241, when he assumed

[37] Lu Xiong, *Suzhou fuzhi* (1379; Seikadō Bunko), *j.*8/5a.

[38] Xia Chengtao, *Tang Song ciren nianpu*, p. 463. The poem, written to the tune *Qi tian yue*, is discussed in chap. 3, sec. 3.

[39] See *Shidao pitai* entry in Zhou Mi's *Qidong yeyu* (*Xuejin taoyuan* ed.), *j.*16/8a–9a. Zhou states that after the incident over the publication of subversive poetry in the *Rivers and Lakes Collection*, the writing of *shi* poetry was suppressed by Shi Miyuan from 1225 to 1227, and that it was due to Shi's son, Shi Zhaizhi, and son-in-law, Zhao Rumei's interest in poetry that the ban was lifted two years later.

his second term of office in Suzhou, until his death in Hangzhou in 1249. When Wu's movements between Suzhou and Hangzhou became discernible in 1243 and 1244, leading to his eventual move from Suzhou in 1244, their relationship to Shi Zhaizhi's departure from Suzhou in 1243 may be seen to be more than merely coincidental.

The two years 1243 and 1244 brought sudden changes and uncertainties. Concerning Wu's life in Suzhou at this time, we no longer know whether he was still employed at the Grain Transport Office. The likelihood is that he was not. The possibility looms large that he had already changed his mode of life to that of a guest poet dependent on the patronage of wealthy notables. Shi Zhaizhi, as we have seen, may have been an important patron whose departure from Suzhou in 1243 could have signaled a serious loss of support.

Owing to the independent preservation of a group of sixteen poems, together with several others dated to these two years, we are able to discern a vague outline of Wu's movements and to posit some of his concerns at this time. The Ming work *Tiewang shanhu* contains a manuscript of sixteen poems by Wu Wenying titled "Draft of New *ci* Poems," and signed "From Wenying with one hundred obeisances in fear and anxiety." [40] Originally in Wu's own handwriting, the manuscript was included in the section *Shupin* as a calligraphic specimen. Though it is impossible now to trace the transmission of this draft from its provenance to its preservation in the *Tiewang shanhu*, the late Qing scholar Zheng Wenzhuo (1856–1918) has argued from circumstantial and textual evidence that these sixteen poems were all composed in the course of the year *guimao*, that is, between January 1243 and February 1244 in the Western calendar. [41]

[40] *Tiewang shanhu*, comp. Zhu Cunli (Rpt. Taipei: Guoli zhongyang tushuguan, 1970), 2:463–70. Also in *Siming congshu*, comp. Zhang Shouyong (1936; rpt. Taipei: Guofang yanjiuyuan, 1970), vol. 1, pt. 2. The *QSC* page references to these sixteen poems are, in the order found in the manuscript: *Ruihe xian* 2876/1, *Qinyuan chun* 2905/5, *Yulou chi* 2909/2, *Gu xiang man* 2941/4, *Qi tian yue* 2884/4, *Si jiake* 2933/1, *Su wu man* 2887/4, *Basheng Ganzhou* 2926/3, *Tan fangxin* 2902/1, *Jiangnan chun* 2900/3, *Shuilong yin* 2879/1, *Bai xingyue man* 2818/4, *Xi ping yue* 2891/1, *Ding xiang jie* 2889/2, *Hua fan* 2893/2, *Huan jing le* 2888/3.

[41] Zheng Wenzhuo, *Mengchuang ci jiaoyi*, in *Siming congshu*, comp. Zhang Shouyong, vol. 1, pt. 2; partially quoted in Xia Chengtao, *Tang Song ciren nianpu*, p. 466.

An examination of the poems yields no special order of ar-
rangement, except for the placement of the first piece, which was
addressed to Fang Wanli (*jinshi* 1211), the recipient of the manu-
script, who held the office of Registrar at one of the Imperial
Courts in Hangzhou at the time.[42] To the tune *Ruihe xian*, the
poem is subtitled "For celebrating your venerable birthday in
the year *guimao*."[43] The poem begins with the lines:

> Like a pulley turning, autumn comes again.
> I remember swiftly jotting down new lyrics,
> Entrusting them to the wild geese by the river.

(QSC 2876/1)

> 轆轤秋又轉。
> 記旋草新詞，
> 江頭憑雁。

Wu Wenying was sending this birthday poem along with a small
collection of his recent compositions to the official Fang Wanli.
Not only is the deferential phrasing of the signature revealing of
Wu's humble status in relation to the addressee, but he also
signed the manuscript with his personal name, which is used
when a person of inferior status is addressing one of greater
prestige; these signs leave little doubt regarding the character of
this manuscript as an instrument of patronage seeking.[44] In
modern parlance, Wu was attempting to "market his talent" by
presenting a manuscript of poems to an official in the capital on a
suitable occasion. The number of poems included (sixteen)

---

[42] Fang was co-author of the gazetteer *Baoqing Siming zhi*, preface dated 1227;
see *A Sung Bibliography*, ed. Yves Hervouet (Hong Kong: The Chinese Univer-
sity Press, 1978), pp. 143–44.

[43] The *QSC* version of the subtitle follows that found in Mao Jin's *Jiguge*
edition, which reads: "In *guimao* (1243) celebrating the birthday of the Court
Registrar Fang Huiyan." The *Tiewang shanhu* version, based on Wu Wenying's
own handwritten manuscript, is more likely to reflect the original text and is
therefore given here. For the same reason, and because it makes better sense in
the context, the *Tiewang shanhu* variant "autumn," rather than the *QSC*
"spring," is adopted in the first line of the poem.

[44] See n. 32 on the various handwritten manuscripts by Wu Wenying appre-
ciated by Zhou Mi and Zhang Yan, which were either in circulation or in private
collections in the late Song and early Yuan. Their existence corroborates the
function postulated here of certain manuscripts.

would also constitute an appropriately sized scroll for presentation. The target may have been Fang Wanli personally or a broader official coterie connected with him. It is of considerable interest that three poems in this group were written to tunes that Wu himself had composed during this year, indicating a marked period of creativity.[45] The term "new lyrics" in the title of the draft and also in the text of two of the poems thus takes on a double meaning, not simply denoting newly written poems but also incorporating the idea of newly composed tunes.[46]

A degree of unrest in Wu's life can be discerned from the prefatory contents of some of these poems. They show, for example, that Wu made at least three trips to Hangzhou this year: once in spring, once in autumn, and then again in winter when he stayed through the lunar New Year.[47] His elder brother Weng Fenglong had also been in Hangzhou this winter.[48] Was Wu Wenying approaching some personal or financial crisis and seeking his brother's help as well? There is no way of telling. Definite answers cannot be provided for many questions concerning concrete details in Wu's life; an evolutionary movement, as it were, is all that can be mapped out.

One thing definite that can be repeated at this point about Wu Wenying is his obvious lack of personal interest in contemporary politics and government, evidenced by a near absence of poems expressing such concerns. This trait is of course a logical extension of that temperament which earlier eschewed the pursuit of a career among the official elite, and which the diverse and more permissive society of the Southern Song could comfortably ac-

---

[45] *Gu xiang man, Tan fangxin,* and *Jiangnan chun.* See n. 40 for page references.

[46] In the same sense as that immortalized by Jiang Kui's usage of the term in his *shi* poem about his two most famous tunes which he had just composed. The relevant lines read: "The rhymes of my newly composed tunes are most charming, while Xiao Hong sings quietly I play the flute." See Shuen-fu Lin, *The Transformation of the Chinese Lyrical Tradition,* p. 53. Wu Wenying's line, in a poem written on New Year's eve in 1243, reads, "Singing my new tunes I see the year off." (*QSC* 2934/6)

[47] The poems indicating his respective presence in Hangzhou are *Xi ping yue man* (spring), *QSC* 2891/1, and *Qinyuan chun* (autumn), *QSC* 2905/5, both in the *Tiewang shanhu* manuscript, and *Liushao qing* (*QSC* 2928/5) and *Si jiake* (*QSC* 2934/6).

[48] See preface to *Liushao qing* (*QSC* 2928/5).

commodate. Xia Chengtao observes that, in the beginning years of the 1240s, while the Mongols were beginning to press southward across the border into Song territories, Wu was singing about a life that was completely divorced from political realities.[49] A poem written on the fifteenth of the first month in 1243 contains these lines:

> I still remember when I first came to Wu Park,
> No frost then, now it has flown
> To startle the hair at my temples.
> Sporting I have passed my time here
> Where the scenery is infinite
> With bright songs and pretty dances.
> Now stale marks on the traveler's robe,
> An old face in the ornate mirror,
> All my happiness is ended.
> Under the fading lamp my dream is brief,
> The morning horn plays "Plum Blossom"—
> For whom does it chant its lament?

(QSC 2880/4)

猶記初來吳苑。
未清霜、飛驚雙鬢。
嬉遊是處，
風光無際，
舞葱歌舊。
陳迹征衫，
老容華鏡，
歡悰都盡，
向殘燈夢短，
梅花曉角，
為誰吟怨。

These lines typically bespeak Wu's aesthetically oriented life of wine and song, his nostalgia for youth, and the absence of reference to Southern Song political realities. However, we may do well to remember that the expression of didacticism and realism is not typical of the *ci* genre, and that in the case of Wu

---

[49] Xia Chengtao, *Tang Song ciren nianpu*, p. 465.

Wenying, his concerns were after all shaped by his role as a literary dependent, rather than as a concerned government official.

III. Emergence of Vanished Love

After a winter, and perhaps spring as well, in Hangzhou, we find Wu Wenying temporarily lodging in the area outside Suzhou's Pan Gate in the early summer of 1244, as he mentions in his preface to *Manjiang hong* (*QSC* 2877/1), written on the occasion of the Double Fifth Festival. The poem reveals a dissolved relationship. Xia Chengtao has observed that all four poems dated to this year contain references to the same tragic event,[50] whose significance, by virtue of its profound influence on the thematic development of Wu Wenying's poetry, can hardly be ignored; nearly one quarter of the total corpus of his poetry is devoted to various explorations on the theme of lost love.[51]

The actual circumstances surrounding the relationship remain vague and shadowy. Nevertheless, a few details can be gleaned from some poems. During his early years in Suzhou, Wu took on a concubine with whom he lived for roughly a decade, and by whom he had more than one child.[52] In the spring of 1244 they separated for reasons unknown. It seems that the concubine was dismissed, but at the same time, a feeling of helplessness can be sensed in the situation, and her departure left a deep wound in Wu's heart, from which many poems of sorrow flowed. As speculated above, Wu's livelihood may have been particularly insecure at this time, and the concubine sent away as a result of some

---

[50] The four poems are, in the order in which they were composed: *Manjiang hong* (*QSC* 2877/1), *Feng qi wu* (2937/5), *Wei fan* (2928/1), and *Xi qian ying* (2918/4). See Xia Chengtao, *Tang Song ciren nianpu*, pp. 467–68.

[51] Termed *huairen ci* in Chinese. Yang Tiefu (*Mengchuang ci quanji jianshi*, pp. 364–67) cites 102 titles pertaining to this category. See also the ones cited in Xia Chengtao, *Tang Song ciren nianpu*, pp. 467–70.

[52] The preface to *Xi qian ying* (*QSC* 2918/4) reads, "In 1244, on the winter solstice I went to live in Yue (Zhejiang), while my sons were left at Xiao Temple in Guajing." Also, line 15 in *Yu zhu xin* (*QSC* 2881/1), "I remember it was when you were tired of embroidery and desired sour things," seems to refer to the concubine's pregnancy, the desire for sour things and fatigue being common symptoms of pregnancy.

unavoidable necessity. Toward the end of the year, even their children were left at a temple in Guajing, a little south of Suzhou, while Wu went to Zhejiang.[53]

Xia Chengtao suggests that Wu's concubine subsequently became a prostitute in Hangzhou. A poem he quotes by Moqi Shaozhi does lend support to this view.[54] To the tune *Jiangshenzi* and subtitled "Presented to a singing girl and sent to Mengchuang," the poem is thought by Xia to have been written for Wu's Suzhou concubine.[55] It is set in her voice and sums up her plight:

1   Ten years—my heart's concern rises to my brows,
       Startled that a dream has faded;
       The latticed window turns chill.
       Like cloud and catkin I follow the wind,
5   For thousands of miles crossing mountains and passes.
       Nowhere can I find
       The soulmate who knew my lute's sound.
       Pale my powdered face,
       Loose the gold bracelet.

10   His poem scrolls in the jade casket
       I am loath to read again.
       Remembering our former joy,
       I shed secret tears.
       I am already crossing over
15   To Chang'an in a flying skiff.
       Please say for me that I am ravaged by grief,
       And seek from him
       A brocade missive in return.

                                    (*QSC* 2948/4)

十年心事上眉端。
夢驚殘。
瑣窗寒。

---

[53] See n. 52. Nothing more is heard about the children.

[54] No information exists concerning Wu's acquaintance with Moqi Shaozhi, whose great-grandfather Moqi Xue was one of the officials who plotted Yue Fei's death with Qin Gui.

[55] Xia Chengtao, *Tang Song ciren nianpu*, pp. 468–69.

雲絮隨風千里度關山。
琴裏知音無覓處，
妝粉淡，
釧金寬。

瑤箱吟卷懶重看。
憶前歡。
淚偷彈。
我已相將，
飛棹過長安。
為說崔徽憔悴損，
須覓取，
錦箋還。

From the content of the poem, it seems that Moqi Shaozhi had encountered the woman who had been Wu's concubine on her journey to Hangzhou after their separation. She spoke grievously of the broken affair and her present fate, and requested Moqi to be the messenger of her affliction. However, it appears that the only sequel was a chance encounter with Wu a year or two later at West Lake in Hangzhou; the separation was to be permanent.[56]

At this point, attention should be drawn to another fatal relationship in Wu's life, one briefly mentioned in our discussion of his early years. The existence of this relationship is unanimously acknowledged in previous studies, but concrete details concerning it are almost entirely lacking and its chronology has never been established. Xia Chengtao, after considerable examination of Wu's poems for clues, was able to determine that Wu Wenying met this mistress in Hangzhou, that she died sometime after he left, and that he learned of her death when he returned to Hangzhou some years later.[57]

The poem *Yingti xu* (*QSC* 2907/4) frames the Hangzhou love affair in a clear narrative sequence. Since the poem itself is not dated, it is not possible to fit the biographical elements it

[56] The second stanza of *Sao hua you* (*QSC* 2886/1) describes what seems to be a chance meeting with his former concubine during the Cold Food Festival. Yang Tiefu dates this poem to 1245; see Yang Tiefu, *Mengchuang ci quanji jianshi*, pp. 54–55.

[57] Xia Chengtao, *Tang Song ciren nianpu*, p. 469.

contains—the meeting, love affair, parting, her death, and his return—into any time slot in Wu's life. In the absence of any dated poems on the subject, I can only hazard the guess, based on the youthful feeling of this romance and the evidence that Wu had spent time in Hangzhou as a young man, that this affair took place before he took up residence in Suzhou as a clerk at the Grain Transport Office.

The information apropos of these two relationships, however meager, does furnish a meaningful context in which to understand an important body of Wu Wenying's poetry.

IV. Late Years: Integrity versus Improbity or a Man without Principles

Evidence for Wu's last sojourn in Suzhou is provided by a poem he wrote in the autumn of 1245 (*QSC* 2921/4) celebrating the birthday of Wei Jun, who was then Administrator of Suzhou.[58] For the next few years, he seemed to have stayed mainly in and around Hangzhou. There are poems from 1246 and 1247 indicating his presence in the area.[59] He continued in much the style of life he had established in Suzhou, playing the poet laureate for officialdom at social functions. Compared with the large number of lower grade officials and private citizens of wealth that comprise his circle of social interaction in his early years in Suzhou, his associations in this period belong more to the established high ranking bureaucracy. In prefaces to poems, we now find names such as Wei Jun, whose wife was Emperor Lizong's sister, and who was recalled to the capital from Suzhou in the spring of 1246 for promotion to Executive of the Ministry of Justice;[60] Li Boyu, the upright Professor of the National University whose fame rose with his memorial in defense of two censors against the accusations of the power-monopolizing chief councillor Shi Songzhi;[61] and an old friend and patron, Yin Huan, whose promotion in 1247 from the Grain Transport Office in the suburbs of

---

[58] For the dating of this poem, see *ibid.*, p. 470.
[59] *Ibid.*, pp. 471–72.
[60] *QSC* 2904/1 and *ibid.*, p. 471.
[61] *QSC* 2911/2 and *ibid.*

the capital to that of Left Division Chief in the central government in Hangzhou was celebrated by Wu in two poems (*QSC* 2889/1, 2902/2).

At the same time, scattered through Wu's collection of poetry are a number of poems addressed to courtesans, Buddhist and Taoist nuns, a palace ritual attendant, a brushmaker, and the bookdealer Chen Qi,[62] showing his contact with people who, like himself, were on the periphery of the elite and yet dependent on this high society for patronage and support.[63] The existence of these poems points to the complex social fabric of urban centers such as Hangzhou of which Wu formed a part.

During the winter of 1249, Wu Wenying appears to have joined Wu Qian's staff in Shaoxing. Sources indicate that Wu Qian had held the offices of Administrator of Shaoxing and Pacificator of Zhedong from the eighth month of 1249 until the beginning of 1250.[64] The poem *Jiangdu chun* coincides with the circumstances; its preface states, "Inscribed on the lantern screen at Penglai Pavilion—Lüweng (Wu Qian) is commanding Yue" (*QSC* 2911/3). Shaoxing prefecture, referred to as Yue, was the site of Penglai Pavilion.[65] Wu Qian we have met many years ago, in 1217, when he and Weng Fenglong both became *jinshi*. The acquaintance between Wu Qian and Wu Wenying goes back at least to 1237 and 1238, when he was Administrator of Suzhou.

It was also during these years after he left Suzhou that Wu Wenying made the acquaintance of Jia Sidao (1213–1275), the "bad last minister" who became the incontrovertible arch-villain

---

[62] *QSC* 2885/4. Chen Qi was the Hangzhou bookdealer who compiled and published the poetic works of his contemporaries in an anthology called the *Rivers and Lakes Collection* from which the "Rivers and Lakes" School derived its name. On the incident over certain subversive political comments in the collection, see Yoshikawa Kōjirō, *An Introduction to Sung Poetry*, pp. 175–77. When Wu Wenying became acquainted with Chen Qi in the late 1240s and early 1250s, the affair lay at least twenty years in the past. Wu's poem alludes to the reclusive life Chen was leading at the time.

[63] The term *guirenjia* (noble or wealthy household), which Wu used a few times, leads one to suspect that he keenly felt the distinction between his own commoner status and the elite status of the wealthy and prestigious. See *QSC* 2938/4, and 2920/4, and 2906/2.

[64] Basic Annals of Lizong, *Song shi*, 43/841.

[65] Wang Xiangzhi, *Yudi jisheng* (preface 1221; rpt. Taipei: Wenhai chubanshe, 1962), 1:103.

in Southern Song history.[66] Because of the animosity which later arose between Wu Qian and Jia Sidao, and of Wu Qian's subsequent demotion, banishment, and supposed murder through the foul machinations of Jia Sidao, much ink has been spilled over eight poems in Wu Wenying's collection, four each addressed to Wu Qian and Jia Sidao, and the possible moral implications of Wu Wenying's involvement with the two political antagonists.[67] The origin of this concern stems from the critical judgment passed on Wu Wenying the man by the editors of the *Siku quanshu* in the eighteenth century when they remarked that "... there are several pieces celebrating the birthday of Jia Sidao. This shows that he (Wu Wenying) probably lost his principles late in life, like Zhu Dunru and Lu You."[68] Subsequent attempts to salvage or condemn Wu Wenying's moral character have hinged on the dating of one particular poem to Jia Sidao (*QSC* 2909/3), on whether or not it was written prior to the final enmity between the two men which led to Wu Qian's exile in 1260. In her definitive study of this aspect of Wu Wenying's life, Yeh Chiaying has proven beyond doubt that this poem was written precisely at the time when Wu Qian was being demoted from the rank of Left Grand Councillor and banished, while Jia Sidao, in his position as Right Grand Councillor, was being recalled to court in the summer of 1260.[69]

The point is not simply that Wu Wenying had compromised his relationship with Wu Qian in particular, as has often been the emphasis in the past, but more fundamentally that Wu Wenying,

---

[66] Biography in *Song shi*, 233/13779–87. Cf. the modern reappraisal by Herbert Franke, "Chia Ssu-tao (1213–1275): A 'Bad Last Minister'?", in *Confucian Personalities*, ed. Arthur Wright (Stanford: Stanford University Press, 1962), pp. 215–34.

[67] Cf. (a) Liu Yusong's long preface in defense of Wu's character in "Mengchuang cigao zhuke xuba" in *Siming congshu*, comp. Zhang Shouyong, vol. 1, pt. 2; (b) Hu Yunyi's disparaging remarks in *Songci yanjiu* (Shanghai: Zhonghua shuju, 1926), p. 179; (c) Xia Chengtao's special essay on the subject, "Mengchuang wannian yu Jia Sidao juejiao bian," in *Tang Song ciren nianpu*, pp. 484–86; and (d) Yeh Chia-ying's detailed examination of this problem in "Chaisui qibaoloutai: tan Mengchuang ci zhi xiandaiguan," in *Jialing tanci* (Taipei: Chunwenxue congshu, 1970), pp. 188–97.

[68] *Siku quanshu zongmu tiyao* (Shanghai: Commercial Press, 1933), 4:4447.

[69] See Yeh Chia-ying, *Jialing tanci*, pp. 231–36.

as his actions and mode of life demonstrate, did not consistently follow a Confucian code of principles and ideals. Furthermore, examination of the "friendship" between Wu Wenying and Wu Qian, which dates back to Wu Wenying's Suzhou days, does not make it at all clear what the real nature of their relationship was. From the poems they exchanged, it can be seen that Wu Wenying accompanied Wu Qian on a number of social occasions, such as outings and banquets, and there is a suggestion of a degree of serious reflection and communication between them, as that conveyed in the poem *Jinlü ge*, subtitled "Viewing plum blossoms at Canglang Garden in the company of Mr. Lüzhai" (*QSC* 2939/5). Unfortunately, the extant poems they exchanged are too few—seven in all—to provide a firm basis for speculation, much less a conclusive statement on their relationship.[70] Even taking into account the positive elements of a plausibly established initial acquaintance through Weng Fenglong and the length of time they had known each other, it is still not certain that, as far as Wu Qian was concerned, Wu Wenying was ever more than a literary guest-friend whose talented and sensitive presence provided occasional desirable company and diversion from the routine of official duties. In other words, there was nothing really indispensible about Wu Wenying; he played a role which could have been filled adequately by any number of people in his class. Wu Wenying's younger brother Weng Yuanlong, for example, also enjoyed some form of patronage from Wu Qian during the latter's administratorship of Qingyuan prefecture (i.e., Siming) from 1255 to 1258.[71] In neither case was there any sign of mutual commitment. Officials, with their frequent transfers from one posting to another, did not as a rule take along the members of their literary entourage. The general practice seems to have been

[70] There are four poems to Wu Qian in Wu Wenying's collection (*QSC* 2893/5, 2905/2, 2911/3, 2939/5), and three to Wu Wenying in Wu Qian's collection (*QSC* 2730/2, 2735/1, 2741/8).

[71] The gazetteer *Baoqing Siming xuzhi* (preface 1259, in *Song Yuan difangzhi congshu*, vol. 8) covers the period from 1255 to 1258 when Wu Qian was Administrator of Qingyuan fu. It contains three *juan* of *shi* poetry by Wu Qian written in that period. There are two *shi* poems addressed to Weng Yuanlong in *j.*10 and four *ci* poems in *j.*11 and 12. Page references for the *ci* poems in the *QSC* are: 2746/4, 2747/1 and 2, 2762/3.

for drifting scholar-artists to seek out aristocrats and high officials as short-term patrons, earning cash and other rewards for a living from their visits to these households. The late Song and early Yuan writer Fang Hui (1227–1307) gives a vivid account of the situation in Wu Wenying's lifetime:

> After the Qingyuan and Jiading reigns (1195–1201, 1210–1225), there began to appear poets acting as visiting guests (of prominent officials). People like Liu Guo of Longzhou were many, and Stone Screen (Dai Fugu) was one of them. These people followed one another to form a fashion to the extent that they would not study for the civil service examination. They sought the letters of one or two people in important positions as a reference, which they called the "broad tablet," to be supplemented with their own poems, and often in one visit obtained several thousand, or even ten thousand cash. For instance, Song Qianfu of Hushan, in one visit paid to Jia Sidao, obtained 200,000 cash, which he used to build a luxurious house. The lakes and hills of Qiantang (i.e., Hangzhou) were full of such people forming groups of tens and hundreds.[72]

Evidence for the nature of the association between Wu Wenying and Jia Sidao is even more tenuous and completely lacking in concrete details. All there is to go on are four poems addressed to Jia by Wu Wenying, two written on the occasion of Jia's birthday and two describing Jia's residences in Hangzhou. Were these poems aimed at gaining some favor from Jia, immediate or otherwise? Jia was known to have been a notorious megalomaniac who relished *ci* poems celebrating his birthday to the extent that he conducted yearly poetry competitions on these occasions. Winners were lavishly rewarded.[73] It is quite conceivable that Wu participated, if not in the actual competitions, then at least in presenting lyrics as a means of obtaining material re-

---

[72] Fang Hui, *Yingkui lüsui* (*Siku quanshu zhenben baji*), *j.*20/73b–74a; trans. Shuen-fu Lin, *The Transformation of the Chinese Lyrical Tradition*, p. 34. I have changed the romanization to *pinyin*.

[73] See entry *Jiaxiang shouci* in Zhou Mi, *Qidong yeyu* (*Xuejin taoyuan* ed.), *j.*12/10b–12b.

wards and patronage or an influential introduction or recommendation from Jia to other prospective patrons. The circumstances of the last years of Wu Wenying's life suggest just such an intermediary function as one that Jia Sidao might have fulfilled.

Wu Qian's fall and Jia Sidao's simultaneous rise to the monopoly of power were tied to the question of selecting an heir to the childless Lizong. When Lizong sought Wu Qian's advice concerning his intention to designate his brother Prince Sirong's son (the future Duzong) heir apparent, Wu Qian not only refrained from giving any advice, but did so in such a blunt manner as to imply that Lizong's own succession to the throne had been questionable, so that he incurred the emperor's great displeasure. Jia Sidao, on learning of the incident, acted opportunistically by memorializing for the naming of the heir apparent, thereby gaining Lizong's confidence.[74]

In the fourth month of 1260, while Jia Sidao was being summoned to the capital, Wu Qian was stripped of his office as chief councillor and demoted. Once back in court, Jia swiftly brought about Wu Qian's exile to Jianchang Commandery in Jiangxi in the seventh month of 1260. Meanwhile, the heir apparent had entered the Eastern Palace and Jia Sidao had been given the additional title of Lesser Preceptor to the Heir Apparent. In the tenth month, Wu Qian was further exiled to Chaozhou in the far south.

Where was Wu Wenying around this time? From all appearances, he was gravitating towards Jia Sidao and his circle. In the autumn of 1259, Wu wrote a farewell poem (*QSC* 2906/1) to Weng Mengyin who was on his way to Jia Sidao's retinue in Hubei. Belonging to the class of "visiting poets" described by Fang Hui, Weng Mengyin was no stranger to Jia Sidao's company and extravagant generosity. Zhou Mi tells of how well Weng Mengyin was received by Jia Sidao in Yangzhou when the latter was administrator there in 1250. Jia was reportedly so pleased with Weng's parting poem that he showered Weng with "tens of thousands" of precious drinking vessels used at the

---

[74] On Lizong's enthronement, see n. 35. The information for the conflict between Wu Qian and Jia Sidao is found in their respective biographies and the Basic Annals of Lizong in the *Song shi*.

banquet.[75] Now in 1259, while Jia was in Hubei as Special Grand Commissioner for Jinghunanbei circuits, Weng Mengyin was perhaps journeying there to seek his fortune again from Jia. Wu Wenying took the opportunity to eulogize Jia Sidao in the poem to Weng by likening him to the talented Han official Jia Yi, playing on their having the same surname. Wu wrote the poem *Jinzhanzi* (*QSC* 2909/3) in the summer of 1260, singing of Jia Sidao's sumptuous lifestyle and residence by West Lake, shortly after Jia's triumphant recall to Hangzhou and during the months when misfortunes were befalling Wu Qian. By the eighth month, Wu Wenying seems to have been securely ensconced as resident poet at the royal estate of the heir apparent's natural parents, Prince Sirong and his wife, in Shaoxing. One can only take a guess at the connections through which he managed to enter into the protection of this aristocratic household.

There are altogether eight poems in Wu Wenying's collection addressed to Prince Sirong and his wife. In view of the unmistakable allusions to the crown prince, five of these poems are to be dated to after the sixth month of 1260, that is, after Prince Sirong's son had been designated heir apparent.[76] That Wu Wenying probably enjoyed at this time the most secure and extended patronage in his life is indicated by his references to Prince Sirong in these poems by alluding to Liang Xiaowang of the Han, who was famous for being a patron to many scholars, and also by the four birthday poems to Prince Sirong and his wife, which can safely be assumed to have been composed on more than one birthday.

Wu Wenying died in the early 1260s.[77] His last years, probably until his death, were spent at the royal residence of Prince

[75] *Haoranzhai yatan* (*Cihua congbian* ed., vol. 1), 174.

[76] *QSC* 2879/4, 2882/5, 2885/2, 2886/5, 2915/2.

[77] The generally accepted date of Wu Wenying's death as suggested by Xia Chengtao is between 1260 and 1262. See Xia Chengtao, *Tang Song ciren nianpu*, p. 480. The reason he gives to support the choice is that important events in the next few years which might have been reflected in Wu's poetry, such as the completion in the first month of 1262 of Jia Sidao's imperially bestowed residence (the Houleyuan by West Lake), Wu Qian's death in the sixth month of 1262, Duzong's enthronement in the tenth month of 1264, and Prince Sirong's investiture as Regional Commandant of Wukang and Ningjiang in the eleventh month of 1264, are completely absent.

Sirong. In retrospect, it can be seen that Wu Wenying had lived for the greater part of his life as a guest-poet supported by the patronage of officials and aristocrats. The class of career poets was a growing phenomenon in the second half of the Southern Song, and, to all appearances, was well accepted by contemporary upper-class society. Some well-known figures of the Rivers and Lakes School lived this mode of life. Among *ci* poets, the most exalted "guest" is undoubtedly Jiang Kui (ca. 1155–ca. 1221), whose celebrated literary association with his one-time patron, the poet-statesman Fan Chengda (1120–1193), was almost a legend in its own time.[78] The nature and extent of these artist-patron relationships varied widely: some link fellow pleasure-seekers at parties; some are between bureaucrat and secretary-cum-literary advisor; others are between close friends and long-term companions. Ironically, of all patrons, Jia Sidao can claim the honor of having had a rare friend in a literary retainer who remained faithful to him even after he fell from power, and who eventually chose suicide rather than humiliation for his association with Jia.[79]

Apparently Wu Wenying did not feel that his relationship with Wu Qian warranted absolute loyalty. Therefore we find an extant poem addressed to Jia Sidao written after Wu Qian had been demoted and sent into exile. There is no indication that Wu Wenying was criticized for this by his contemporaries. Zhou Mi, who recorded gossip and opinions current in the late Song, certainly made no mention of it and thought only the best of Wu Wenying as a *ci* poet. This breach of integrity was first commented on by the editors in the *Siku quanshu zongmu tiyao*, which was written in a period when the issue of loyalty was a sensitive one.[80] Even so, no literary critic during the Qing paid any heed to this alleged moral blemish on Wu Wenying's life. Only with the growing repute of Wu Wenying's *ci* in the late Qing did this

---

[78] See Shuen-fu Lin, *The Transformation of the Chinese Lyrical Tradition*, pp. 53–54.

[79] A scholar by the name of Liao Yingzhong. See the biographical note and two *ci* by him (one is a birthday poem to Jia Sidao) in *QSC* 5/3318. See also Herbert Franke, "Chia Ssu-tao," in Wright, *Confucian Personalities*, pp. 232–33.

[80] For the historical background of the *Siku quanshu*, see L. C. Goodrich, *The Literary Inquisition of Ch'ien-lung* (Baltimore: Waverly Press, 1935).

biographical detail make its appearance in prefaces written to several editions of his *ci* printed in the period.[81]

Although Wu Wenying's ambiguous relationship with both Jia Sidao and Wu Qian may be a point of biographical interest, it does not in itself have any relevance to the study of his poetry. It is rather the mode of life he adopted as poet in the late Song period which is of significance. This mode of life is often reflected in the subject and occasion of his composition. As a period phenomenon, it fostered particular concerns in the writing of *ci*. Wu Wenying's *ci* stand in the fore of developments in Southern Song *ci* poetry that mirror aesthetic tendencies in the late Song. These are areas that will be explored in the following chapters.

[81] These prefaces are collected in *Siming congshu*, comp. Zhang Shouyong, vol. 1, pt. 1.

*2. THE ART OF SOUTHERN
SONG* CI

I. Introduction

By the time Wu Wenying wrote his *ci* poems in the mid-
thirteenth century, the *ci* genre had evolved from its origins in
popular lyrics in the late Tang and Five Dynasties period to a
highly refined and sophisticated art form toward the end of the
Southern Song. The process of transformation in the hands of
innovative *ci* poets who brought new stylistic and thematic di-
mensions to the genre through their practice has been delineated
in several modern studies. Most studies, however, focus on the
germinal period in the development of the *ci*, that is , from the
late Tang through the Northern Song period. Therefore only
works by significant poets of that time of generic innovation are
dealt with.[1] The transition from Northern Song to Southern
Song in the development of the *ci* is often regarded by modern
Chinese literary historians, albeit implicitly, as a transition from
maturity to decadence, from creativity to stagnation and artifici-
ality, or at best, to a mannered and overwrought sophistication.
The account given by Liu Dajie in his standard, often-quoted
History of the Development of Chinese Literature, after drawing on

[1] See for example James J. Y. Liu, *Major Lyricists of the Northern Sung*
(Princeton: Princeton University Press, 1974); Kang-i Sun Chang, *The Evolution
of Chinese Tz'u Poetry from Late T'ang to Northern Sung* (Princeton: Princeton
University Press, 1980); and Marsha L. Wagner, *The Lotus Boat: the Origins of
Chinese Tz'u Poetry in T'ang Popular Culture* (New York: Columbia University
Press, 1984). An exception is Shuen-fu Lin's study of Jiang Kui, *The Transforma-
tion of the Chinese Lyrical Tradition*.

various views of past critics, concludes with the judgment that: "The Southern Song produced many musicians; therefore its *ci* poetry has beauty of musical rhythm and of diction, formalistic elegance and antiquarian flavor. But it lacks life and character."[2] Lu Kanru and Feng Yuanjun in their work *History of Chinese Poetry* describe the state of *ci* poetry in the Southern Song as having gone from its zenith to its decline.[3] Hu Shi calls it disparagingly the *ci* of craftsmen,[4] and Wang Guowei is well known for his bias against Southern Song *ci*.[5]

The adverse view is by no means the only view. Southern Song *ci* poetry has had its share of enthusiasts and defenders as well. The Qing scholar and poet Zhu Yizun claimed that "only in the Southern Song did the *ci* attain perfection, and only at the end of the Song did it exhaust its transformations."[6] Wang Guowei complains that *ci* poets who came after Zhu Yizun too often succumbed to his opinion.[7]

Literary history indicates that the evaluation of a genre, a period style, a particular school or poet is never absolute. Aesthetic standards are often a matter of changing taste, and change implies a relativity of values. What is appreciated and praised by one group or one age may be condemned by others. Often, neglected authors are resurrected after long eclipse and given places of prominence in the literary pantheon. A given literary phenomenon, be it a particular genre, style, or school, may pass out of fashion, indeed become obsolete, but changed circumstances may bring about its revival. A case in point is the *ci* genre. After the Mongols conquered the Song, *ci* gradually fell out of fashion as an effective poetic medium. Through the Yuan and Ming dynasties, few poets wrote *ci* and scarcely any critical work on *ci* was produced during these centuries. With the revival of

---

[2] Liu Dajie, *Zhongguo wenxue fada shi* (Rpt. Taipei: Zhonghua shuju, 1962), 2:120.

[3] Lu Kanru and Feng Yuanjun, *Zhongguo shishi* (Beijing: Zuojia chubanshe, 1956), 3:670.

[4] Hu Shi, *Cixuan* (Shanghai: Commercial Press, 1928), p. 10.

[5] Wang Guowei, *Renjian cihua* (*Cihua congbian* ed., vol. 12).

[6] Zhu Yizun, "Cizong fafan," in *Cizong* (1691; rpt. Shanghai: Shanghai guji chubanshe, 1978), 1:10.

[7] Wang Guowei, *Renjian cihua* (*Cihua congbian* ed., vol. 12), p. 4263.

interest in *ci* poetry during the Qing dynasty, the Southern Song style as realized in the works of several representative poets came to be dominant. The poets and critics of major Qing schools upheld its several representatives as unquestioned models for emulation in the writing of *ci* poetry.

What then characterizes this Southern Song style, which is at once decadent and seminal? What were the concerns of *ci* poets at that time? Who were the influential figures and in what manner were they influential? How did Wu Wenying come to be regarded as a representative of this style? How does his poetry stand in relation to the poetics current in his time? And what stylistic characteristics constitute outstanding features of his poetry? Even if the *ci* had indeed ended with the Song dynasty these questions would still have relevance in an examination of generic demise, but in the light of the renaissance of *ci* in the Qing dynasty, their literary-historical significance is all the more crucial.

To answer some of the questions posed above, we must investigate the broader issue of period style and the specifics of Wu Wenying's style. Period style in *ci* involves trends in Southern Song poetics, and I shall survey developments in the Southern Song poetic scene in addition to examining two important late Song treatises on *ci* poetry, the *Yuefu zhimi* and the *Ciyuan*. I believe the controversy surrounding Wu's style, especially among late Qing and modern critics, is a reflection of the larger split between partisans and detractors of the Southern Song style versus the Northern Song style; an examination of the controversy will elucidate some of the broader issues involved. The final chapter discusses critical views on Wu Wenying's poetry.

I shall first of all define the term "Southern Song" as a designation of a literary style. Politically the Southern Song begins in 1127 with the fall of the Northern Song capital, Kaifeng, and the loss of the entire northern half of China to the Jurchens and ends in 1279, when the Mongols completed their conquest of the whole of China. Literary history, however, does not necessarily parallel political history. As defined by Wellek and Warren, "a period" in literary history "is a time section dominated by a system of literary norms, standards, and conventions, whose introduction, spread, diversification, integration, and disappearance can be traced."[8] Developments in the *ci* genre did not occur overnight with the political changeover. *Ci* poets such as Li Qingzhao (1084–1147) and Zhu Dunru (ca. 1084–ca. 1175), who lived through the traumatic political transition, continued to write in a style that is relatively straightforward and allusion-free and generally associated with the overall Northern Song style, though their themes and tone might have changed. Conversely, the roots of what is now commonly referred to as the Southern Song style are recognized as being traceable to the works of the Northern Song master Zhou Bangyan. The Southern Song style should properly be called the late Southern Song style, since its normative poetics did not crystallize until the generation of poets who wrote after the turn of the century, in the 1200s. Even when the prefix is not applied, in speaking of a Southern Song style, literary critics and historians are usually referring to the "late" style.

II. *Trends in Southern Song* Ci *Poetry—Late Twelfth Century*

The political situation in the first half of the Southern Song period produced *ci* poets with a distinct voice; these were the "patriotic poets," thus designated during the new dawn of Chinese nationalistic consciousness in the twentieth century. These poets often wrote in a grand and heroic manner (*haofang*) lamenting the fall of the Northern Song and expressing their pain and frustration at the Southern Song government's failure to recover the lost territory. Although the thematic and linguistic scope of the *haofang* style was developed and established in the Northern Song, notably by the versatile genius Su Shi (1036–1101),[9] as a period style, Southern Song patriotic-heroic

[8] Rene Wellek and Austin Warren, *A Theory of Literature* (New York: Harcourt, Brace & World, 1962), p. 265.

[9] For Su Shi's contribution to the development of the *ci* genre, see Kang-i Sun Chang, *The Evolution of Chinese Tz'u Poetry from Late T'ang to Northern Sung*, pp. 158–206, and James J. Y. Liu, *Major Lyricists of the Northern Sung*, pp. 121–60.

poetry is constituted by the expressive voice of the poets, which reveals a common concern and emotion. Shuen-fu Lin observes that "during the beginning decades of the Southern Song period, songwriters tended to adopt a strong rhythm and an intensely propositional language."[10] He cites the prolific Xin Qiji (1140–1207) as the prime example of this trend toward a discursive style. What is here called the "expressive voice" and Lin's "strong rhythm and propositional language" are evidently two sides of the same coin. *Ci* poems in this "expressive" mode tend to exhibit hypotactic syntax—the necessary linguistic medium for propositional language, the incorporation of many prose elements such as pronouns and particles, a "masculine" vocabulary with an abundance of historical allusions, and hyperbolic diction. The following anthology piece by Xin Qiji exhibits almost all the characteristics enumerated above:

To the tune *Yongyu le*
Recalling ancient times at Beigu Pavilion in Jingkou

1   Amid mountains and rivers of a thousand ages
    No hero can be found
    In the domain of Sun Zhongmou.
    Dance pavilions and song-filled terraces—
5   All romance and charm in the end are
    Beaten by rain, swept away by the winds.
    Weeds and trees in twilight
    Along common streets and lanes—
    People say this is where Jinu lived.
10 I imagine in those years, with golden spears and
                armored horses,
    Their force like tigers would swallow up ten thousand
                miles.

    In the Yuanjia reign, carelessly
    They offered sacrifice on Mount Langjuxu,
    Gaining only panic-stricken glances to the north.
15 Forty-three years since,

---

[10] Shuen-fu Lin, *The Transformation of the Chinese Lyrical Tradition*, p. 183.

Gazing at the scene I still recall
Beacon fires along the road to Yangzhou.
How can I bear to look back?
20   Beneath the shrine of Bili,
A strain of temple crows and ritual drums.
Who can I depend on to ask: Lian Po is indeed old,
Can he still eat that much rice?

(*QSC* 3/1954)

京口北固亭懷古

千古江山，
英雄無覓，
孫仲謀處。
舞榭歌臺，
風流總被，
雨打風吹去。
斜陽草樹，
尋常巷陌，
人道寄奴曾住。
想當年，
金戈鐵馬，
氣吞萬里如虎。

元嘉草草，
封狼居胥，
贏得倉皇北顧。
四十三年，
望中猶記，
烽火揚州路。
可堪回首，
佛狸祠下，
一片神鴉社鼓。
憑誰問，
廉頗老矣，
尚能飯否。

   This poem is replete with historical allusions, in particular
those with reference to military-political figures or events as-
sociated with Jingkou (present day Zhenjiang in Jiangsu

province) from the Six Dynasties period.[11] Xin Qiji, while reflecting on the political situation in the divided China of the Six Dynasties, implies an uncanny parallel between it and that of his own day. The diction is masculine: we find hyperbole, references to heroes and villains, and images of martial fanfare. What it expresses are the intense feelings of a frustrated heroic temperament. The emotional content of the poem is reinforced by the syntactic rhythm. To see this, we should be aware of the common practice of poets writing in the tune pattern *Yongyu le* to begin the first strophe, which consists of three lines of four characters each, with the first two lines syntactically parallel (4//4/4), as exemplified by all three poems Wu Wenying wrote to this tune pattern.[12] Moreover, these parallel lines would be end-stopped sentences. The structure of the strophic unit is balanced, with rhetorical and semantic pauses coinciding with the syntactic and metrical breaks. The slow movement thus created allows the reader to concentrate on the images presented line by line, as in Su Shi's beautiful opening to his *Yongyu le*:

> The bright moon is like frost,
> The fine wind like water—
> Infinite is this pure scene.

(QSC 1/302)

> 明月如霜，
> 好風如水，
> 清景無限。

Or in Wu Wenying's lines:

> Storing snow, the clouds are low,
> Sweeping sand, the wind is gusty;
> Startled wild geese lose their formation.

(QSC 4/2910)

> 閣雪雲低，
> 捲沙風急，
> 驚雁失序。

[11] For an explanation of the allusions see Zheng Qian, *Cixuan* (Taipei: Huagang chubanshe, 1970), pp. 100–101, and Irving Y. Lo, *Hsin Ch'i-chi* (New York: Twayne Publishers, 1971), pp. 71–72.

[12] *QSC* 4/2910.

In contrast, Xin Qiji opens his poem with three run-on lines which must be read in full to arrive at semantic completion. Thus in contrast to the others, Xin's syntactic rhythm has a forceful, sweeping movement that accords well with the intense emotional undertone. The second strophe, with a 4/4/5 metrical division, again provides a choice between two structures: 4//4/5 or 4/4/5, and Xin rushes on with his continuous rhythm. In Xin's poems of the *man* type (long tunes),[13] he very often employs this discursive syntax in which strophic units are enjambed until the rhyme word is reached.

These characteristics as exemplified by Xin Qiji became the stock-in-trade of the *haofang* mode of *ci* poetry. With the conventionalization of the original stylistic impulse, which was directed towards expression of masculine, heroic sentiments, be they anger or grief, there was a tendency among later practitioners and imitators of this style toward further amplification, often resulting in a gratuitous gruffness.[14] Liu Kezhuang (1187–1269), Wu Wenying's slightly older contemporary, was a dedicated heir of this school whose work clearly shows the limits of the style; his collection of *ci* poetry is replete with examples written in the heroic mode. Liu Kezhuang was himself a great admirer of Xin Qiji, and by that yardstick he is judged by later critics to be inferior.[15] Among his own contemporaries, Liu Kezhuang was something of an anomaly in his consistent practice of this style. For the next wave of the heroic style only arose with the fall of the Song when the voice of patriotism was again heard in the *ci* poetry of Confucian-minded men such as Liu

---

[13] Traditional criticism divides *ci* patterns according to length into *xiaoling* (short lyrics under 58 characters) and *manci* (slow or long tunes between 59 and 240 characters). The *manci* are further divided into *zhongdiao* (medium length tunes with 59 to 90 characters) and *changdiao* (long tunes over 90 characters). See Wang Li, *Hanyu shilü xue* (Shanghai: Shanghai jiaoyu chubanshe, 1963), p. 518. Since the popularization of *manci* among the literati after Liu Yong (985–1053), it remained the dominant form used throughout the Song.

[14] This is a common view among Qing critics. See for example Zhou Ji's comment, "Later poets tried to imitate Jiaxuan (Xin) by using crude heroics," *Jiecunzhai lunci zazhu* (*Cihua congbian* ed., vol. 5), p. 1627.

[15] Although the Qing critic Chen Tingzhuo thought that Liu Kezhuang was far inferior to Xin, he still considered Liu one of the more able *ci* poets of this style. *Baiyu zhai cihua* (*Cihua congbian* ed., vol. 11), p. 3818.

Chenweng (1232–1297) and Wen Tianxiang (1236–1283). Even then the heroic mode was far from being the mainstream of *ci* practice at the time.[16]

Toward the last years of the twelfth century, among such aging luminaries of the scholar-official circle of poets as Xin Qiji and Fan Chengda (1120–1193) there moved a younger literary figure whose slim volume of eighty-odd surviving *ci* poems (reinforced by his almost legendary image as a bona fide poet whose life was completely devoted to the art of poetry) has secured him the reputation as a major poet of the late Southern Song style. This figure is Jiang Kui. Jiang Kui's significance in the development of Southern Song *ci* is twofold. First, with his profound knowledge of music, he redirected attention to the musical technicalities of *ci*. Second, the literary aspect of his *ci* poetry exhibited certain incipient tendencies away from the language and style of the heroic mode still prevalent in his day. As important as these two traits are in Jiang Kui's *ci*, before elaborating on them it is necessary to point out the transitional and hybrid character of his style.

Jiang Kui's small collection of *ci* poetry contains numerous examples of linguistic and stylistic features more akin to the heroic mode than to the late Southern Song style; particularly in diction and syntax, of prose features found in the more explicit rhetoric of the heroic mode. Occurrences of personal pronouns—*wo* and *wu* ("I"), *jun* and *gong* ("you"), and *yi* ("he, she, it")—are common; there is a high incidence of sentence final particles such as *zai, yi, ye, yu, ye*, and of conjunctions—*ran, er, ji*—used in prose; and also of function words (*xuzi*). An extremely unpoetic phrase such as *ran ze fei yu* ("But then is it not so?") may be rare, and perhaps imitative of Xin Qiji's style since it occurs in a poem written to match Xin's rhymes (*QSC* 3/2188). But prosy lines such as the following are common:

---

[16] By the late Southern Song, the language of the *ci* had evolved a metaphorical and allegorical dimension, and major poets of the time such as Zhou Mi, Zhang Yan, and Wang Yisun chose to express their lament over the collapse of the Song in an oblique or allegorical mode rather than the heroic and expressive *haofang* style. See their relevant works contained in Huang Zhaoxian, *Yuefu buti yanjiu ji jianzhu* (Hong Kong: Xuewen chubanshe, 1975).

I am drunk and want to sleep, it keeps me company.

(QSC 3/2177)

我醉欲眠伊伴我

Master Wei has gone.

(QSC 3/2181)

韋郎去也

My inspiration is also vast.

(QSC 3/2187)

吾興亦悠哉

Deictic and modal elements bring semantic explicitness to the poem by imparting an immediacy to its tone. The former points directly to the speaker or to the recipient or reader of the poem or to the thing spoken about; the latter indicates the mental and emotional state of the speaker: by indicating a statement of fact, an expression of doubt or surprise, the speaker lets his mood be known and establishes a point of contact with the reader. Function words, often used in lead-word (*lingzi*) positions, fulfill a similar function by contributing semantic explicitness. (This category will be examined in the next section.)

What Jiang Kui's poetry is noted for, almost to the exclusion of the features we have examined above, is the emergence of a new poetic sensibility, which in time came to characterize the late Song style. Stylistically this poetic sensibility is most apparent in a certain semantic ambiguity arising from the implicit embodiment of emotion in imagery, the use of a more complex language involving frequent allusions and metonyms, and a denser syntax, elements all contributing to the quality of "opacity" (*ge*) Wang Guowei found so objectionable in Southern Song *ci* poetry.[17] In order to see these stylistic elements in context, let us look at *Shuying*, one of Jiang Kui's two famous pieces on the plum blossom:

1   Mossy branches adorned with jade—
        They are tiny green birds roosting together on a branch.
        Meeting her on a journey

---

[17] Wang Guowei, *Renjian cihua* (*Cihua congbian* ed., vol. 12), pp. 4250–51.

5   At twilight by the corner of a fence,
Where wordless she leans next to tall bamboos.
Zhaojun unaccustomed to tartar sands far away
Only longed in secret for her native Southland.
I imagine the one with jade pendants returning on a
        moonlit night,
10   Transformed into this flower, hidden and solitary.

I still recall in the old tale of the secluded palace,
That beauty was asleep then
When one alighted beside her dark moth-eyebrows.
Don't be like the spring wind,
15   Heedless of beauty in full bloom,
But early arrange for it a gold chamber.
If you let one petal flow away with the waves,
You will be resenting the sad tune for the Jade Dragon
        flute;
If one waits till then to seek again the subtle scent,
20   It will have entered the horizontal scroll by the small
        window.[18]

(QSC 3/2182)

苔枝綴玉。
有翠禽小小，
枝上同宿。
客裏相逢，
籬角黃昏，
無言自倚修竹。
昭君不慣胡沙遠，
但暗憶、江南江北。
想佩環、月夜歸來，
化作此花幽獨。

猶記深宮舊事，
那人正睡裏，
飛近蛾綠。
莫似春風，
不管盈盈，

---

[18] Cf. Shuen-fu Lin's discussion on this poem, *The Transformation of the Chinese Lyrical Tradition*, pp. 172ff.

42

早與安排金屋。
還教一片隨波去，
又卻怨、玉龍哀曲。
等恁時、重覓幽香，
已入小窗橫幅。

The syntactic structure of the poem remains on the whole hypotactic and explicit, particularly toward the end when the lines are structured with conjunctions. The complete suppression of subjective emotional expression, however, produces an ambiguity in the overall meaning. One is left with a series of images and allusions connected by grammar without ever being shown the private emotion that should unify them. Traditional critics have always been eager to go hunting for allegory in obscure poems that offer isolated hints. In this case, the allusion to Wang Zhaojun, the Han palace lady who was married off to a Xiongnu chieftain and spent her life in exile in barbarian desertlands triggers a forced comparison with the last Northern Song emperor who was captured and taken north along with his imperial concubines by the Jurchen invaders. A more plausible interpretation is offered by modern scholars who read in it the poet's reminiscence of a woman associated in his mind with the plum blossom.[19] Certainly the first stanza is pervaded by feminine presence—the personification of the plum tree as a beautiful woman and the blossoms seen as the incarnation of Wang Zhaojun. The poem, however, is not structured on the theme of reminiscence; it belongs to a poetry of mood in which certain generalized moods and feelings are represented in a metaphorical and allusive language. The pervading mood in the first stanza is one of solitariness and seclusion, and in the second, regret at the transience of beauty symbolized by the fading plum blossoms.

At this stage, a unified metaphorical dimension in the *ci* (particularly in the *yongwu* subgenre to which this poem belongs) was still in the process of development. Therefore, there was as yet insufficient ground for integral hermeneutics. Since the linguistic appurtenances are there, we will first proceed to examine what they are before seeing how they are used to create a new

[19] *Ibid.*, pp. 172–77.

mode in Southern Song *ci* poetry, particularly in the *yongwu* subgenre as it came to be treated in the late Song.

III. The Yuefu Zhimi *and* Ciyuan: *Poetics and Aesthetics in the Late Song Style of* Ci *Poetry (Thirteenth Century)*

Wu Wenying did not leave to posterity any critical theoretical writings on *ci* poetry. But fortunately his views on the matter have been recorded in a small treatise on the art of *ci* writing entitled the *Yuefu zhimi* [*A Guidebook to Song-lyrics*] written by a contemporary fellow poet Shen Yifu (?–after 1279) some time in the second half of the thirteenth century.[20] The *Yuefu zhimi* is an extremely terse work containing a brief introductory section followed by twenty-eight items, each consisting of a few sentences at most, on various aspects of the composition of *ci* poetry. The stylistic principles it espouses evidence current tastes in late Southern Song *ci* poetics, indicating the prevalence of an aesthetic formalism represented by Wu Wenying's style of *ci* poetry. This work is therefore very valuable both for the insights it offers into aesthetic preferences in late Song *ci* and for its exposition of the characteristics of Wu Wenying's style. The other treatise to be examined, the *Ciyuan*, was written by Zhang Yan and dates from the early 1300s.[21] It is in two *juan*: the first deals entirely with the musical composition of *ci*; the second concerns itself with the literary craft of the *ci* and is similar to the *Yuefu zhimi* in format.[22] While the *Ciyuan* affirms and elaborates some of the same concepts found in the *Yuefu zhimi*, it supplements the

[20] Shen Yifu was a native of Zhenze in Jiangsu. His reputation rested on being a neo-Confucian scholar of some learning. He had lectured at the White Deer Grotto Academy where Zhu Xi had taught. None of Shen's other writings have survived, the *Yuefu zhimi* being his only extant work. See Xia Chengtao and Cai Songyun, *Ciyuan zhu Yuefu zhimi jianshi* (Beijing: Renmin wenxue chubanshe, 1981), p. 89. There are three poems in Wu's collection addressed to Shen (*Jiangnan hao*, *QSC* 2903/2, *Yongyu le* 2910/3 and *Shengsheng man* 2930/5). In all three Wu matched the rhymes used by Shen in his poems.

[21] Preface by Qian Liangyou dated 1317, see Xia Chengtao and Cai Songyun, *ibid.*, p. 50.

[22] For a summary of the *juan* on music, see Rulan Pian, *Sonq Dynasty Musical Sources and Their Interpretation* (Cambridge: Harvard University Press, 1967), pp. 21–22.

44

Yuefu zhimi by postulating what is in effect an opposition poetics to that embodied in Wu Wenying's *ci* style and expounded by Shen Yifu. Both because of the similarities and differences in their aesthetic emphases and because of their relative proximity in time of composition, these two works are extremely important for an understanding of both prevailing and evolving poetic tastes and norms in the late Song and immediate post-Song era.

In the introductory section of the *Yuefu zhimi* Shen Yifu begins by recounting his first meeting in 1242 with Wu Wenying's younger brother Weng Yuanlong, and in 1243 with Wu himself, and their subsequent discussions on the art of writing *ci*. Shen, in all modesty as a late beginner in the genre, acknowledges the difficulties of this art and his indebtedness to the two brothers. He next explains that he was recording their views on writing *ci* to refer to when students began to seek advice from him on the subject. He then sets forth the four tenets to be observed in the writing of *ci*.

It is obvious both from the phrasing of the introduction and from corroborating features in Wu Wenying's poetry that Shen's statements on the four tenets, if not quoted verbatim from Wu, are certainly based on the views of Wu and his brother. As pointed out in the biographical chapter, Wu Wenying ranked higher as a *ci* poet than his younger brother; furthermore, judging from the close relationship between the theories expressed in this work and Wu's practice in his *ci* composition, it can safely be assumed that Wu Wenying is the voice of authority behind these words. The four principles on the composition of *ci* enumerated by Shen Yifu are:

> The tones of words should be in harmony with the music; if they do not harmonize, the result would be just *shi* poetry in lines of unequal length. The diction should be elegant, otherwise it would resemble that of popular songs. The use of words should not be too explicit, as explicitness is blunt and abrupt and lacks deep, prolonged aftereffects. The expression of sentiments should not be too grandiose; otherwise you end up with wildness and eccentricity and lose sensibility.[23]

[23] *Yuefu zhimi* (*Cihua congbian* ed., vol. 1), p. 229.

From the above formulations we can extrapolate the key concepts of musicality, elegance, indirection, and sensibility. Among these, sensibility can be subsumed under elegance as they both deal with language and expression; though indirection begins with how poetic language should be used, it concerns the ideal method or manner of representation. In the following sections, these concepts will be correlated with critical comments in the two works and examined in the context of the development of *ci*.

Music was an integral part of the *ci* genre as it was practiced in Song times,[24] yet it became a problematic aspect quite early on in the development of the *ci*. Already in Su Shi's time, critics were gibing at the unwieldiness of some of his *ci* poetry for singing; it was said that the tonal patterns of the words often did not accord with the notes of the melody.[25] Shortly after, the poetess Li Qingzhao, who had an expert knowledge in music, criticized the unmusicality of *ci* written by literati scholar-officials such as Su Shi and Ouyang Xiu, saying that their song lyrics were but *shi* poetry, which does not repeat phrases and lines (of equal length). The crux of the matter, as she saw it, seemed to lie in the much finer tonal and harmonic distinctions and interrelations that exist in *ci* poetry. Practitioners of *shi* poetry, accustomed to the simple distinction between level and oblique tones, could be guilty of neglecting these.[26] Li Qingzhao's disapprobation may have been part of a general reaction against a perceptible decline in the musicality of *ci* poetry. Her near contemporary Zhou Bangyan, the expert musician and *ci* poet who came to be highly revered

[24] Song *ci* poetry was written to music and sung. But the practice from the inception of the genre for poets to write words to existing tunes instead of always inventing new ones led to increasing attention being paid to the number of characters and the sequences of tones and rhymes used in the tune patterns, thus laying a foundation for the separation of music from the metrical pattern. After *ci* music was lost, the post-Song practice of "filling in words" became and continues to be the only procedure in writing *ci* poetry. As my focus is on the literary aspect of the *ci*, discussion of music will be limited to the literary-historical perspective, omitting the theoretical. For writings on the music of *ci*, see Rulan Pian, *Sonq Dynasty Musical Sources and Their Interpretation*.

[25] Wu Zeng, *Nenggaizhai manlu* (*Cihua congbian* ed., vol. 1), p. 83.

[26] Li Qingzhao's "Cilun," recorded in Hu Zi, *Tiaoxi yuyin conghua* (Beijing: Renmin wenxue chubanshe, 1981), 2:254.

and imitated in the late Southern song, devoted considerable effort to examining and determining correct versions of old music scores while he served as Director of the Bureau of Music from 1116 to 1118 during the last years of the Northern Song.

In the wake of the flight south after the Jurchen invasion, it was inevitable that numerous *ci* music scores would be lost. When the Southern Song populace finally settled down to a comfortable life in the lush environment and thriving economy of the south, poets again began paying attention to the technical aspects of *ci* music. Toward the end of the twelfth century, Jiang Kui and the circle he moved in (including Fan Chengda and his highly trained singing girls) pursued the matter with avid dedication. Jiang Kui's long prefaces to his *ci* poems often contain his musings on music, harmony and prosody, and describe the process by which he resolved certain difficulties in the musical score.[27] The music of *ci*, however, had become such a specialized and intellectual art that it necessarily remained confined to members of the cultured elite who had the leisure, learning, and inclination to pursue its intricacies.

The preoccupation of *ci* specialists with the music and language of *ci* was in inverse proportion to the popularity of their *ci* in society at large.[28] By Shen Yifu's time, the process of separation between the text and the music of *ci* was becoming acute, as each tended to fall into the "possession" of discrete social groups. Shen observed that no one would sing literary *ci* because they did not fit the music, while on the other hand the *ci* that were sung— written by professional musicians and entertainers—entirely lacked literary merit.[29] Toward the end of the Song, when the *ci* musical tradition was still alive but becoming an esoteric subject, it was natural for concerned *ci* poets to emphasize what was in fact a defining generic characteristic. By the end of the Song and into the early years of the Yuan dynasty, this preoccupation

---

[27] For example, see the prefaces to *Manjiang hong* (*QSC* 3/2176), *Zhizhao*, (*QSC* 3/2182–83), and *Qiliang fan*, (*QSC* 3/2183–84).

[28] The divergence between *ci* and popular songs in the Southern Song can be deduced from Shen and Zhang's admonitions to *ci* writers not to be influenced by popular songs in language or music.

[29] *Yuefu zhimi* (*Cihua congbian* ed., vol. 1), pp. 232–33.

sometimes became an obsession, as exemplified by Zhang Yan. The entire first *juan* of the *Ciyuan* consists of a most thorough erudite treatment of musical theory. Zhang Yan has often been faulted by later critics for his fastidious concern with music to the detriment of the literary aspect of the *ci*.[30]

Wu Wenying, in his own time and after, was known and admired for his expertise in music. He created a number of new tune patterns and his *ci* are praised as musically correct.[31] This pronouncement in the *Yuefu zhimi* on the importance of strict adherence to musical structure underlines his concern for formal perfection.

As crucial as harmony between words and music was tantamount to an authentic practice of writing *ci* composition, that is, *ci* as song words should be singable, it is clear that the practitioners of the genre at large were focusing on the literary aspects of the genre. In the main, late Southern Song *ci* poets paid meticulous attention to form (structure) and language (various aspects of style), as both the *Yuefu zhimi* and the *Ciyuan* indicate. Both contain discussions of such structural aspects of the *ci* as stanzaic transition, opening, closure, and line structure; literary devices such as allusion, metonymy, and rhyme; and critical theories on diction, elegance and so on.[32] And, as we will see, the remaining three tenets set down by Shen Yifu all relate to the literary-textual composition of *ci* poetry.

The second tenet states that the diction of *ci* should be elegant (*ya*). The concept of elegance had by this time become central to Southern Song views of the *ci*. It had appeared earlier in South-

---

[30] The passage often cited for criticism relates how Zhang Yan's father Zhang Shu, whom he regarded an exemplary *ci* writer, had changed one character in a line three times before he felt that it agreed with the music. Meaning hardly seemed to matter as the sentence went from "The latticed window is deep" to "The latticed window is dark" to "The latticed window is bright." See *Ciyuan* (*Cihua congbian* ed., vol. 1), p. 203.

[31] In discussions of tonal and musical aspects of *ci* poetry, Wu Wenying is often cited for illustration along with Zhou Bangyan and Jiang Kui as good models. See for example Wu Mei, *Cixue tonglun* (Hong Kong: Taiping shuju, 1964), pp. 10–11 and p. 41.

[32] For further reference, see the convenient headings in the table of contents made for the annotated edition of the two works in Xia Chengtao and Cai Songyun, *Ciyuan zhu Yuefu zhimi jianshi*.

ern Song remarks on *ci*, and the term *yaci* ("elegant *ci*") was incorporated into the titles of several collections and anthologies of *ci* poetry.[33] Its importance was in a sense fortuitous—it arises from the character's original definition as *zhengsheng* ("correct, proper tone") and its classical association with music: *yayue* was the proper music of ancient times. From this primary meaning derives the secondary meaning of culture and refinement, which became the principle behind a poetics of elegance.

Of the six poets on whose *ci* poetry Shen Yifu proffered pithy evaluative comments, four were criticized for varying degrees of vulgarity, the antithesis of elegance.[34] Invariably they were faulted for the incorporation (inadvertent or otherwise) of "low vulgar" language in their *ci*. Basically this vulgar language breaks down into colloquial expressions and hackneyed clichés in the vocabulary of popular singers and musicians.[35] It is interesting to note that this colloquial style of *ci*, which first raised a few eyebrows among the literati when the Northern Song *ci* poet Liu Yong (985–1053) practiced it with enormous popularity, had persisted down to the end of the Song despite all the criticism leveled at it from more orthodox quarters. Li Qingzhao for one said of Liu Yong that his language was "below dust." Wang Zhuo

[33] Li Qingzhao in her "Cilun" had appraised the *ci* poetry of the Southern Tang kingdom of the Five Dynasties period as having "cultured elegance." See Hu Zi, *Tiaoxi yuyin conghua*, 2:254. Wang Zhuo recorded in his *Biji manzhi* that Moqi Yong (ca. 1050–ca. 1130), Zhou Bangyan's colleague in the Bureau of Music, divided his *ci* poetry into two categories: "elegant *ci*" and "erotic *ci*." See *Biji manzhi* (*Cihua congbian* ed., Vol. 1), p. 33. Wang Zhuo also remarks that *ci* poetry should exhibit the elegance and correctness of ancient music. See Luo Genze's discussion of Wang Zhuo's critical bias in his *Zhongguo wenxue pipingshi* (Shanghai: Gudian wenxue chubanshe, 1957), 3:252–53. The modern scholar Zhao Wanli has observed that elegance in *ci* was highly esteemed in the Southern Song. He demonstrates this self-conscious concern regarding elegance among Southern Song *ci* poets and anthologists by quoting several titles of *ci* collections using the character *ya*. See Zhao's preface in his *Jiaoji Song Jin Yuan ren ci* (Taipei: Tailian guofeng chubanshe, 1971), 1:2a.

[34] They are the Northern Song poet Liu Yong and the three Southern Song poets Kang Yuzhi, Shi Yue, and Sun Weixin.

[35] Shen used the term *shijing ju* ("market place expressions") and *jiaofang zhi xi* ("usage of professional musicians") in his criticism of Sun Weixin and Shi Yue respectively. See also Cai Songyun's discussion of *bisu yu* ("vulgar language") in Xia Chengtao and Cai Songyun, *Ciyuan zhu Yuefu zhimi jianshi*, p. 47, n. 4.

(fl. 1149) caustically compared the "substandard" but influential popularity of Liu's style to the "poison in the saliva of a wild fox." [36] This persistence of the "vulgar" is a sign of the complex and unstable nature of the *ci* genre, of its reversible metamorphosis from popular song to literary genre, and of the resultant ambivalent boundary between the two that our experts were attempting to define clearly. At the same time, prosaic elements derived from the language of the classics and histories, prominent in the heroic style, are considered stiff and affected, and therefore also inappropriate for the delicate and elegant diction expected in *ci*.

In the above, elegance in diction is negatively defined: the avoidance of colloquialisms and banal clichés forms the basis for elegance. Beyond this, affirmative statements on elegance in diction are disappointingly meager and singularly uninspiring in both the *Yuefu zhimi* and the *Ciyuan*. Both authors express the opinion that it derives from the skillful integration of lines of *shi* poetry, especially those by Tang poets. On this point, Shen Yifu opines that "in seeking [material for] diction, one should look for fine and unvulgar lines from the poetry of Wen Tingyun, Li He and Li Shangyin," while Zhang Yan praises Wu Wenying and the Northern Song poet He Zhu for their skill in creating a refined, polished diction by adapting lines from the poetry of Wen Tingyun and Li He.[37] The ornamented style of the late Tang obviously had great appeal to Southern Song taste. To them Zhou Bangyan, who continued to be admired after the Song for his "craft" above all else by generations of *ci* critics, epitomized the artful technique of borrowing.[38] The poem most often quoted for illustration of this technique is among Zhou Bangyan's most famous pieces. Written to the tune pattern *Ruilong yin*, the poem is almost a pastiche of adapted lines from

---

[36] Li Qingzhao, "Cilun," in Hu Zi, *Tiaoxi yuyin conghua*. Wang Zhuo, *Biji manzhi* (*Cihua congbian* ed., vol. 1), pp. 34–35.

[37] *Yuefu zhimi* (*Cihua congbian* ed., vol. 1), p. 231. *Ciyuan* (*Cihua congbian* ed., vol. 1), pp. 206–7.

[38] *Yuefu zhimi, ibid.*, pp. 229–30. *Ciyuan, ibid.*, p. 201. N.B. The term *shiju* is misprinted as *ciju* in this edition.

poems and prefaces to poems of no less than four Tang poets.[39] The adapted lines, however, are woven so naturally into the context that the result is a stylistically unified poem highly admired by discerning readers of the *ci*. Elegance, then, is sophistication and refinement grounded in a literary tradition. That what nowadays would be regarded as a kind of plagiarism was looked upon as a primary technique of achieving poetic elegance should not be too surprising in view of a predominant traditional Chinese attitude towards literary creation that is essentially backward looking—it seeks to build on, echo, and transform an older tradition. During the Song, this attitude was particularly pronounced in the poetic theory and method of the influential Jiangxi school of *shi* poetry.[40] Since a few prominent Jiangxi school poets wrote in both genres, it is conceivable that their views had some impact on the general approach to poetry.[41]

As we have seen, the concept of elegance goes beyond the domain of diction; it also governs music and the expression of sentiment, areas in which its application reflects the original meaning of *ya*. Speaking of music, Shen Yifu advised that *ci* poets of his "generation should choose tunes of classic elegance as models and should not write [words] to those that have been popularized."[42] Concerning sentiment, Zhang Yan admonished

---

[39] Xia Chengtao gives the sources for Zhou's adapted lines in Xia Chengtao and Cai Songyun, *Ciyuan zhu Yuefu zhimi jianshi*, p. 30, n. 1. See also James Liu's explication of this poem in *Major Lyricists of the Northern Sung*, pp. 165–73.

[40] Their poetics of *duotai huangu* ("creative imitation") stated simplistically— to express a new or different idea based on an old word formula and conversely, to express a similar idea (to an old one) in different words—rests heavily on a revered pre-existing body of poetry. On the origins of these concepts in Huang Tingjian (1045–1105), see Adele A. Rickett, "Method and Intuition: The Poetic Theories of Huang T'ing-chien," in *Chinese Approaches to Literature from Confucius to Liang Ch'i-ch'ao*, ed. Adele A. Rickett (Princeton: Princeton University Press, 1978), pp. 97–119.

[41] In the Southern Song, the influence of Jiangxi School poetics was pervasive. *Shi* poets often began their poetic careers as apprentices in this school, though just as often they rejected it later (e.g., Yang Wanli, Lu You, and Jiang Kui). Jiangxi School poetics emphasizes technique; many terms from their critical vocabulary, such as *jufa* ("line structure"), *juyan* ("eye of the line"), and *shiyan* ("eye of the poem"), were adopted by *ci* critics. See Zhu Dongrun, *Zhongguo wenxue pipingshi dagang* (n.p.: Kaiming shudian, 1944), p. 202.

[42] *Yuefu zhimi* (*Cihua congbian* ed., vol. 1), pp. 234–35.

that "when *ci* poetry becomes the slave of passion, it loses its elegant and correct tone." The lines he quoted for criticism, such as "For her my tears fall," "I am afraid that she will ask and ask for news, / Thinness will ruin the lustre of her looks," and "A lot of trouble / All because at the time, / For a moment I sowed love," are by no less a poet than Zhou Bangyan.[43] What is lacking in these lines for Southern Song taste is art and subtlety. According to the late Song ideal of elegance, they all fall short because of the overly simple and direct manner in which excessively emotive statements are made, some to the point of sounding facile. Though Zhang Yan did not comment on it, the heavily colloquial tone of these lines would render them twice removed from elegance. In the same vein, Zhang Yan also criticizes the Southern Song heroic mode practiced by Xin Qiji and his followers for being inelegant.[44] Obviously the virile spirit and assertive language of the *haofang* style are too direct. As noted above, Shen Yifu's fourth tenet, concerning sensibility, really pertains to an aspect of elegance and, what is more, it is directed against the same virility of expression, characteristic of the heroic mode, that Zhang Yan censures. Both Shen and Zhang's injunctions on music and the various aspects of elegance are at bottom reactions by critics who followed and tried to uphold the orthodox line against the expressivity in both the heroic and popular trends in the *ci* genre.

Elegance in *ci* poetry meant to these poets and critics an aesthetic quality that can be best achieved by indirection, both in manner of expression and in the creation of an allusive and connotative language. This poetic language functions like a prism refracting a source of light into a rich spectrum of colors—the surface text of the poem is extended and enriched by levels of intertextual meaning. So that in fact if we were to point to an underlying stylistic principle in the *Yuefu zhimi*, it is that of indirection as stated in the third tenet: "The use of words should not be explicit, as explicitness is blunt and abrupt and lacks prolonged aftereffects." *Lu* means literally "exposed"

[43] *Ciyuan* (*Cihua congbian* ed., vol. 1), p. 218.
[44] *Ibid.*, p. 219.

or "open," therefore "overt" or "explicit." Its opposite is advocated by Shen Yifu, spokesman for the poet whose style is an extreme embodiment of this principle. Shen's discussions of closure, allusions to names, metonyms (*daizi*), and poems on objects all relate to the principle of indirection on one level or another. The passage on closure is interesting for its expression of Chinese poetic sensibility:

> Closure should evoke endless reverberations. It is best to conclude a poem with a scene which embodies emotion, for although a closure which expresses emotion is acceptable, it can easily sound trite and explicit.[45]

That is to say, an image that conceals and hints at the emotion is preferred to undisguised emotion. The assumption is that a feeling stated directly is apprehended at once, leaving no scope for further evocation, whereas the successful merging of a concrete image and an unstated emotion creates an elusiveness that expands the reader's experience of the poem. If we look at the example he cites of the closure to Zhou Bangyan's aforementioned *Ruilong yin*, "Heartbroken in the courtyard, / A curtain full of windblown catkins," we will see that the visual image of the last line is neither random nor purely descriptive; it is selected to elicit emotional response and interpretation. Its representational ambiguity, however, makes the image not an obvious, definite symbol but the nucleus of a range of possible associations in a complex network of echoes and correspondences both within the text of the poem itself and intertextually. In this case, a sense of confusion, separation, forlornness are all suggested by the profusion of detached, floating catkins. Traditional Chinese critics value this kind of elusive closural imagery highly for its rich suggestiveness;[46] it has become an artistic means to be consciously followed.

---

[45] *Yuefu zhimi* (*Cihua congbian* ed., vol. 1), pp. 230–31.

[46] Traditional Chinese poetics has placed great importance on the proper distribution between *jing* ("natural scene") and *qing* ("lyrical feelings"), i.e. on the interaction between image-oriented and expression-oriented language. Shen's stress on the treatment of closure is but a specific application of this general principle. In traditional criticism, critics have drawn attention to, but have not explicated, poetic segments which fulfill this criterion. One can compare

About allusions to names, metonyms, and poems on objects, what Shen has to say sounds rather pedantic and superficial. For instance, in alluding to names, one is adivsed not to use the full name without some form of alteration, especially when it is used in a parallel structure with another name. He disapproves of Zhou Bangyan's frequent use of full names in parallel lines, as in "Yu Xin's sorrows are many, / Jiang Yan's regrets are extreme." [47] As a modern scholar has noted, in Wu Wenying's *ci*, in allusions names are usually altered (often by reduction to one character), as in the following lines: "So many times passing winecups around we mourned Fu (i.e., Tu Fu), / Holding chrysanthemums we summoned the spirit of Qian (i.e., Tao Qian)." [48] In this way, the allusion is not obtrusive and there is literally more word space to develop semantic and imagistic interplay.

With regard to poems on objects Shen admonishes that words contained in the title of the poem should not be used in the text of the poem, and metonyms are deemed an indispensable device for poetic representation. In other words, the ideal language of the *ci* should be oblique: so far as possible nothing should be stated directly. One can easily see the inherent pitfall of obscurantism in this principle when it is carried too far. Significantly, elsewhere in the *Yuefu zhimi* Shen Yifu points to Wu Wenying's occasional obscurity in diction and use of allusion as his stylistic weakness. [49]

Although Zhang Yan maintained many of the same aesthetic values expressed in Shen's treatise, his own *Ciyuan*, written somewhat later, represents a reaction to the crystallization of the poetics of indirection found in Wu Wenying's poetic style. In Zhang's own introductory remarks in the second *juan* of the *Ciyuan*, Wu is cited among five poets—including Jiang Kui—as

---

the different interpretations to which Zhou Bangyan's implicit imagery has given rise to in modern exegesis. Cf. James J. Y. Liu, *Major Lyricists of the Northern Sung*, p. 173; and James R. Hightower, "The Songs of Chou Pang-yen," in *HJAS* 37 (1977), p. 245.

[47] *Yuefu zhimi* (*Cihua congbian* ed., vol. 1), p. 234.

[48] The lines are from *Shengsheng man* (*QSC* 2/2930). This observation is made by Wu Mei in his preface to the *Yuefu zhimi jianshi* quoted in Xia Chengtao and Cai Songyun, *Ciyuan zhu Yuefu zhimi jianshi*, pp. 90–92.

[49] *Yuefu zhimi* (*Cihua congbian* ed., vol. 1), p. 230.

well-known poets who had developed their own individual style. Wu is further cited favorably in the three sections on line structure, diction, and short lyrics. It is clear that in the late Song and early Yuan, Wu Wenying was a major influence to be reckoned with. A statistical analysis of the poets Zhang Yan refers to in the *Ciyuan* makes the shift in taste quite apparent. Zhou Bangyan, while still regarded as a great master, is by no means held up as the perfect or only model. Frequent positive references are made to other Northern Song *ci* poets—in particular Su Shi and Qin Guan—hardly mentioned in the *Yuefu zhimi*.[50] These Northern Song poets stand for a more natural, flowing style before Zhou Bangyan initiated the trend towards "subtlety and sophistication," to use James Liu's terminology,[51] in verbal structures and the expression of sentiments.

In the final analysis, Zhang Yan sought a style that retained some of the rhythmic flow of the Northern Song style and at the same time exhibited certain desirable Southern Song sensibilities. He found this in the *ci* of Jiang Kui. His concept of *qingkong* ("transparency"), which he formulated with Jiang Kui's *ci* as the ideal model, forms the core of his opposition to certain aspects of Wu Wenying's poetics of indirection, which he characterized as *zhishi* ("density"). Consequently there is no special discussion of metonyms in the *Ciyuan*, and his advice on the use of *xuzi* ("empty words") is antithetical to Shen Yifu's.[52] In his famous statement on *qingkong* versus *zhishi*, he pits Jiang Kui against Wu Wenying in a passage that has come to occupy the controversial starting point for any critical evaluation of Wu Wenying's style:

> *Ci* poetry should be transparent and not dense. If transparent, it will have archaic elegance and vigor; if dense, it will be stagnant and obscure. Jiang Kui's *ci* are like a wild cloud that flies alone, coming and going without a trace, and Wu Wenying's *ci* are like a many-jewelled edifice

[50] Su Shi is mentioned only once in the *Yuefu zhimi*. Shen conceded that some of Su's *ci* poems written in the non-heroic mode did accord with music. *Yuefu zhimi* (*Cihua congbian* ed., vol. 1), p. 234.

[51] James J. Y. Liu, *Major Lyricists of the Northern Sung*, p. 161.

[52] Their differing views on the subject will be taken up in the next section.

which dazzles the eye, but when taken apart does not form clauses or sentences.[53]

This statement perhaps says as much about the critic as about the poet criticized. Its intensely metaphorical mode, as we shall see, only amounts to Zhang Yan's concern for the linguistic aspect of the *ci*. Both Shen Yifu and Zhang Yan noticed the brilliant surface structure of Wu Wenying's poetry (e.g., in praising the beauty of his diction) and seem to have missed the emotional depth underneath and therefore the holistic art which comes from a fusion of dazzling sensuousness of imagery with flights of imagination and a palpable depth of feeling.

IV. The Poetics of Density

Zhang Yan's characterization of Wu Wenying's style as "dense" is unquestionably perspicacious. That he is critical towards this characteristic reflects his personal taste and preference. However, his incisive view provides a useful perspective from which to examine the poetics of Wu Wenying's *ci*. The opposition that Zhang Yan set up between *qingkong* ("transparency") and *zhishi* ("density") revolves around the use of *shizi* ("full words") and *xuzi* ("empty words"), grammatical categories under which words were traditionally classified. These two terms have been used in discussions of poetry since Song times.[54] Current Song usages of the terms *shizi* and *xuzi* indicate that the two terms already constituted an implicit binary system of word classification. Song definitions of these terms are rare, but the neo-Confucian philosopher Lu Jiuyuan (1139–1193) left one in his collected works: "The ideas words represent can be empty or full. In the case of empty words we can only speak of the meaning in the word, whereas in the case of full words we can speak about something real or concrete (*shi*) that the word refers to." [55] The

---

[53] *Ciyuan* (*Cihua congbian* ed., vol. 1), p. 207.

[54] I am indebted to Professor E. G. Pulleyblank for alerting me to this fact. For a convenient list of Song and post-Song sources in which the terms *shizi* and *xuzi* occur, see *Guhanyu yufaxue ziliao huibian*, comp. Zheng Dian and Mai Meiqiao, (Beijing: Zhonghua shuju, 1964), pp. 91–104.

[55] From *Lu Xiangshan quanji*, quoted in Zheng Dian and Mai Meiqiao, p. 95.

definition suggests that words with a perceptual or image content are considered full words, and words devoid of such concrete referents are considered empty.[56]

In the late Qing, Ma Jianzhong wrote his pioneering comprehensive grammar of classical Chinese, the *Mashi wentong*. In it he defines full words as "those which refer to some definite phenomenon that can be explained" and empty words as "those which refer to no definite phenomenon but which modify the nature and condition of full words."[57] A functional criterion for distinguishing the two word classes is provided by the contemporary Chinese linguist Zhou Fagao: full words can function as the subject or predicate of a sentence whereas empty words cannot. With respect to their functions, Zhou subdivides full words into substantives (nouns) and predicatives (verbs and adjectives), and other lesser categories; and empty words into adverbs, connectives, prepositions, interjections, and particles.[58] In an article entitled "Full Words, Empty Words, and Allusions," the modern scholar Yuan Zhai notes that in traditional discussions of poetry, nouns and some verbs and adjectives are counted as full words, the rest fall into an undifferentiated category of empty words.[59] These modern extrapolations of the meaning and scope of full words and empty words agree on the basic difference in semantic content and grammatical function between the two word classes. In poetry, this difference between words with an image content and those which express primarily grammatical relationships affects the syntactic and semantic flow in the poetic structure.

[56] This difference is borne out by the examples of verse lines quoted in the *Shiren yuxie*, a Southern Song work containing comments and critiques on poetry. The examples are pentasyllabic and heptasyllabic lines illustrating the use of full words and empty words in different positions in the line. Nouns with physical correlates are clearly considered to be full words; function words such as prepositions and adverbs are empty words; but the status of verbs and adjectives is not so clear and consistent. See Wei Qingzhi, *Shiren yuxie* (Preface 1244; rpt. Shanghai: Gudian wenxue chubanshe, 1958), 1 : 77–80; also quoted in Zheng Dian and Mai Meiqiao, pp. 93–94.

[57] Ma Jianzhong, *Mashi wentong jiaozhu* (Beijing: Zhonghua shuju, 1961), 1 : 1.

[58] Zhou Fagao, *Zhongguo gudai yufa: zaoju bian*, vol. 1 (Taipei: Institute of History and Philology, Academia Sinica, 1961), p. 22.

[59] Yuan Zhai, "Shizi xuzi yu yongdian," *Yilin conglu*, 4 (1964), p. 52.

In the concentrated, image-oriented language of poetry, the use of empty words is usually reduced and particles in particular are avoided, except in instances when the poet is aiming for a special effect, such as a colloquial, discursive, or erudite tone. Yet, even in *shi* poetry, in which structural progression is at least organized on the repetition of the couplet, the presence of empty words in strategic positions is often vital to the flow and meaning, for empty words are grammatical markers, which function to create hypotactic syntax and semantic coherence between lines and couplets by making causal links and logical transitions. Stated inversely, the coherence and flow of a poem is more difficult to achieve in a proportionate absence of empty words. Yuan Zhai, in the article mentioned above, quotes a poem by the Tang poet Wei Yingwu as an example in which there is a relatively high percentage of empty words, and they are used effectively to bring out the emotional flow.[60] The poem, written in pentasyllabic regulated form, is titled "I rejoiced in encountering an old friend from Liangzhou on the Huai River." Liangzhou is an archaic name for the southwestern part of Shaanxi around the Han river.

> *Once* sojourners on the Yangzi and Han Rivers,
> *Each time* we met we returned drunk.
> Floating clouds—*after* we parted,
> Flowing water—a *period* of ten years.
> Happy and laughing, our friendship *same as* in the past,
> Sparse and thin, our hair is *already* spotted with grey.
> *Why* do I *not* return?
> *There are* autumn hills around the Huai.[61]

江漢曾爲客，
相逢每醉還。
浮雲一別後，
流水十年間。
歡笑情如舊，

---

[60] *Ibid.*, p. 53.

[61] *Quan Tang shi* [hereafter *QTS*] (Beijing: Zhonghua shuju, 1979), 6: 1898; the version quoted in Yuan Zhai has "green hills" instead of "autumn hills" in the last line; see "Shizi xuzi yu yongdian," p. 53.

蕭疏鬢已斑。
何因不歸去？
淮上有秋山。

Upon scrutiny, many of the empty words pointed out by Yuan Zhai in this poem turn out to be adverbs and prepositions denoting temporal relationships, which together produce a smooth temporal transition. A mutually reflective comparison between the past and present is expressed through the temporal framework set up by the use of these empty words. The poet's happy sentiments—his fond memories of a past friendship and joy in the present meeting—are combined in a deceptively simple and natural manner with a certain wistfulness at the passage of time.

In the case of *ci* poetry, and we are here primarily concerned with the *manci* form prevalent in the Southern Song,[62] both the relative structural complexity (irregularity of line lengths, strophic and stanzaic divisions) and the musical accompaniment generated new metrical and structural developments that involve specific usages of empty words. Of course the overall distribution of empty words in a piece continued to have an important influence on the flow of these *ci* poems, just as it does in *shi* poetry. But the length and asymmetry of *manci*, relative to *xiaoling* ("short *ci* lyrics") and regulated *shi*, required means of structural organization other than paratactic and hypotactic parallelism and couplet movement. The most notable new feature introduced in the structural poetics of *manci* was a class of "empty words" in prescribed tones and used in prescribed positions in *manci* tune patterns, designated by the term *lingzi* ("leading-word").[63] The Northern Song *ci* poet Liu Yong is credited with having been instrumental in popularizing the use of *manci* tune patterns and in developing this new feature.[64]

---

[62] See n. 13.

[63] For a general discussion of *lingzi*, see Xia Chengtao and Wu Xionghe, *Duci changshi* (Beijing: Zhonghua shuju, 1962), pp. 94–99. Shuen-fu Lin also provides an informed discussion of the subject in *The Transformation of the Chinese Lyrical Tradition*, pp. 131–41.

[64] On Liu Yong and the development of *lingzi*, see Kang-i Sun Chang, *The Evolution of Chinese Tz'u Poetry*, pp. 122–47; and Winnie L. Leung, "Liu Yung and His *Tz'u*" (Master's thesis, University of British Columbia, 1976), pp. 149–66.

These positioned "empty words" in *manci* form a specialized group, which includes conventional empty words from the grammatical word class, but which includes certain verbs as well. They consist of segments ranging from one to three characters, invariably occupy the initial position in a line, and may govern from one to four consecutive lines. For this reason they are called in Qing and post-Qing *ci* poetics *lingju zi* ("line-leading words") or simply *lingzi* ("leading-words"). During the Southern Song, no special terminology existed for lead-segments; they were referred to as "empty words" or "empty words at the beginning of the line,"[65] perhaps because many lead-segment words do belong to the grammatical class of empty words.

When *ci* were actually being written to existing tunes and sung, as it was the practice during the Song, the prescribed syntactic position and strict tonal restriction governing lead-segments suggest that they bore an integral relation to the musical pattern. Not only do lead-segments occupy the initial position in a line, but they occur in the first or second line of a strophic unit, indicating some correspondence to rhythmic stress or transition. This hypothesis is supported by the predominant use of characters in the falling tone for lead-segments.[66] Xia Chengtao has observed that "the falling tone has a special status in *ci*; it is used in places where the musical pitch plays a critical role in the tune."[67] The heavy stress of the falling tone is considered vigorous and expressive;[68] thus this tonal characteristic is exploited in lead-segments, in relation to both the musical and the poetic structures. It should be noted that the prescribed initial position for lead-segments makes for syntactic flexibility, often resulting in lines whose syntax would otherwise appear to be ungrammatical. This is a common feature unique to the structure of *manci*.[69]

[65] See *Ciyuan* and *Yuefu zhimi* (*Cihua congbian* ed., vol. 1), pp. 207 and 233 respectively.

[66] Some characters in the rising tone are also used, but these form a small minority.

[67] Xia Chengtao and Wu Xionghe, *Duci changshi*, p. 59.

[68] *Ibid.*, p. 60. Shen Yifu also stresses the importance of the falling tone in tune patterns; see *Yuefu zhimi* (*Cihua congbian* ed., vol. 1), p. 232.

[69] For examples of syntactic abnormalities in *manci*, see Wang Li, *Hanyu shilü xue* (Shanghai: Shanghai jiaoyu chubanshe, 1963), pp. 659–61.

Liu Yong's germinal practice of using lead-segments estab-
lished a structural principle that came to be carefully observed,
not only in that set positions are followed in a particular tune
pattern, but also in the general choice of words to be used as lead-
segments. By far the great majority of lead-segments are mono-
syllabic. They average two to six occurrences in a *manci* tune
pattern and their prescribed positions are rigidly followed. Pre-
vious studies have noted that most lead-segments tend to con-
sist of adverbs and verbs, which often serve as conjunctives
and interrogatives; some, especially polysyllabic lead-segments,
are colloquial expressions.[70] The structural function of lead-
segments is to effect an integration of expressive and imagistic
language and to produce a sense of transition as well as flow and
continuity. In the following example from a *ci* by Liu Yong, the
lead-segment connects the two lines by linking the content of
perception to the verb in the preceding line; it also gives contex-
tual qualification to the images it governs:

> [On] the homeward journey:
> Even where I gaze intently,
> *Only* / sunset and dusky haze fill the grassy plain.[71]
>
> 歸途。 *(Mulanhua man, QSC* 1/47)
>
> 縱凝望處,
> 但斜陽暮靄滿平蕪。

Another illustrative example is Liu Yong's much admired sec-
ond strophe in his poem to the tune *Basheng Ganzhou*; in it a
preposed adverb governs three consecutive lines and so unifies a
series of images by providing a temporal context:

> *Gradually* / the frosty wind [becomes] chilly and harsh,
> The mountain pass and river desolate,
> The fading twilight [falls] on the pavilion.   *(QSC* 1/43)
>
> 漸霜風淒慘,
> 關河冷落,
> 殘照當樓。

---

[70] Kang-i Sun Chang, *The Evolution of Chinese Tz'u Poetry*, pp. 128–29; and
Winnie L. Leung, "Liu Yung and His *Tz'u*," p. 150.
[71] The virgule indicates the caesura after the lead-segment.

By far the most common verbs used as lead-segments are those denoting perception, mentation, or emotion. In revealing the subjective lyrical experience of the poet, these verbal lead-segments also act as structural links both by indicating shifts in experiential state between strophes and by setting off the lines they govern as the content of the experience. The opening strophe of *Basheng Ganzhou* begins with a lead-segment, and Liu Yong begins it with a verb revealing his perception:

> I *face* splashing / rain at dusk sprinkling river and sky,
> Once more cleansing clear autumn.

(QSC 1/43)

對蒲蒲、暮雨灑江天，
一番洗清秋。

Then he proceeds to the second strophe quoted above, led by an adverb that lends a temporal dimension to his experience. The two strophes suggest that the persona's perception of the autumn evening landscape was a prolonged act. The transition between the strophic units and the linkage of the lines are so skillfully structured on these two lead-segments that they are almost seamless. Of the four strophic units in the second stanza of *Basheng Ganzhou*, each of the first three contains a lead-segment position.[72] Liu Yong uses three consecutive verbal lead-segments, which indicate respectively perception, emotion, and mentation: first, the verb "gaze upon" (*wang*) elicits the content of his perception, which in turn causes him to "lament" (*tan*) about his present condition of being away from home and his lover; then he "imagines" (*xiang*) the state of his lover faraway (*QSC* 1/43). Again, the twists and turns of the lyrical consciousness are presented distinctly by the use of such verbal lead-segments. We will later have occasion to compare the lead-segments in Wu Wenying's *Basheng Ganzhou* with this model by Liu Yong.

That the use of empty words and lead-segments had become an established structural device of importance can be surmised from the discussions on this topic contained in both the *Ciyuan*

---

[72] I am following Kang-i Sun Chang's count, *The Evolution of Chinese Tz'u Poetry*, p. 128. Strictly speaking, the line immediately following the one with the third lead-segment should also be considered as starting with a lead-segment.

and *Yuefu zhimi*. As we have seen, the views expressed in these two treatises accord with each other on most matters concerning the aesthetics and poetics of *ci*, but this is one area in which they decidedly diverge. First, let us examine Zhang Yan's comments in the *Ciyuan*:

> *Shi* and *ci* are different. Lines in *ci* can have anywhere from two to eight characters. If one piles up full words, [the *ci*] will not even make smooth reading, how can one then give it to a singing girl to perform? One should coordinate it with empty words, those of one character such as "now" [*zheng*], "but" [*dan*], "it is that/why" [*shen*], and "let" [*ren*], those of two characters such as "is it not that" [*moshi*], "then again" [*huanyou*], and "what's more" [*nakan*], and those of three characters such as "moreover how can one bear" [*gengnengxiao*], "most unreasonable that" [*zuiwuduan*], and "yet again it is" [*youqueshi*]. However, these empty words should be used appropriately in places where they belong. If as many as possible of these empty words are used, the language will naturally come alive; it certainly will not be dense, and the reader will not scoff at it by closing the book. [Variant reading of the last section: If one uses all empty words, the language would be vulgar. Though it certainly will not be dense, one cannot avoid being mocked at by the reader closing the book.][73]

Zhang Yan's discussion at once concerns the overall use of empty words and the use of empty words as lead-segments. The latter point may not be immediately apparent due to the lack of a specific term for lead-segments. But it can be inferred from the examples of empty words cited by Zhang Yan, as they are mostly used in lead-segment positions, and also from his qualification that "these empty words should be used appropriately in places where they belong." From the list, we can also see that these "empty words" are nearly all adverbial conjunctions, interroga-

---

[73] Xia Chengtao and Cai Songyun, *Ciyuan zhu Yuefu zhimi jianshi*, p. 15 and p. 16, n. 2. The *Cihua congbian* edition of the *Ciyuan* adopts the variant reading, 1:207.

tives, and colloquial expressions; by employing them a poet can create hypotactic syntax and explicit rhetoric. The importance placed by Zhang Yan on the use of empty words, or lead-segments, in fact constitutes the backbone of his poetics of transparency. Lead-segments, as we have seen, are denotative links, which thread together and make manifest the varied dimensions of image, thought, and feeling in a *manci*, thus enhancing its flow and continuity. Therefore, Zhang Yan asserts that the frequent use of empty words in proper places will make the language "come alive." The variant reading is noteworthy for pointing out the undesirable effect of vulgarity produced by an excessive use of empty words: fluency is desired, not an overly colloquial tone. Even more significant is the point made in both readings that the language "certainly will not be dense" if empty words are employed. This discussion immediately precedes the famous passage criticizing the "density" of Wu Wenying's *ci*. Although Zhang Yan never states explicitly that Wu Wenying's density hinges on the use of empty words, or want of it, at least half the explanation lies precisely in this point.

We may recall that the model Zhang Yan upholds for his poetics of transparency is Jiang Kui's *ci*. Jiang Kui does tend to use conjunctive lead-segments and empty words within lines to effect hypotaxis and concatenation. All the same, as we have seen in the previous section, in his representative works the emotional and conceptual processes remain suppressed, and the flow is maintained primarily on the syntactic and structural level. Wang Guowei's summary comment on Jiang Kui reflects this dual aspect in Jiang's *ci*: "Baishi (Jiang Kui) has style but no feeling."[74] Critics and readers who appreciate Jiang's *ci*, do so perhaps at least in part for the ambiguity and elusiveness produced by this union of opposites.

Zhang Yan should have used himself as an example of his own poetics; he is a critic who does put theory into practice. His *ci* are sometimes transparent to the point of being naked. Not only do his poems exhibit an extremely fluent structure using lead-

---

[74] Wang Guowei, *Renjian cihua* (*Cihua congbian* ed., vol. 12), p. 4252.

segments and a high ratio of empty words, but these structural elements also lay bare his heart and mind. One example will suffice, for Zhang Yan is quite consistent stylistically. On taking leave of an old friend after a chance visit, Zhang elaborates on his reluctance to leave his companion with the aid of many empty words:

> Didn't plan to meet each other on an old path.
> Just when I was wondering if it was a dream, I was then
>   again startled awake.
> Light breeze on the willows,
> The river sways with white waves,
> The boat leaves at the break of dawn.
> Even if I could come again,
> It is better not to depart,
> How can I bear this feeling in my bosom?
> Who will know that once again the gate with the five
>   willows will be deserted
> Where I had heard the cuckoos cry.
>
> (*Shuilong yin, QSC* 5/3471)

不擬相逢古道。
纔疑夢、又還驚覺。
清風在柳，
江搖白浪，
舟行趁曉。
遮莫重來，
不如休去，
怎堪懷抱。
那知又、五柳門荒，
曾聽得、鵑啼了。

Aside from the strophe evoking the scene of departure and the closure, the stanza is somewhat devoid of images. With the hypotactic conjunctions *cai ... youhuan* ("just when ... then again"), *zhemo ... buru* ("Even if I could ... it is better"); and the interrogatives *zenkan* ("how can I bear") and *nazhiyou* ("who would know that") the stanza acquires a prosy syntax and a conversational tone. This is further enhanced by Zhang Yan's propensity for verbal resultatives; the stanza ends with two of his favorites—*de* in *tingde* ("had heard"), and *liao* in *tiliao* ("had cried").

Wu Wenying's practice is diametrically opposed to that of Zhang Yan. The two men represent antithetical extremes in late Southern Song structural poetics. For Wu's theory, we shall again turn to Shen Yifu's record in the *Yuefu zhimi*:

> Tunes often have lines which should begin with an empty word, such as: "to lament" [*jie*], "how can one bear" [*nai*], "how much more"[*kuang*], "even more" [*geng*], "then again" [*you*], "to imagine" [*liao*], "to think, imagine" [*xiang*], "just when" [*zheng*], and "it is that" [*shen*]. These can be used without harm. However, it will not be good if they are used two to three times in one *ci*, in which case they will be called "empty head-words" [*kong-tou zi*]. It is far better to use instead a "static word" [*jingzi*] right at the beginning [of the line] to lead the following; then the line structure will be vigorous. Yet they should not be used too often.[75]

This passage on the use of monosyllabic lead-segments directly contradicts Zhang Yan's advice. Whereas Zhang Yan encourages the use of empty words in lead-segment positions, Shen Yifu cautions against their repeated use. Perfunctory and redundant use of empty words as lead-segments result in "empty head-words," meaningless repetition, and Shen suggests the substitution of a "static word" in place of an empty word in a lead-segment. In this context "static word" clearly means full word.[76] The fact that Shen does not provide any examples of static words also suggests that they refer to a broad lexical category under-

[75] *Yuefu zhimi* (*Cihua congbian* ed., vol. 1), p. 233.

[76] In Cai Songyun's annotation of the *Yuefu zhimi*, he explains *jingzi* as "full words which convey the form of things and is used in opposition to *dongzi*. *Jingzi* express an accomplished scene or condition, and *dongzi* an action to be accomplished" (Xia Chengtao and Cai Songyun, p. 74). This explanation is taken verbatim from Ma Jianzhong's definition of *jingzi*, a term which Ma uses to stand for adjectives. See *Mashi wentong*, p. 5. In Shen Yifu's passage, the term is used in opposition to *xuzi*, and appears to imply a broader range than adjectives.

stood as full words. Since nouns cannot function structurally as monosyllabic lead-segments, static words for this purpose must be chosen chiefly from verbs and adjectives. But Shen's list of empty words includes one emotive verb ("to lament") and two verbs of mentation ("to imagine" and "to think"), thus excluding two of the common categories of verbs used as lead-segments from his intended range of static words. By inference, we arrive at verbs that denote a more "visible" semantic content. The possibilities would still be endless were it not for the tonal restriction, which limits the number of such verbs (and adjectives) available as lead-segments. Shen also warns against overusing this technique of substitution.

Shen's advice is supported by Wu Wenying's practice. To be sure, Wu Wenying for the most part employs the more common adverbs and verbs in the accepted repertory of lead-segments. But his deviations from accepted norms are what contribute to the density of his style. He uses a number of stray verbs, which he varies judicially with the more commonly used lead-segment words. The following are some illustrative examples:[77]

1. River herons just began to fly;
    Drifting / thousands of miles—white clouds,
    The horizon seems bathed.

    (*Sanbu yue, QSC* 4/2874)

    江鶂初飛 ，
    蕩萬里素雲 ，
    際空如沐 。

2. *Moistening* / cold plum blossoms—a fine drizzle,
    It puts out lamplights, in darkness the dust is scented.

    (*Mulanhua man, QSC* 4/2917)

    潤寒梅細雨 ，
    捲燈火 ，
    暗塵香 。

[77] All examples of lead-segments are given in the context of the strophe in which they occur. For practical purposes, I take the rhyme positions as marking strophic divisions.

3.   *Passing* / a few drops of rain at sunset,
Weeping on silk, traces of cold powder.

(Faqu xianxian yin, QSC 4/2888)

過數點斜陽雨，
啼綃粉痕冷。

4.   The chilly sky is pale blue;
Girdled with / light clouds screening the willows,
And deep mist protecting the flowers.

(Sao hua you, QSC 4/2886)

冷空澹碧，
帶翳柳輕雲，
護花深霧。

5.   I detest spring for being too jealous,
Splashing / her outing skirt, I regret even more
Her phoenix shoes soiled by dust.

(Sao hua you, QSC 4/2886)

恨春太妒。
濺行裙更惜，
鳳鉤塵汙。

6.   *Imprinted* / on the lichen her paired lovebird shoes,
I recall our walks through the deep woods.

(San shu mei, QSC 4/2923–24)

印蘚迹雙鴛，
記穿林窈。

Invariably the use of these verbs in lead-segment positions high-lights the sensuous aspect of the images; they do not "lead" or link the lines structurally in an obvious way. Moreover, since many lead-segment verbs are intended as signposts of the lyrical voice, their displacement cannot but submerge it to some degree. Instead of being made explicit by verbs indicating subjective experience, it remains implicit in the poetic structure. In the last two examples, the presence of the lyrical voice is clearly discernible through the use of the verbs "detest," "regret," and "recall;" but interestingly, though "detest" and "recall," being in the falling tone, can be used as lead-segments, they are displaced from these structurally prominent positions. It is especially clear in the last example that the image is what the poet wants to stress.

What is rare and quite unorthodox in Wu's choice of words for monosyllabic lead-segments is the use of adjectives. In a structurally prominent position, an adjective intensifies the imagistic aspect of the line(s) it modifies, but does not satisfy the pivotal function usually expected of a lead-segment. For that reason, adjectives form only a small portion of lead-segment words in Wu's corpus; they are nevertheless significant for contributing to the impact of sensuousness and density in his *ci*:

1. *Placid* / her springtime pose and snow-white beauty,
    [Like] cold plum blossoms fresh and pure.

    (*Ruihe xian, QSC* 4/2876)

    澹春姿雪態，
    寒梅清泚。

2. *Far off* / misty sands—a flying sail,
    Dusky hills display their green.

    (*Qi tian yue, QSC* 4/2885)

    渺煙磧飛帆，
    暮山橫翠。

3. *Resplendent* / dragon rays suddenly soaked,
    Cloud vapors on apricot-wood rafters.

    (*Sao hua you, QSC* 4/2886–87)

    燦驪光乍溼，
    杏梁雲氣。

4. Ten years by the river maples,
    Cold / frosty waves turn into patterned silk.

    (*Wei fan, QSC* 4/2927)

    十載江楓，
    冷霜波成縠。

5. Teardrops stretch to the lone city wall,
    Endless / grassy plain, extending mist.

    (*Wei fan, QSC* 4/2927)

    淚接孤城，
    渺平蕪煙闊。

6.   I imagine at the villa by West Lake, love is most
        fervent,
    Luminous / the painted boat in the moonlight,
    [And you] drunk with your palace robe of brocade.

(Dong xian ge, QSC 4/2904)

料別館、西湖最情濃，

爛畫舫月明，

醉宮袍錦。

It is particularly noticeable in translation that these adjectival
lead-segments tend to blend in as part of the description of the
image and lose the distinct character of lead-segments as direc-
tives and connectives. In the original, some of the lines that begin
with adjectival lead-segments form curious syntactic inversions
of normal pentasyllabic lines. For instance, (1) would normally
read "Her springtime pose and snow-white beauty are placid"
(*Chunzi xuetai dan*), (4) may be construed as "Frosty waves,
frozen into patterned silk" (*Shuangbo leng cheng ji*), and
(6) "The moon being bright, the painted boat is luminous"(*Yue
ming huafang lan*). Number (5) can be thought of as both inver-
sion and ellipsis combined, the normal syntax being: "The grassy
plain endless, the mist extending" (*Pingwu miaomiao yan kuo*).[78]
In all cases, the syntactic disruption, the "static" quality of
descriptive lead-segments, and the relative lack of internal empty
words, while making for imagistic density, at the same time
interrupt the normal fluency of language expected in recitation.
Thus Zhang Yan can say that "if one piles up full words, the *ci*
will not even make smooth reading," much less can it be given
"to an ordinary singing girl to perform." The statement of
course first speaks for Zhang Yan's preference for a fluid style
enhanced by the use of empty words. Theoretically, the musical
tune should carry the words along; the metrical conformity of the
lines to the musical pattern must have effected a degree of tran-
sition and flow in the performance of a *ci*. We should also
remember that Wu generally uses the more common lead-
segment words and only occasionally varies them with "static"
words.

[78] This is pointed out by Wang Li in *Hanyu shilü xue*, p. 660.

70

The lead-segments in the poem Wu wrote to the tune *Basheng Ganzhou* illustrate well his variation of "static" and "empty" lead-segments, though even this work is exceptional among Wu's poems in its "static" preference in regard to lead-segments. The poem is about an excursion to Mount Lingyan near Suzhou, the ancient palace site of King Fucha of Wu. It has come to be one of Wu's most well-known works and is typical of his condensed style in its use of allusions and of unusual and complex imagery, and in its general eschewal of empty words.[79] As previously noted in the example by Liu Yong, the first two strophes of the tune pattern *Basheng Ganzhou* both begin with a monosyllabic lead-segment position. Liu Yong's handling presents a distinct lyrical presence and temporal progression by means of the lead-segments "I face" and "gradually." In Wu Wenying's version, each of the consecutive strophes begins with a descriptive lead-segment:

> *Endless* | void and mist to the four distances,
> What year was it the meteor fell from a clear sky?
> *Illusory* | green crags and cloud trees,
> Celebrated beauty's chamber,
> Failed Leader's palace wall.[80]

(QSC 4/2926)

> 渺空煙四遠，
> 是何年、青天墜長星。
> 幻蒼厓雲樹，
> 名娃金屋，
> 殘霸宮城。

Clearly, "endless" and "illusory" do not provide structural links in the obvious sense. Rather, they impart the paradoxical qualities of timelessness and illusion to the images they modify (three lines in the case of "illusory"). In fact, the opposition

---

[79] This poem is analyzed in detail in Chia-ying Yeh Chao, "Wu Wen-ying's *Tz'u*: A Modern View," in *Studies in Chinese Literary Genres*, ed. Cyril Birch (Berkeley: University of California Press, 1974), pp. 179–91. See also chap. 3, sec. 3 for complete translation and further discussion.

[80] This is adapted from James Hightower's translation in Chia-ying Yeh Chao, "Wu Wen-ying's *Tz'u*," p. 179–80. The version here aims to highlight the presence of the monosyllabic lead-segments.

posed by the lead-segments "endless" and "illusory" is crucial
to the meaning of the poem. The poet is not concerned with a
sequential presentation of an experience but with the presenta-
tion of the tension and interaction between continuity and
discontinuity, reality and illusion, seen in the relics from a
bygone age. It has been said of Wu Wenying's *ci* that, due to the
lack of empty words, structure and flow are maintained through
the "method of internal transition of hidden forces."[81] The
technique sounds rather mystical; but we do get a sense of Wu's
alchemy in this poem wherein the surface links are deempha-
sized and the coherence derives from an underlying idea.

Through the more conventional verbal lead-segments em-
ployed in the second stanza, past history gives way to lyrical
presence in a complex process of transformation:

> In the palace the King of Wu is dead drunk,
> *Sending* | the weary traveler of Five Lakes
> To angle alone, cold sober.
> [I] *ask* | the blue waves: they won't talk;
> How can white hair cope with the mountain's green?[82]

> (QSC 4/2926)

> 宮裏吳王沈醉，
> 倩五湖倦客，
> 獨釣醒醒。

The weary traveler, while alluding to the historical figure Fan Li,
also takes on shades of a persona, a transformation that is com-
pleted in the next strophe. "White hair" is clearly a metonym for
the poet, but it also echoes the image of the weary traveler.[83] It is
the poet who asks the blue waves, and the question underlies the
poem's concern with the impermanence of man as contrasted
with the permanence of nature.

Where Liu Yong begins the next strophe with a lead-segment,
"I *imagine* the fair one | gazing hard from her boudoir chamber"
(*QSC* 1/43), Wu replaces it with an image:"Water enveloping the
void | from the balcony's height." On the level of structural
poetics, this poem shows that the image content of full words,

---

[81] Xia Chengtao and Cai Songyun, *Ciyuan zhu Yuefu zhimi jianshi*, p. 75.
[82] See n. 80.
[83] See Chia-ying Yeh Chao, "Wu Wen-ying's *Tz'u*," pp. 188–89.

especially in the case of descriptives used as lead-segments, has a function within the poetic structure different from that of normative lead-segments. It does not "move" the poem along but instead increases the visual "density" by focusing on the images in a poetic structure already inclined toward "piling up full words." However, this poem also shows that the transitions are effected on a deeper structure of thought through an imagistic presentation that underscores the meditation on reality and illusion, continuity and discontinuity.

Compared to most Southern Song *ci* poets, Wu Wenying relies much less on empty words to achieve flow, whether throughout the text of the poem or specifically in lead-segment positions. Sometimes he even dispenses with monosyllabic lead-segments. The ten poems he wrote to the tune pattern *Shuilong yin* provide an extreme example. The last strophe of the first stanza should begin with a monosyllabic lead-segment that directs two tetrasyllabic lines. In five of the ten poems Wu wrote to this tune, he does without this lead-segment, producing normal pentasyllabic lines.[84] He of course observes the falling / rising tone rule governing that position. The second stanza begins with an optional disyllabic lead-segment position;[85] of the ten, in only three does he opt for a disyllabic lead-segment. In contrast, Xin Qiji employs a disyllabic segment in seven out of the eleven poems he wrote to this tune, almost the exact reverse of the ratio in Wu's poems. Xin Qiji, writing in the *haofang* style, naturally tends to use more empty words in the poem and in lead-segments. Yet, when Wu Wenying's *manci* poems are compared to those written to the same tunes by Zhou Bangyan and Jiang Kui, the results show Wu to prefer full words.[86]

Wu's handling of trisyllabic lead-segments also corroborates

---

[84] *QSC* 4/2879: the first, third, fourth, and eighth poem listed under *Shuilong yin*; and *QSC* 4/2935.

[85] Disyllabic lead-segments seem to be the least clearly defined. This disyllabic lead-segment position is pointed out in Xia Chengtao and Wu Xionghe, *Duci changshi*, p. 95. Generally speaking, polysyllabic lead-segment positions are less scrupulously observed; they may be "filled" with full words instead. But the choice would of course affect the relative density of the style.

[86] See for example the following tune patterns: *An xiang*, *QSC* 4/2902 (Wu), 3/2181 (Jiang); *Yan Qingdu*, 4/2882–83 (Wu), 2/604 (Zhou); *Faqu xianxian yin*, 4/2888 (Wu), 2/602 (Zhou), 3/2178 (Jiang).

his preference for semantic and imagistic density. Trisyllabic lead-segments occur in lines of longer length, the most common being heptasyllabic and octosyllabic. In order to function metrically as a lead-segment, the initial character of the trisyllabic cluster has to be in the falling (or rising) tone, and it is often followed by one or two more oblique-tone characters.[87] Moreover, many standard trisyllabic lead-segments comprise empty words that form colloquial expressions, as in the examples offered by Zhang Yan. Their colloquial tone lends a characteristic expressiveness and flow to the line(s). Wu Wenying employs a number of them in his *manci*. But he more often than not takes the alternative of using a monosyllabic segment to lead the line, with the caesura maintained after the third syllable. It is obvious that this allows for more development of imagery. As an illustration, let us examine the trisyllabic lead-segments in the five *ci* Wu wrote to the tune pattern *Xi qiuhua*. Of the tunes Wu himself composed this is the one to which he wrote the greatest number of poems. The third strophe in the first stanza and the fourth strophe in the second both contain trisyllabic lead-segments in all five poems.[88] None of them is a trisyllabic colloquial formula. The trisyllabic clusters all begin with monosyllabic lead-segments that can be divided into three categories. The first consists of the more conventional adverbial and verbal lead-segments:

1.   Lady Autumn's tears dampen the evening;
     Once again over the whole city / light rain and slight
     wind.

(QSC 4/2912)

秋娘淚溼黃昏，
又滿城、雨輕風小。

---

[87] See Wu Mei, *Cixue tonglun* (Hong Kong: Taiping shuju, 1964), p. 45.

[88] There are some variations in line division in this pattern that affect lead-segments. For example, the opening strophe varies between having a trisyllabic lead-segment, a monosyllabic lead-segment, or no lead-segment. The two trisyllabic lead-segment positions chosen for illustration do occur in all five poems. Furthermore, not all post-trisyllabic pauses mark the occurrence of lead-segments. It has been pointed out that trisyllabic lead-segments usually have the first two or all three characters in oblique tones; see Wu Mei, *Cixue tonglun*, p. 45.

2.   On earth the dream is on the other side of the west
            wind,
      I *reckon* that in heaven / a year is just the blink of an
            eye.

                                                    (*QSC* 4/2912)

人間夢隔西風，
算天上、年華一瞬。

3.   In great haste we pour the farewell cup,
      I *regret* our meeting / [is like] the gathering and
            dispersing of clouds and duckweed.

                                                    (*QSC* 4/2913)

忽忽便倒離尊，
悵遇合、雲銷萍聚。

4.   A tiny boat lodged at night on the Wu River,
      Just at a time when water pendants and rainbow skirts
            are countless.

                                                    (*QSC* 4/2913)

扁舟夜宿吳江，
正水佩寬裳無數。

5.   With my grief dusk gathers into emerald clouds,
      I *Have it be* chanted into / the music of the "*Liu yao*"
            tune.

                                                    (*QSC* 4/2913)

愁邊暮合碧雲，
倩唱入六么聲裏。

This type of lead-segment, as expected, performs the primary
function of structural linkage. These lead-segments correlate the
two lines of the strophe with a logical connection as well as
impart a forward movement to the lines in which they occur. In
the second category, we find verbal lead-segments that are visu-
ally oriented, and the structural function is less obvious:

1.   The Autumn Goddess, endowed with leisured feeling,
      Leaning on the jade cup / tiny brows just raised.

                                                    (*QSC* 4/2912)

秋娥賦得閒情，
倚翠尊、小眉初展。

2.   The mirror of West Lake covered by dust and sand,
     Dimming the dawn reflection / of the hill's coiffure
             ruffled by clouds.

(QSC 4/2912)

西湖鏡掩塵沙，
翳曉影、秦鬟雲擾。

When we come to the third category of adjectival lead-segments, a descriptive and qualifying function prevails:

1.   Penglai Pavilion across rises in dark clouds,
     Placid the rustic scene / the hill's mien gathers in
             sadness.

(QSC 4/2912)

蓬萊對起幽雲，
澹野色、山容愁捲。

2.   All frail flowers cannot endure autumn,
     Illusory glossy jade / Luscious red [so] bright and
             lovely.

(QSC 4/2913)

凡花瘦不禁秋，
幻膩玉、腴紅鮮麗。

The last example in particular is packed with color and texture, and generally perceptual qualities. It occurs in a poem on the autumn-flowering hibiscus. The line thus maximizes the sensuousness of this showy flower. Next to all the wilted and wilting flowers, its voluptuous glamor must appear incredible and unreal. "Illusory," in the way it emphasizes this contrast established in two lines, can be said to fulfill a structural function in the transition. But this is by no means apparent when such an unusual word is encountered in a lead-segment position, followed by a string of metonyms. Immediate understanding is deferred, however slightly, in the absence of explicit rhetoric. If we replace "illusory" with a more common and perfectly tenable verbal lead-segment such as *guai*, producing "I *marvel* at the glossy jade / luscious red [so] bright and lovely," the meaning of the line is somewhat more transparent. But not much more, for it is also deferred by the metonymic components that require a process of translation to arrive at their referents. However spontaneous this process of translation may be in the case of well-versed readers of *ci* poetry, it is nonetheless there.

If the basic function of empty words and lead-segments is to effect a kind of structural kinetics, this kinetics is often the result of the externalization of subjective states and of sequential progression achieved through normative applications of these structural elements. Wu Wenying's radical tendencies in the use of lead-segments and his corresponding reduction of empty words represent a reversal of the normative structural poetics developed and perfected by Liu Yong. His deviations produce the opposite result of internalization of subjective elements and ambiguous temporal structures. However, these traits alone do not adequately account for the density, or complexity, of Wu Wenying's *ci*. It is when they are combined with his proclivity for an image-oriented language—a metonymic and allusive diction—that the effects of density are most visible. Metonymy, in its substitution of an image by associations of attributes and qualities, tends to anatomize the image into its sensuous components of color, shape, and texture. In a literary genre as inbred as the *ci* had become in the late Song, metonymy creates a connotative textual surface whose constituents often have definite associations and evocative power. Similarly, the skillful use of allusions, by condensing and implicating dimensions of thought and meaning from a body of intertexts, imparts added depth and complexity to the poem. But behind all the artifice, there is the artificer, and one with a sensitive heart and mind. We should therefore turn to look at how these disparate elements contribute toward an individual style and result in a compelling poetry.

3. THE POETRY OF WU WENYING:
MAJOR THEMES AND SUBGENRES

I. Yongwu Ci: *Poem as Artifice and Poem as Metaphor*

The term *yongwu* means to celebrate objects in poetic discourse. When it was used in the sixth century by the great anthologist Xiao Tong (502–531) in the preface to *Wenxuan*, it referred to an already well-established subgenre[1] in the *fu*, or rhymeprose: "When it comes to *fu* describing one event or celebrating a single object (*yong yi wu*), such as those on wind, clouds, plants and trees, or the ones about fish, insects, birds, and beasts, considering their range, it is quite impossible to list them all."[2]

As Xiao Tong's statement suggests, the category of objects suitable for description in the *fu* is almost infinitely expandable: any living thing, natural phenomenon, or artifact is a potential candidate for poetic elaboration. This is certainly the case with the category *yongwu fu* (or *fu* on objects) as its repertory grew from the Han through the Six Dynasties period. Although it would be an exaggeration to say that by Xiao Tong's time there hardly remained an object in the natural world that had escaped treatment in the *fu*, one could safely say that the range of the form

---

[1] I follow Stephen Owen's use of the term subgenre "to designate the classification by subject matter and occasion and the term genre for the formal, metrical classification." In *Poetry of the Early T'ang*, (New Haven: Yale University Press, 1977), p. 445, n. 13.

[2] Trans. James R. Hightower in "The *Wen Hsuan* and Genre Theory," *HJAS*, 20 (1957), p. 520.

had become truly encyclopedic.[3] Nor is this surprising in view of the nature of the *fu*, a genre characterized by exhaustive and extravagant descriptions of a topic. Insofar as its origin lies in the *fu*, the *yongwu* mode has at its center the element of description. The cumulative descriptive technique and epideictic rhetoric of the *fu*, by which details are enumerated in lush verbiage in an effort to capture the appearance as well as the essence of a thing, were modified in *shi* and *ci* poetry and in *yongwu fu* of the late Six Dynasties to effect a more selective portrayal of the object.

Thus as the *yongwu* subgenre evolved across generic boundaries, certain conventions associated with the *yongwu fu* were carried over, while each genre in turn also imposed its own rules and requirements on the *yongwu* mode. We find, for example, that the kind of *yongwu* poetry that constitutes a staple subgenre of palace style poetry, notably as practiced by the Liang court aristocracy, is sharply curtailed in subject matter and length and is written for the most part in short pentasyllabic *shi* with an economy and preciosity of language undreamed of by the exuberant and effusive Han *fu* writer.[4] These changes reflect developments brought about by both social and literary historical factors. In the case of the palace style *yongwu*, the sheltered lives of prince and courtier and a growing sense of normative aesthetics both contributed to a narrowing of the poetic world to the man-made luxuries and tamed aspects of nature found in the palace environment. *Yongwu* then became a perfect vehicle for verbal ingenuity and display; self-conscious artistry flirted with such poetic devices as parallelism, paronomasia, and tonal euphony, all then in vogue.

The very practice of writing about a specific object in a high poetic tradition demands that appropriate rhetorical and figurative devices be used and formal rules of versification adhered to. The literary conventions expected in *yongwu* render it an ex-

---

[3] Even a brief glance through the table of contents of the *Lidai fuhui* demonstrates this fact.

[4] For an informed discussion of the development of *yongwu shi* in the Six Dynasties, see the chapter on Xie Tiao (464–499) in Kang-i Sun Chang, *Six Dynasties Poetry: From T'ao Ch'ien to Yü Hsin* (Princeton University Press, 1986).

tremely self-conscious art form. Artifice becomes its inevitable hallmark. When *yongwu* poetry serves the additional function of social occasional poetry, as it often did in the course of its history, the element of craft is particularly dominant.

The *yongwu* subgenre was firmly transplanted into *shi* poetry during the age of palace style poetry (roughly corresponding to the last three Southern Dynasties, the Qi, Liang, and Chen), when under aristocratic patronage poetry was for the first time totally divorced from politics and from moral intent and was indulged in as an art for its own sake. To the court poets and their royal patrons, epitomized by the coterie surrounding Xiao Gang (who later became Emperor Jianwen of the Liang), nothing seemed more suitable as a literary pastime than a form of verse that afforded the participants communal delight in an object and enhanced with recherché descriptions in a prescribed mode the pleasure derived from the object. In the anthology *Yutai xinyong* [New Songs from a Jade Terrace], commissioned by Xiao Gang, *yongwu* poems fill more than a few pages.[5] Among the favorite objects for celebration are certain upper-class luxury articles— carved candles, bronze mirrors, musical instruments, and the like—and such poetic clichés from the natural world as wind, moon, and flowers. The conscious artistry in the treatment and the unabashed sensuality generally exhibited have earned their courtly authors the opprobrium of later serious-minded critics as effete and decadent.

The descriptions in these poems generally present a series of the attributes, striking effects, and unusual properties of the object celebrated, often in florid and ornate diction with set associations and poetic figures. Since the aim is to display wit and refinement, the majority of the poems are adroitly executed "sensuous word-pictures"[6] lacking deeper emotional or intellectual significance that would involve the reader. The following succinct little piece is by He Sun (ca. 480–ca. 530), who was much admired by his contemporaries. It is written in pentasyllabic

[5] For a complete translation of the *Yutai xinyong*, see Anne Birrell, *New Songs from a Jade Terrace* (London: George Allen & Unwin, 1982).

[6] John Marney, *Liang Chien-wen ti*, Twayne's World Author Series (Boston: G. K. Hall & Co., 1976), p. 108.

form with two parallel couplets, the second of which anticipates
Tang regulated verse in its perfect tonal antithesis. Structurally,
the first couplet tries to capture the essence of the object while the
second depicts some of the wondrous effects that have caught the
poet's fancy:

"On Spring Breeze"

Audible yet invisible,
May be heavy, may be light.
Before the mirror spilled powder swirls,
Across the lute lingering notes are echoed.[7]

詠春風

可聞不可見，
能重復能輕。
鏡前飄落粉，
琴上響餘聲。

The word-game nature of the piece is apparent: the mysterious
entity of the wind is not named in the lines themselves. The
wind, as observed or imagined by a courtier, does not rustle
through a hermit's bamboo grove but mischievously scatters the
cosmetic powder a palace lady is using and at the same time plays
with the strings of the idle lute probably lying by her side.

Despite the charge of decadence made during the Confucian
reforms of Emperor Wen of the short-lived Sui dynasty,[8] this
tradition of the courtly *yongwu*, along with other poetic norms
and models developed during the period, continued into the
early Tang. Tang Taizong (r. 627–649), for example, took in-
genuous delight in writing in the ornate palace style, to the
consternation of his more morally inclined courtiers.[9]

Yet, in the seventh century, even while many *yongwu* pieces

---

[7] *Yutai xinyong* (Shanghai: Shijie shuju, 1935), p. 281. Translation adapted
from Anne Birrell, *New Songs from a Jade Terrace*, p. 278.

[8] For the extent and duration of Emperor Wen's reform measures affecting the
literary heritage, see Arthur Wright, *The Sui Dynasty* (New Haven: Yale Univer-
sity Press, 1978), pp. 122–25.

[9] See Liu Su, *Da Tang xinyu* (*Congshu jicheng chubian* ed., vol. 2741), p. 28; and
Ji Yougong, *Tangshi jishi* (Beijing: Zhonghua shuju, 1965), 1:6.

were still being turned out on the numerous courtly occasions when poems were written on imperial command, poets, when writing poems of a more personal and self-expressive nature, began to subject the *yongwu* subgenre to conscious experimentation in an allegorical mode.[10] In such poems, the object is no longer simply described with artful dexterity for literary entertainment. The description now serves to signify something outside itself. In Luo Binwang's (ca. 640–684) dense and allusive poem on the cicada, the insect, which is nourished on the wind and dew, is used as a symbol of the poet's own purity.[11] Another early example is Chen Ziang's (661–702) allegorical poem on the fragrant orchid in his *Ganyu* 'Stirred by things encountered' series (No. 2):

> The fragrant orchid grows in spring and summer,
> How brightly luxuriant in its prime.
> Hidden and alone in the empty woods,
> Vermilion blossoms appear on its purple stems.
> Slowly the bright day turns to evening,
> Softly the autumn winds begin to rise.
> When the year's flowering has all fallen away,
> What becomes of its fragrant intentions?[12]

> 蘭若生春夏，
> 芊蔚何青青。
> 幽獨空林色，
> 朱蕤冒紫莖。
> 遲遲白日晚，
> 嫋嫋秋風生。
> 歲華盡搖落，
> 芳意竟何成。

[10] In the Chinese poetic tradition, allegory has the narrower sense of possessing a specifically moral or political tenor. The allegorical mode was first consciously employed in some of the *Chuci* poems, and allegorical interpretation, a hermeneutics with pre-Qin origins specifically applied to the *Book of Odes*, was first fully established in the Han with the systematic distortion of the *Shi jing* poems to elucidate their moral or political message. In later ages, allegorical interpretation was of course not restricted to the *Shi jing*.

[11] "Zaiyu yong chan," *QTS*, 3:848.

[12] *QTS*, 3:890. Trans. adapted from Stephen Owen, *Poetry of the Early T'ang*, p. 218.

The statement is quite obvious: the flower so often emblematic in the "Li Sao" stands as a symbol of high-minded men whose virtues and talents go unrecognized.

As Chen Ziang's use of "Li Sao" symbolism suggests, the allegorical mode was by no means new in the Chinese poetic tradition, nor was it without precedent in the *yongwu* subgenre. Allegorical *fu* on objects had been written in the late Han,[13] and poets with a penchant for allegory, such as Cao Zhi (192–232) furthered its development. By the late third century *yongwu fu* had become a common allegorical medium. The various *fu* on musical instruments or natural phenomena often aimed to express ideas beyond the immediate limits of their subject.[14] The trajectory of *yongwu fu* from objective description to descriptive symbolism was later paralleled by the course of its counterpart in the *shi* genre, which similarly moved from the intricate word-pictures of the palace style to the allegorical *yongwu* of the early Tang and beyond.[15]

This development in *yongwu* poetry can be seen as a reflection of the tendency in verse to move toward complexity and so-phistication in methods and modes of representation. Yet in a specifically Chinese context, it also bears a crucial relationship to the dominant concept of poetry inherited from antiquity, one which bears the mark of the Confucian ethos. From the *Shangshu* dictum "poetry expresses intent" (*shi yan zhi*) and its elabora-tion in the Great Preface to *Shi jing*, poetry was given a didactic definition from which it never entirely freed itself. Although *zhi* ("intent") was equated with *qing* ("emotion") in the great Pre-face, thus making the lyrical expression of emotion a prominent feature of poetry, in the depths of the Chinese poetic conscious-ness, the tenacious notion persisted that poetry, to be of true value, should somehow serve ethics; failing this, it should at least

[13] Mi Heng's (ca. 173–198) "Yingwu fu" for example; see William T. Graham, Jr., "Mi Heng's 'Rhapsody on a Parrot'," *HJAS*, 30:1 (1979), pp. 39–54.

[14] Xi Kang's "Qin fu" is a good example; see *Xi Kang ji jiaozhu* (Beijing: Renmin wenxue chubanshe, 1962), pp. 82–109. In this piece Xi Kang is not just interested in describing the external attributes of the *qin* and its music, but in expressing certain truths about the nature of music, human emotion, and the Tao.

[15] I am indebted to Stephen Owen's discussions of Tang *yongwu* poetry in *Poetry of the Early T'ang*; see in particular, pp. 281–93.

not subvert it. The Han *fu* was criticized in its day for extravagance in language and content, which was judged to have the effect of encouraging the very vices it was to restrain. Clearly, the moral message commonly tagged on at the end of a *fu* did not suffice to right the balance after prolonged indulgence in tantalizing descriptions. However, if the descriptive process itself could serve to articulate the author's serious thoughts and emotions, thus creating an extra-literal or metaphorical dimension, the resultant composition would serve to "express intent." The great sixth-century critic Liu Xie's elucidation of the nature of the *fu* as "writing intent by embodying an object" testifies to the theoretical merging of the boundaries of the object and intent in allegorical *yongwu fu*.[16]

Palace style verse remained outside this relation between allegory and content. We need only go to the preface of the *Yutai xinyong* to confirm this. Xu Ling, the compiler, avowed that the purpose of the anthology was for the distraction of beautiful palace ladies from their boredom.[17] To "express intent" was simply not the court poets' concern when writing palace style verse; they made no pretensions to it, and it is not surprising that *yongwu shi* in the palace style failed to develop an allegorical dimension.

This historical perspective on the *yongwu* subgenre as it evolved in the *fu* and *shi* suggests that similar patterns of development in the *ci* may also be found. The dual potentiality of the *yongwu* mode as a vehicle for literary amusement and for symbolic expression was bound to have an influence on the evolution of *yongwu ci*. However, before going into the subject of *yongwu ci* proper, a few salient aspects of the *ci* genre, and its relation to *shi* and the orthodox concept of poetry should be considered. *Yongwu ci*, as we shall see, eventually came to occupy a significant place in a complex configuration of literary-historical relationships.

[16] Liu Xie, *Wenxin diaolong zhu* (Beijing: Renmin wenxue chubanshe, 1958), p. 134.

[17] This preface has been translated by James R. Hightower in "Some Characteristics of Parallel Prose," in *Studies in Chinese Literature*, ed. John L. Bishop (Cambridge: Harvard University Press, 1966), pp. 108–39.

The *ci*, originating as it did in a new song form, which first became popular in the entertainment quarters during the Tang, did not have the prerogatives of orthodox poetry, or *shi*, as a time-honored vehicle for personal and ethical expression. The heterodox status of *ci*, however, conveniently freed those literati interested in the form from any didactic obligations when trying their hands at writing lyrics to the popular tunes. With their literary training and skill, they created song-poems in a refined and elegant diction, which courtesans and singing girls performed. The lyrics closely reflected the psyche of these denizens of the demimonde and their boudoir environment, with the result that *ci* from the late Tang through the Five Dynasties focused on exploring the moods and emotions of the fair and often languishing female persona. Such an emphasis was in marked contrast to the predominantly "human-equals-man" world of *shi* poetry. One of the consequences was that *shi* and *ci* began to assume distinct generic roles. The late Tang poet Wen Tingyun (813?–870), the first acknowledged master of the *ci*, for example, dealt with significantly different themes in his *shi* poetry. The *ci* subsequently evolved its own poetic conventions, by which the poet evokes moods and feelings through imagistic diction with little regard for mimetic realism or logical development of thought. Song poets of the tenth and eleventh centuries who wrote *ci* inherited this poetics of mood and realized more of its possibilities for emotional projection, whether of the subtle and elusive variety of the Yan Shu-Ouyang Xiu style or of the more personal and direct Li Yu-Liu Yong type.[18] *Shi* poetry, meanwhile, as is well known, took the opposite direction, toward increasing realism and discursiveness.

In an aesthetics of *ci* wherein a premium is placed on the emotional association and resonance of images, often at the expense of their logical and descriptive unity, the unsuitability of descriptive *yongwu* should be apparent. And indeed for almost

---

[18] The following works contain discussions on the styles of these four *ci* poets: Kang-i Sun Chang, *The Evolution of Chinese Tz'u Poetry* (Princeton: Princeton University Press, 1980); James J. Y. Liu, *Major Lyricists of the Northern Sung* (Princeton: Princeton University Press, 1974); and Yeh Chia-ying, *Jialing tanci* (Taipei: Chunwenxue congshu, 1970).

two centuries following the adoption of *ci* by the literati in the late Tang, except for isolated examples, *yongwu* poems were absent from the corpus of *ci*.[19] The first epoch of *yongwu ci* began in the second half of the eleventh century with *ci* written by the many-faceted genius Su Shi and his circle of scholar-official poets. Typical of his general daring and innovative spirit in artistic matters, Su Shi demolished some of the established generic boundaries between *shi* and *ci* poetry by using *ci* for purposes previously restricted to *shi*. Su wrote *ci* poems with philosophical and historical themes and introduced the frequent use of allusions, even from the classics and histories, practices avoided by more orthodox writers of *ci*. Su Shi's unorthodox approach has elicited both praise and blame from his contemporaries and later critics, but the important point for us in Su Shi's departure from tradition is his introduction of the *yongwu* subgenre into *ci* poetry.

It is no doubt the social occasional function that *ci* poetry now assumed in the hands of Su Shi and his friends that in part stimulated a sizeable quantity of *yongwu* poems. In the preface they often provided for their *ci* poems, itself a new feature, one sees the multifarious occasions—farewells, banquets, excursions—on which *ci* poems are now composed. In a social milieu where literati gatherings of all descriptions were frequent, the *yongwu* mode came into favor again when extemporary poems were called for. The object furnished a common theme for individual efforts, and the finished products in *ci* form could then be sung. Incidentally, the popularity of flower viewing and tea drinking in Song life precipitated a great number of *yongwu* poems, with those on flowers outnumbering all the others. Once

---

[19] In the earliest anthology of *ci* poetry, the *Huajian ji*, there are certain tune titles that still served as the subject matter of the poems, thus giving us some poems on objects. The small number of poems written to the tunes *Liuzhi* and *Yangliu zhi* are usually about willows. Huang Qingshi, in his essay "Tan yongwu ci," does not mention any of these willow poems, but quotes Niu Qiao's *Meng Jiangnan* on the swallow and mandarin ducks as being the first example of *yongwu ci*; *Yilin conglu*, 5 (1964), pp. 84–91. Before the mid Northern Song period, examples are rare indeed; there is one in Ouyang Xiu's corpus, *Liangzhou ling* (*QSC* 1/146), and four in Liu Yong's: *Huangyinger* (*QSC* 1/13) and *Mulanhua* (three) (*QSC* 1/52).

instituted, the *yongwu* remained a major and staple subgenre in the *ci*, throughout the Southern Song. As an index of its continued popularity in the Southern Song, we can turn to the reign of Emperor Gaozong (1127–1162), when not long after the 1127 loss of the northern half of the empire to the Jurchens, *yongwu ci* poems written to imperial command and *ci* poems celebrating imperial birthdays were happily produced by his court officials.[20] In a Southern Song sheltered by an expensive peace bought from the Jurchens, *yongwu ci* thrived among the entertainments the cultured upper classes devised for themselves. The phenomenon of *ci* poetry clubs (*cishe*) also made its appearance at this time, providing yet another congenial environment in which *yongwu* figured as an eminently appropriate literary form.[21]

The above account suggests a causal relationship between the function of *ci* poetry as occasional verse and the rise of the *yongwu* subgenre, but it does not follow that all *yongwu ci* are occasional poems. In fact, a great majority of those *yongwu ci* for which the preface simply gives the name of the object are not occasional. In many instances they belong to the category of personal *yongwu*.[22]

What approach did a poet take when writing a *yongwu* poem in the *ci* genre? By definition the *yongwu* mode takes the object as the organizing principle and, on the most elementary level, the *ci* poet readily subscribes to the conventions of the subgenre by

---

[20] See the *ci* collections of Cao Xun (1098–1174), in *QSC* 2/1206–39, and of Kang Yuzhi (fl. 1140s) in *QSC* 2/1302–10. Although only a few of Kang Yuzhi's *ci* poems survive, he is known in the Southern Song for having produced great numbers of them. See Huang Sheng's comment in *Zhongxing yilai juemiao cixuan*, in *Hua'an cixuan*, p. 161.

[21] Xue Liruo in his *Songci tonglun* goes so far as to characterize Southern Song *ci* of the middle and late period (i.e., beginning in the late twelfth century) as the product of *ci* poetry clubs (Taipei: Kaiming shudian, 1958), pp. 50–52. Some of the earliest occurrences of the term *sheyou* ("club friends") are found in Shi Dazu's (1155–1220) prefaces to his *ci*, e.g., *Dian jiangchun* (*QSC* 4/2337) and *Long yin qu* (*QSC* 4/2345).

[22] William T. Graham, Jr., in his article on Mi Heng's rhapsody (p. 51), divides *yongwu fu* into two broad categories of the social and personal. He suggests that in writing social pieces the poet adhered to strict conventions, whereas in the personal he was afforded almost unlimited license in approaching the subject. While the distinction may not be as clear-cut in the case of *yongwu ci*, the same general tendencies can be observed.

manipulating the common lore of poetic images, allusions, and stock symbols associated with the particular object in fashioning his lyric. Inevitably a great many insipid descriptive pieces were produced. If we examine stylistic elements of *yongwu ci*, however, we can discern a shift—with gradations—in the *yongwu* mode, a shift that epitomizes the general transition from the relatively direct and explicit rhetoric of the Northern Song *ci* style to the dense and allusive mannerism of the Southern Song style.

At its most typical, the Northern Song *yongwu ci*, from Su Shi to Zhou Bangyan, maintains a poetic voice independent of the object. Both Su Shi and Zhou Bangyan often employed the technique of sustained personification—hitherto little explored but a principal device in later *yongwu ci*—to project the object onto the human plane for poetic effect. By conceiving of the object as having human attributes, the poet asserts his own self as the lyrical consciousness musing on the object. This is particularly true of Su Shi's *yongwu ci*, in which his personality dominates as observer. Examples are his famous anthology piece written to the tune *Shuilong yin* on the willow catkin (*QSC* 1/277) and the following short lyric on the red plum blossom:

To the tune *Ding feng bo*
On red plum blossoms

1   Fond of sleep, too lazy to bloom, don't mind her being
            late,
     Too bad if her icy face is out of season.
     At times she puts on little red blossoms, in the color of
            peach-and-apricot.
     Easy and graceful
5   She still maintains her lonely and slim posture of snow
            and frost.

     Don't let your idle heart follow the manner of others;
     For what
     Did the wine make you somewhat flushed, tinting your
            pure complexion?
     The old poet does not know where the spirit of the plum
            blossom lies,

As he chants
10   He keeps looking for green leaves and new branches.[23]

(QSC 1/289)

詠紅梅

好睡慵開莫厭遲。
自憐冰臉不時宜。
偶作小紅桃杏色，
閒雅，
尚餘孤瘦雪霜姿。

休把閒心隨物態，
何事，
酒生微暈沁瑤肌。
詩老不知梅格在，
吟詠，
更看綠葉與青枝。

Through the poet's lively imagination, the flowering plum is depicted as a woman, with the flower's traditional symbolic values made over as attributes of the woman. The personification makes it possible for the poet to address the plum tree in the second stanza, further highlighting its red color through the conceit of a wine-flushed face. Su's presence as animator is strongly felt in the second stanza as he delineates an essential image of the flower by his commanding presence.

The voice of the persona is also maintained in many of Zhou Bangyan's *yongwu ci*, but the relationship between the subject and object in the poem begins to change in some of them. Rather than maintaining the distinct roles of observer and observed, an empathic correspondence is developed between the lyrical self and the object sung about. In other words, through the subject's encounter with the object, various nuances of subjective feeling are evoked, echoed, and finally embodied by the object. For example, in Zhou Bangyan's *Liu chou*, on faded roses, the poet begins by lamenting the transience of life, shown by the passing of spring. This regret finds its objective correlative in the faded flowers, personified as palace beauties, dead and buried. The

---

[23] Trans. adapted from Kang-i Sun Chang, *The Evolution of Chinese Tz'u Poetry*, p. 178.

poet's regret and longing are further amplified by sad images: bees and butterflies that still seek the vanished flowers, the branches, now bare of blossoms, that try to "detain" the poet, as if seeking some solace for their loss, and the wilted rose he puts in his turban, a foil to the remembered rose in full bloom worn in his lover's hair.[24] In such a poem, it is the mood and emotional associations roused by the object rather than any realistic description or intellectual contemplation of the object that form the core of the lyric.

This objectification of one's personal moods and sentiments, whose beginnings can be seen in some of Zhou Bangyan's *yongwu ci*, is developed into an extreme interiorization of subjective sensibility in the *yongwu* works of major Southern Song *ci* poets such as Jiang Kui, Wu Wenying, Zhou Mi, Zhang Yan, and Wang Yisun. With the *yongwu* mode thus turned into a metaphoric projection of the private realm, ambiguity and obscurity inevitably result. Since the poet's intentionality is no longer directed solely towards a descriptive rendering of the object, but aims to metaphorize some personal emotion through the object, even familiar allusions and kennings available for a given object may prove to be semantically elusive in the particular context. We are no longer sure of their true referent: they signify some aspect of the object that is itself in turn only a signifier, whose ultimate referent may remain conjectural. The highly complex referential structure of these late Song *yongwu ci* is compounded by the then current poetics of indirection—a poetics that favors allusive and connotative language—to produce a dense, sometimes almost opaque, texture and meaning. It is easy to see how these have offered critics in the tradition of *ci* hermeneutics fertile ground for enthusiastic exegesis as well as for pejorative criticism.

It is true that these late Song poets continued to write *yongwu ci* of a descriptive or occasional nature, in which case a clever, literary description of the object remained a priority. But their most representative *yongwu* pieces show an unmistakable tendency toward extreme subjectivity. The object merely provides a

---

[24] *QSC* 2/610. See also James J. Y. Liu's analysis of this poem in *Major Lyricists of the Northern Sung*, pp. 173–78.

tenuous thread on which the poet strings together glimpses of past memories, elusive thoughts, and subtle emotions through a partly formal (i.e., object-oriented) and partly personal (i.e., self-oriented) associative process.[25] In other poems, the subjective voice of the poet disappears from the surface of the poem altogether; there is no longer a subject / object dichotomy and the object takes on the full weight of actualizing private moments and emotions.[26]

I have selected three *yongwu* poems from Wu Wenying's collection for exegesis, each exemplifying a different aspect of the *yongwu* subgenre: artifice, lyricism, and metaphor. The first poem is a model of an occasional *yongwu*:

To the tune *Shengsheng man*
> A friend entertained guests with a display of plum blossoms, orchids, daphnes and narcissi, which he named the Four Fragrances. In the distribution of rhymes I received the character *feng*.

1   In mountain valleys deep in clouds,
Or river marshes chilled by mist,
Rare it is in life to meet one another.
Smiling together before the lanterns,
5   Springtime faces arranged in rows of two.
Pure fragrances vie by night in their true forms,
Stirring fresh scents to confuse the east wind.
The hand that gathered the flowers
Must arrange for them a golden chamber:
10   The romantic official is at a loss.

Haggard are the slanting feathers and wilted girdle-pendants,
How sad the Jade Maiden has grown thin,
Drifting to follow the light swan.
I ask my bosom friend:
15   At the party who is the most affectionate?
We keep calling for Purple Cloud to get drunk with us.

---

[25] Examples are Jiang Kui's *Shu ying* (*QSC* 3/2182) and Wu Wenying's *Xinghua tian* (analysis to follow).
[26] An example is Wu Wenying's *Suochuang han* (analyzed below).

The little clove, only just revealing a faint red;
If it understands words,
I will take it home to make rain in a dream.

(QSC 4/2920)

友人以梅、蘭、瑞香、水仙供客，曰四香，
分韻得風字

雲深山隖，
煙冷江皋，
人生未易相逢。
一笑燈前，
釵行兩兩春容。
清芳夜爭眞態，
引生香、撩亂東風。
探花手，
與安排金屋，
懊惱司空。

憔悴敲翹委佩，
恨玉奴銷瘦，
飛趁輕鴻。
試問知心，
尊前誰最情濃。
連呼紫雲伴醉，
小丁香、纔吐微紅。
還解語，
待攜歸、行雨夢中。

The preface furnishes the details regarding the occasion of the composition; it was a literary gathering to view flowers, to which the poet had been invited. This prefatory information orients the reader to a particular way of reading and interpreting the poem. On one level at least, the entire poem can be read as referring to the social event: the poet will perform the feat of magically bringing to life the unique floral assembly of plum blossom, orchid, daphne, and narcissus. To do so only, however, is to miss half the meaning, or perhaps half the fun, of the poem, for Wu Wenying skillfully combines apt allusions with personification to produce a poetic structure with two simultaneous sets of referents. To be sure, the formal description of objects is there, but through the description, the poet aims at portraying another reality.

The poem unfolds as a narrative, moving spatially from the natural environment of the flowers to the lively scene at the party where they are the main attraction. At this point, the identity of the flowers undergo a metamorphosis—personified, they now also represent real women, singing girls or entertainers brought together for the occasion. Their competing charms ironically are causing some confusion to the host who has brought them together. The allusion that comes at the close of the first stanza consolidates the flowers' personification and relationship to the host. "Gold chamber," a term originating in a story about the love of Emperor Wu of Han as a child for his cousin Ajiao, is a conventional figure symbolizing the care and protection a man should give to the woman he loves.[27]

In the new stanza we witness in the wilting of the narcissus, orchid, and plum, how some of the singing girls lost in the competition for favor. True to *yongwu* conventions in occasional verse, the flowers are deftly referred to by familiar allusive kennings, which are also, appropriately, feminine accessories, and by a woman's name, thereby maintaining the twofold description of flowers and women. By using the character *qiao* (line 11), which means long feathers as well as a woman's hair ornaments, the poet by a metonymic trope refers to both the narcissus, with its long, feather-shaped leaves, and a woman with a disarrayed headdress. In the term "wilted girdle-pendants," the orchid is thinly disguised by an allusion to the "Li sao" line, "I strung together autumn orchids for girdle-pendants."[28] By describing the orchid-pendants as wilted, one of the "Li sao" themes—being out of favor—is borrowed, minus its allegorical significance, to amplify the dejection felt by some of the singing girls, already suggested by the word "haggard." Thus the lapidary craft of *yongwu* poetry is applied meticulously. The precedent for using the name Jade Maiden to refer to the plum blossom comes

---

[27] Ban Gu, *Han Wu gushi*, in *Xu tan zhu* (*Congshu jicheng chubian* ed., vol. 272), p. 64.

[28] Zhu Xi, *Chuci jizhu* (Shanghai: Shanghai guji chubanshe, 1979), p. 3.

93

from Su Shi. In one of his *shi* poems on the plum blossom, Su personifies the plum blossom as the beautiful concubine of a nobleman of the Southern Qi, whose name was Jade Maiden.[29] Wu here describes the fading and falling of the plum petals in the image of an ethereal maiden so slender that she floats away, her motion in harmony with the graceful movements of a swan.

With the disposal—on literal, metaphorical, and structural levels—of three out of four of his subjects, Wu devotes the rest of the poem to the handling of the daphne, whose attributes are manipulated by ingenious wordplay to complete the verbal artifice. By the association of color, the daphne is personified as Purple Cloud, the name of a singing girl desired by the Tang poet Du Mu,[30] and perhaps one whom our poet desires on the present occasion, as the last line seems to suggest. Line 17 sustains the personification by a metonymic substitution. By association through color and shape, the daphne is referred to as the clove, which is, conveniently, the conventional figure for a woman's tongue. The line may be paraphrased as "Her small clovelike tongue, only just revealing its faint red." The note of eroticism thus introduced is consummated in the last line; "cloud and rain" or "moving rain," especially in a dream, is a stock image for sexual intercourse whose *locus classicus* is in the "Gaotang fu" attributed to Song Yu.[31] The reference to a dream in the last line, moreover, alludes obliquely to the daphne, whose alternative name is *shuixiang* ("sleep fragrance"), thereby artfully maintaining the relevance of the actual flower to the end of the poem.

Such an involuted system of signification in an occasional *yongwu* serves as an erudite literary embellishment in a poem that is otherwise devoid of deeper meaning. Here is a poem of artifice par excellence, and one that is reminiscent of the gloss and wit of its Southern Dynasties antecedents.

In Wu Wenying's use of the *yongwu* mode when the occasion is not a social one, there is a tendency to violate the primary convention of the subgenre by deviating from the declared topic.

---

[29] Su's poem is entitled *Ci yun Yang Gongji fengyi meihua* "After the rhymes of Yang Gongji's poem on the plum blossom;" Wang Wen'gao's annotations in *Su shi bianzhu jicheng* (1888 ed.), *j*.33/1b–2a.

[30] Ji Yougong, *Tangshi jishi*, p. 849.

[31] Xiao Tong, *Wenxuan* (Hong Kong: Commercial Press, 1978), 1 : 392.

The following poem on medicinal broth is an example:

To the tune *Xinghua tian*
On broth

1   Southern ginger and cardamon—the taste of love,
      I reckon it was in the spring breeze beneath her tongue.
      River's purity tenderly given to dispel a lingering
            drunkenness,
      A haggard Wenyuan rose from illness.

5   I stopped my neighing horse—the singer's brows
            conveyed her feelings,
      I remember dawn colors in a dream by the eastern city
            wall.
      Purple sandalwood, hazy and light, fragrant glances so
            delicate,
      Heartbreak in the little quarter with weeping willows.

(QSC 4/2933)

詠湯

蠻薑豆蔻相思味。
算卻在、春風舌底。
江青愛與消殘醉。
悴憔文園病起。

停嘶馬、歌眉送意。
記曉色、東城夢裏。
紫檀暈淺香波細。
腸斷垂楊小市。

This is hardly what one would expect to find in a *yongwu* on medicinal broth. There should have been some more elaboration on the preparation of the broth and more praise of the broth's healing properties and magical effects. For comparison, we can take a look at a short *ci* poem by Zhang Yan on the same subject, which does exactly what the form requires:

To the tune *Ta suo xing*
On broth

1   Collecting fragrances of rare herbs, gathering mercury
            from immortal flowers,

Where the ice wheel grinds, scented dust is stirred.
On a stove with bamboo the broth warms over a
    reddening flame.
After the blending by jade hands, it was delivered with
    song.

5   I wave away the Classic of Tea, hide the Eulogy of wine,
Enjoying a cup of pure flavor with wonderful guests.
Immortality has always been gained by gathering herbs,
Don't be fooled by the love potion at Indigo Bridge.

(QSC 5/3510)

詠湯

瑤草收香，
琪花采汞。
冰輪碾處芳塵動。
竹鑪湯暖火初紅，
玉纖調罷歌聲送。

庵去茶經，
襲藏酒頌。
一杯清味佳賓共。
從來采藥得長生，
藍橋休被瓊漿弄。

The methodical description in the first stanza of Zhang Yan's poem makes for a flat reading and, together with the little Taoist injunction at the end, give it a discursive flavor more characteristic of trends in Song period *shi* poetry than *ci*.

Wu Wenying, for his part, used this topic as a warp on which to weave a small but touching human incident; the poem becomes a vehicle for the memory of a tender experience. The poet, suffering from illness and a hangover, was nursed back to health by a pretty and loving singing girl in the brothel district in the eastern part of Hangzhou.[32] Then came the parting inevitable in all such encounters, made sad here by a genuine appreciation of her tenderness and care.

[32] Hangzhou in Song times had a brothel district in its eastern section. See entry on *Wazi xiang* in Li E, *Dongcheng zaji* (*Congshu jicheng chubian* ed., vol. 3174), p. 43.

There is very little description of the object itself except that the broth, made of ginger and cardamon, is clear like a river and regenerative like love. The ingredients of the broth also allude to the tender age and beauty of the girl who made it. The term *doukou* ("cardamon") has stood for an attractive young girl ever since one was celebrated by Du Mu:

> Delicate and pretty, a little over thirteen,
> The tips of cardamon branches at the start of March.[33]

娉娉嫋嫋十三餘，
豆蔻梢頭二月初。

The epithet for ginger, *man* ("southern"), may echo the name of Bai Juyi's young concubine, Xiao Man, who has become a stock poetic figure for a charming young mistress. These literal and literary ingredients impart an ambiguous and mildly erotic tone to the first two lines. The taste of love is the girl herself, experienced by the poet through the "spring breeze beneath her tongue," that is, the pleasing songs and words which come forth from her mouth. Concealed in this image is also the possibility that the taste of love is derived from the manner in which she feeds him the broth—with her mouth. "Spring" here is read with its romantic and erotic connotations.

The parting and heartbreak in the second stanza, seemingly far removed from the surface topic, hinge on an implied analogy between the singing girl and medicinal broth—both are curative and beneficial but not everyday fare.

As befits the personal nature of this poem, Wu Wenying resorts less to rhetorical tropes or embellishments. The allusions to Du Mu's poem and to Bai Juyi's concubine fit into the text of the poem very naturally. The only other allusive name, Wenyuan, is derived from the title of the Han poet Sima Xiangru. It is a popular reference rich with the associations of literary talent, romantic disposition, and failing health, and Wu often uses the term for his persona.

What becomes apparent in reading this *yongwu* poem is that the violation of form may serve as an assertion of lyricism in a

---

[33] From the first of two poems entitled "Written at parting," *QTS*, 16:5988.

poetic mode that otherwise could tend toward excessive imper-
sonality and artificiality in language and sentiment.

The last poem we shall consider is written to the tune *Suo-
chuang han* and is simply subtitled "The Magnolia":

1   Magenta strands on layers of cloud,
      Clear cheeks of moist jade—
      The Woman Adrift first appears,[34]
      Southern stench not yet washed off,
5   The seafarer's heart is full of sad regret.
      Far they journeyed on the magic raft to ride on high
            winds.
      Possessing the noblest fragrance in the kingdom, her
            secret heart opens.
      [One character missing] leaving sweet scent but
            concealing color,
      Her real beauty is quiet and subdued—
10   A resurrected soul from the land of Sao.

      One glance
      Exchanged for a thousand pieces of gold.
      Then smiling she accompanies Master Leather-flask,
      Together they return to Wu Park.
15   Amid separating mists and sorrowful waters
      She dreams of faraway southern skies on an autumn
            evening.
      Frail when she came, more so now,
      Cold fragrance seeping into her bones she grieves at the
            distance of her native soil.
      Saddest of all is seeing the guest off in Xianyang,
20   Sash tied to the plaint of the west wind.

                                   (*QSC* 4/2873–74)

玉蘭

紺縷堆雲，
清頲潤玉，

---

[34] The felicitous rendering of the term *fanren* as "Woman Adrift" comes from
James R. Hightower; see Chia-ying Yeh Chao, "Wu Wen-ying's *Tz'u*," pp.
162–63.

汜人初見。
螢腥未洗，
海客一懷悽惋。
渺征槎、去乘閬風，
占香上國幽心展。
□ 遺芳掩色，
眞姿凝澹，
返魂騷畹。

一盼。
千金換。
又笑伴鷗夷，
共歸吳苑。
離煙恨水，
夢杳南天秋晚。
比來時，瘦肌更銷，
冷薰沁骨悲鄉遠。
最傷情、送客咸陽，
佩結西風怨。

The overt subject of the poem is the magnolia, but even an initial reading reveals that the image of the flower is inextricably bound up with and superseded by the image of a woman in the poet's vision. The discussion here will not aim to explicate the meaning of the poem so much as to show how the metaphoric dimension is brought about in the *yongwu* mode.

The poem begins with the personification of the flower as the Woman Adrift. Behind this figure is a strange tale of romance from the Tang set in the south of China and concerning an ill-fated love between a water nymph from the dragon palace and a young scholar.[35] The figure of the Woman Adrift is not uncommon in poems on flowers. Wu Wenying uses it elsewhere in his poetry, and so does Zhou Mi.[36] But in all cases it is used for

[35] Recounted by Shen Yazhi as *Xiang zhong yuan jie* ("An Account of the Unhappy Person by the Xiang River"), in *Shen Xiaxian ji* (*Sibu congkan chubian* ed.), *j*.2/14a–b. A translation of the story by James R. Hightower is found in Chia-ying Yeh Chao, "Wu Wen-ying's *Tz'u*," pp. 162–63.

[36] Wu's poems with the term "Woman Adrift" are *Qitian yue* (*QSC* 4/2884) and *Qiliang fan* (*QSC* 4/2927); and Zhou Mi's is *Yizeshang guoxiang man* (*QSC* 5/3290).

flowers that grow in water, such as the lotus and narcissus. The fact that the magnolia is a tree or shrub that does not even have to grow near water destroys the mimetic correspondence of the personification and throws into relief another element associated with the Woman Adrift tale. It is the setting in the tale: the uncivilized and barbaric south, a mysterious water country criss-crossed with rivers and lakes.

The south is the native growing range of the magnolia, and here again it is the setting for a poetic reenactment of the sad romance. The first stanza tells of a seafarer's meeting with a flower-woman and their journey together to a distant kingdom where her fragrance and beauty are enhanced by the happiness she feels. With the stanzaic change the personification of the flower is reiterated in the figure of Xi Shi, the legendary "kingdom-toppling" beauty. One tradition has it that she wandered off with Fan Li (Master Leather-flask), the Yue minister who had engineered the ruse to use her beauty to defeat the kingdom of Wu.[37] Except for the equation between the beauty of Xi Shi and that of the flower-woman, any mimetic correspondence to the magnolia has all but disappeared in this personification. This does not, however, affect the structural progression in this *yongwu* as it is clearly not activated by a description of the object, but by the quasi narrative made possible by the personification. The personification at the beginning of the second stanza repeats the journey motif only to dramatize the final denouement: the rest of the poem abruptly turns into a tale of grief, decline, and parting.

Even in this seemingly bizarre account of the magnolia, *yongwu* conventions are still observed. The description of the Woman Adrift in the first two lines of the poem is also a perfect description of the magnolia. Through the highly connotative diction of *ci*, in which terms like cloud and jade can have a wide range of referents depending on the context, the woman with a cloudlike coiffure adorned with red ribbons is also the magnolia with its cloudlike white petals marked with purplish red streaks at the base; the soft delicate texture and white color of the petals

[37] See Liu Wenying, "Xi Shi di xialuo wenti," *Yilin conglu*, 5 (1964):315–20.

are likened to the woman's soft, nephrite white cheeks. These first two lines actually establish a strong mimetic correspondence, but one that is frustrated as the poem immediately veers into the strange realms of the poet's private world, metaphorized in a quasi narrative. Much of the power and movement (and perhaps obscurity) of the poem derives from this tension between the *yongwu* demand for mimesis and the poet's own metaphorizing impulse. Ultimately, mimesis, in the narrow sense of reproducing the object verbally, is maintained only in the surface text.

On one level, the poem develops the imagistic possibilities in the name of magnolia. Since the magnolia, unlike the plum blossom and other flowers with impressive *yongwu* portfolios, lacks even a literary antecedent, the poem's figural references to the magnolia are derived from its constituent characters, *yu* and *lan* ("jade-orchid"). These two characters denoting the special characteristics of the magnolia—its white color and orchidlike scent—are amply exploited; in a sense we can read the entire poem, with the exception of a few strophic units, as a series of descriptions generated by *yu* and *lan*. We have already looked at an example of the amplification of *yu* in the opening two lines. As for *lan*, there is the allusion at the end of the stanza: "the land of Sao" is the "many an acre" on which the Li Sao poet tended his beloved orchids;[38] and in the closing lines of the poem, there is an oblique reference to the wilted orchid of the powerful couplet by Li He (791–817) on the grief of parting: "The wilted orchid sees off the guest on Xianyang road, / If heaven had feeling, heaven too would grow old." [39]

When the poem is thus analyzed solely on the level of adherence to the *yongwu* topic, it does stand in danger of falling into dazzling fragments of jade and orchid. But as we have already seen, the real code is not the magnolia as object but the magnolia as metaphor or private symbol of a woman, with the poem expressing a metaphoric tale of love. The unifying principle is

[38] The line is "I had tended many an acre of orchids." Trans. David Hawkes, *Ch'u Tz'u: Songs of the South* (Oxford: Oxford University Press, 1959), p. 23.

[39] The last couplet of the poem "Song of the Bronze Immortal bidding farewell to the Han," (*QTS*, 12:4403).

located in the poet's metaphorizing impulse, which merges the *yongwu* texture and the structure of events and emotions into an organic whole. It may be useful here to recall Su Shi's poem on the red plum blossom for comparison. Even though Su Shi describes the plum blossom through its personification as a woman, he remains mimetically committed to the actual object, and we do not suspect for a moment that he is writing about anything but a particular species of prunus. In Wu Wenying's poem, the subversion of true mimetic involvement creates a metaphoric dimension no longer commensurate with the physical object. This change constitutes a decisive turning point in the development of Southern Song *yongwu ci*. In the *yongwu* works of *ci* poets a generation before Wu Wenying, signs of this dissociation from the object can already be detected;[40] in some of Wu's *yongwu ci* the dissociation is radical and complete.

Less than two decades after Wu Wenying's death, the Southern Song fell to the Mongols. During 1279, a group of men gathered in secret to mourn the Mongol-instigated looting of the Song imperial tombs and the desecration of imperial corpses. Among them were the *ci* poets Zhou Mi, Wang Yisun, and Zhang Yan. The medium they chose for the expression of their thoughts and emotions about this humiliating incident was the *yongwu ci*, written in the allegorical mode.[41] This choice is significant in two respects. First, with respect to the *yongwu* subgenre, it represents a logical conclusion to the development of *yongwu* in *ci* poetry from description to allegory, comparable to its evolutionary patterns in the *fu* and *shi*. And second, with respect to the *ci* genre, it demonstrates concretely the elevation of the generic status of *ci* in the literary orthodoxy to a form considered proper for the

[40] Jiang Kui is of course the most obvious example; see Shuen-fu Lin, *The Transformation of the Chinese Lyrical Tradition*. But even some *yongwu ci* by Xin Qiji exhibit this dissociative trend.

[41] In all, fourteen men participated on different occasions and wrote a total of thirty-seven *ci* using five tune patterns on five different objects. The poems were assembled in a collection entitled the *Yuefu buti*. See Xia Chengtao, "*Yuefu buti* kao," in *Tang Song ciren nianpu*, pp. 376–82; Huang Zhaoxian, *Yuefu buti yanjiu ji jianzhu*; Chia-ying Yeh Chao, "On Wang I-sun and His *Yung-wu Tz'u*," *HJAS*, 40:1 (1980):55–91; and Kang-i Sun Chang, "Symbolic and Allegorical Meanings in the *Yueh-fu pu-t'i* Poem-Series," paper presented at the Workship on Issues in Sung Literati Culture, Harvard University, May 17–18, 1985.

expression of intent. Both processes had been evolving all along. On the first point, we have seen how, by certain stylistic and structural changes, the *yongwu* mode gradually evolved from the time it was first taken up by *ci* poets. On the second, it was the violation of generic boundaries between *shi* and *ci* practiced by Su Shi and his friends that marked a definite step in the elevation of *ci* to a serious literary genre, an elevation brought to completion in the *ci* occasioned by the tomb incident.

The process was not rapid, and the goal perhaps never wholly achieved. From extant critical comments, it seemed that Su's contemporaries and near-contemporaries, governed by a strong generic expectation that *ci* should be delicate, subtle, and musical, were more critical of the technical faults of his new *ci* than aware of his contributions in widening the subject matter of *ci*. Yet, as *ci* became more established as a literary genre in the hands of literati scholar-officials, the moral demands of the literary tradition began to make themselves felt in the minds of its critics and practitioners. In the early Southern Song, the critic Wang Zhuo, who expressed the highest esteem for Su Shi's *ci*, began a discussion of the origin of *ci* by quoting the *shi yan zhi* "poetry expresses intent" dictum.[42] Coming at the end of the Song, Zhang Yan similarly states in his critical treatise, the *Ciyuan*, that "*ci* should be elegant and proper; it is where the heart's intent goes," also taking the Great Preface as his authority ("Poetry [*shi*] is where the heart's intent goes").[43] In using the orthodox definition of *shi* for their discussion of *ci*, these critics and practitioners of *ci* eagerly subscribed to the orthodox concept of poetry and sought to elevate *ci* to the same status as *shi* poetry. That they did not entirely succeed is reflected both in the renewed efforts of their Qing successors to legitimize *ci* along the same lines and in the ambivalent and sometimes depreciative attitude toward the genre expressed by some Qing period *ci* practitioners. But this properly belongs to another chapter in the history of the *ci*. *Yongwu ci* poetry as written in the allegorical mode at the end of the Southern Song was both a confirmation in practice of what *ci*

---

[42] Wang Zhuo, *Biji manzhi* (*Cihua congbian* ed., vol. 1), p. 19.
[43] Zhang Yan, *Ciyuan* (*Cihua congbian* ed., vol. 1), p. 218.

critics held in theory—the higher function of *ci* poetry—and an illustration of the evolutionary possibilities of the *yongwu* subgenre.

II. Poems in Remembrance of Love

Memory is vicarious experience in which there is all the emotional value of actual experience. —John Dewey

Of the 340 extant poems by Wu Wenying, close to one-third are poems written in memory of his two mistresses.[44] An account of the events in Wu Wenying's life that gave rise to the outpouring of these poems of remembrance has been given in Chapter One. To recapitulate the essentials: in his youth Wu Wenying had an ill-fated romance with a singing girl in Hangzhou, which ended tragically with the girl's death while he was absent. Later on in his life, during his sojourn in Suzhou (early 1230s to 1240s), Wu lived with a mistress for a number of years, but for some reason that remains unclear they were eventually forced to part. These two losses left him with memories, indelibly beautiful, and therefore all the more sad. Remembrances and longings for his vanished loves became almost obsessive themes in his poetry.

In the wake of late Qing interest in Wu Wenying's *ci* style, there was a renewed effort among *ci* specialists in the earlier part of this century to carry out biographical and exegetical studies on Wu Wenying and his poetry in the traditional formats of bio-chronology and annotated editions.[45] It was in these works that the existence of these love poems was first systematically noted and their significance duly acknowledged. A few decades later, in an isolated brief article on Wu Wenying, a mainland scholar made the astute comment that "[Wu's] love and longing for the departed mistresses . . . are great sorrows in his life and constitute the very core of emotion in his poetry."[46] In view of the sheer

[44] For a list of tunes cited as love poems, see Xia Chengtao, *Tang Song ciren nianpu*, pp. 467–69; and Yang Tiefu, "Wu Mengchuang Shiji kao," in *Mengchuang ci quanji jianshi*, pp. 364–67.

[45] Besides the above two works, see also Chen Xun's commentaries on a selection of Wu Wenying's poetry in his *Haixiao shuoci* (*Cihua congbian* ed., vol. 12), pp. 4401–43.

[46] Chen Lianzhen, "Du Wu Mengchuang ci," first published in *Guangming Daily*, 28 April 1957; rpt. in *Tang Song ci yanjiu lunwenji* (n.p., 1969), p. 189.

quantity and exceptional quality of these love poems, it is inevitable that any serious attempt to examine Wu Wenying's poetry will involve examples from this corpus. Indeed, the most recent crop of articles on Wu Wenying by mainland scholars, with their marked focus on the *nouvelle vague* aspect of Wu's poetic style—notably in their penchant for characterizing it as the Chinese thirteenth century prototype of twentieth century stream-of-consciousness technique—select examples for illustration or generalization that are most often from among his love poems.[47] This attempt is symptomatic of a certain trendiness in the resurgent critical climate of the post-Mao years, but it does reflect a recognition of Wu's individual style, which is perhaps most readily discernible in the love poems.

A common attribute of Wu's love poems that encourages this sort of analysis is their distinctive hallucinatory ambience (to some extent this can be said of his poetry as a whole). Frequent transposition between reality (actual experience) and the illusory experience of dream and reverie, vision, and flashback is a pronounced feature in the morphology of these love poems. As the development, or movement, of the poem is primarily guided by memory, emotional association, and sense perception (image-making), rather than by any apparent logic, time sequence is often disrupted and spatial viewpoint shifted without any clear demarcation: the poem moves back and forth between reminiscence and description, between the past and the present. The first stanza of *Shuang ye fei*, a poem written on the Double Ninth festival, is an extreme example of these traits:

1 Intervening mist and parting feelings,
   Things that concern the heart.
   The setting sun's redness hides behind frosty trees.
   Half a jar of autumn water I offer to the yellow flower,
5 Its fragrance sprays the west wind and rain.
   I let go the jade rein—lightly flies a swift bird.
   So desolate, no one mourns for the antiquity of this
    deserted terrace.

---

[47] See in particular Tao Erfu, "Shuo Mengchuang ci *Ying ti xu*," in *Wenxue yichan*, no. 3 (1982), pp. 110–19; and Xu Yongduan, "Xuan ren yanmu di jingjie," in *Cixue*, no. 1 (1981), pp. 176–79.

I remember drunkenly treading on Nanping Hill:
The painted fan sobs, the cold cicada is weary of
dreaming,
10   Not knowing Man or Su.

(*QSC* 4/2874–75)

斷煙離緒。
關心事，
斜陽紅隱霜樹。
半壺秋水薦黃花，
香噀西風雨。
縱玉勒、輕飛迅羽。
淒涼誰弔荒臺古。
記醉蹋南屏，
緲扇咽、寒蟬倦夢，
不知蠻素。

Notes

l.8 Nanping Hill is in the southern outskirts of Hangzhou.

l.10 "Man-Su" is an acronym made from the names of the Tang poet Bai Juyi's two concubines, Xiao Man and Fansu. It stands for Wu's long departed mistresses.

The poem moves from an internal reflection (lines 1–2) to external description (lines 3–5), to flashback (lines 6–8), and fantasy (lines 9–10). The only overt indication of time and space is line 8: "I remember drunkenly treading on Nanping Hill," except what follows is hardly a sensible recollection of the hike. What links the succession of scenes and images is the *concern*, the emotional current, expressed at the beginning of the poem. In the inability to forget this concern with the past, an acute appreciation is born for a moment of autumnal beauty, as well as a solicitude for the autumn chrysanthemum, and a lament associated with the Double Ninth for the past (historical). But in the end it is the obsession with a personal past that reasserts itself, expressed in strangely surreal images.[48]

Wu handles the theme of love in a variety of modes and settings; chief among them are the metaphorical *yongwu* mode

---

[48] Cf. Chia-ying Yeh Chao's analysis of these two lines in "Wu Wenying's *Tz'u*," p. 160. Though my translation follows the different punctuation in the *QSC*, the imagery of these two lines is not any less strange.

(discussed in the previous section), lyrical and narrative modes, and seasonal and festival settings. The festivals most frequently used as settings in Wu's love poems are the Qingming festival in spring, the Double Fifth in summer, and the Double Seventh and Double Ninth in autumn. It is a universal feature of festivals that they involve families and groups in communal ritual observances and celebrations. Thus for those who are alone or away from home, festivals become times when they may feel a strong longing for friends and loved ones. Chinese poets over the centuries have had a penchant for composing festival poems, which express their thoughts of home and family when away; the general flavor can be seen captured in the Tang poet Wang Wei's famous lines written on a Double Ninth, "Alone, a sojourner in a strange land, / Whenever a festival comes around, thoughts of kin increase manifold."[49] In Wu's love poems, the constant interweaving of festival motifs with the theme of remembrance and yearning constitutes a unique feature, one that deserves study. Xia Chengtao has further noted that these love poems record distinct memories of the two women by means of different seasonal and geographical indicators: spring and Hangzhou allude to one, summer, autumn and Suzhou to the other.[50]

In the ensuing discussion, examples will be selected from the different modes and settings used in this corpus of poems. Attention will be paid to the analysis of key images and motifs whose vital presence marks these poems as superbly crafted and moving love lyrics. Moreover, since most of these love poems lack true referential prefaces, interpretation of the entire series depends upon a proper understanding of their code, one based on the characteristic recurrence of leitmotifs. Despite its brevity, the following unprefaced poem, written to the tune *Feng ru song*, contains a number of such leitmotifs:

1   Listening to wind, to rain, I pass Grave-sweeping Day,
      Too weary to write an epitaph for buried flowers.
      Before the pavilion, green shade obscures our path of
              parting—
      One sprig of willow, one inch of tender feeling.

[49] *QTS*, 4:1306.
[50] Xia Chengtao, *Tang Song ciren nianpu*, p. 469.

5   Chilly in the spring cold I got drunk ...
       The chirping orioles mingle in my daybreak dream.

       Day after day I sweep the wooded arbor in the West
              Garden,
       Relishing the new clear weather as in the past.
       Again and again yellow bees strike the swing's ropes
10   Where fragrance from her delicate hands still clings.
       Grieved that her mandarin-duck shoes do not come,
       Overnight, moss has grown on the secluded steps.

                                                   (*QSC* 4/2906)

聽風聽雨過清明。
愁草瘞花銘。
樓前綠暗分攜路，
一絲柳、一寸柔情。
料峭春寒中酒，
交加曉夢啼鶯。

西園日日掃林亭。
依舊賞新晴。
黃蜂頻撲鞦韆索，
有當時、纖手香凝。
惆悵雙鴛不到，
幽階一夜苔生。

The Qingming festival—"Grave-sweeping Day"—in spring is
when the Chinese traditionally make their annual visits to the
family grave sites to clear them of weeds and make ritual offer-
ings. Thus this festival often serves in Wu Wenying's love poems
as an apt device to call up poignant memories of his deceased
lover. The association with death evoked in the opening line is
immediately reinforced by "epitaph" and "buried flowers" in
line 2; the image of the fallen flowers of spring, ravaged by wind
and rain, acts then as an implied metaphor for the young lover
who died in the spring of life. In another poem, Wu Wenying
employs a similar metonymic figure, "interred jade and buried
fragrance," in referring to her.[51]

The element of time plays an important role in these poems of

[51] In *Ying ti xu*, the next poem to be discussed.

reminiscence: its irrevocable passage often forms an antithesis to the ironic persistence of memory. While the lapse of time obliterates the past as empirical reality, its failure to erase the stubborn traces of memory becomes a source of bittersweet pain. Wu Wenying in these love lyrics will typically use images that emphasize the remoteness of time past, and then contrast, almost defy, them with images that signify undying emotion. This poem contains a series of binary images which express this tension. Sometimes one and the same image embodies the polarity, as for example the willow (lines 3–4), which through time has grown physically to the extent of blocking out a scene of the past. And yet, paradoxically, its very growth and proliferation is a measure of the proportionately increased emotion (tenderness and love) associated with the past.

The entire second stanza brings to the foreground this counterpoint between time and feeling. The persona encloses himself in the West Garden, the symbolic world of the past in which he persists in living. Sweeping its grounds becomes a psychologically pregnant act of clearing away what is on the surface to reveal what is hidden, to push aside present reality in order to recreate the past. The verb "to sweep" is modified by the adverbial phrase "day after day," emphasizing the persistence of the action. In another poem also set at the time of Qingming, images of the past are conjured up through the same act of sweeping the ground:

> Kiosks and arbors newly swept,
> Imprinted on the lichen, traces of her paired lovebird
>   shoes,
> I recall our walks through the deep woods.
>
> *(San shu mei, QSC 4/2923–4)*

曲榭方亭初掃。
印蘚迹雙鴛，
記穿林窈。

In lines 9 and 10, the poet projects his own persistent longing for the past onto the fragrance-seeking bees, which "again and again" alight on the swing's ropes where the perfume from the dead lover's hands is imagined to still remain. This vivid and haunting imagery has been very much admired by traditional critics for its beauty and power of evocation.[52] In the closural image, however, even the illusory presence of the lover is negated by the accumulation of moss, which suggests the contrary truth of her long absence. That the moss seems to have grown overnight conveys the intensity of his unfulfilled longing and desire. The imagery of the gardenscape is infused with emotional symbolism.

In this short poem we have encountered three of the most common metonyms Wu Wenying uses for the lover—her delicate hands, her shoes or footprints, and her perfume. These often constitute hallucinatory, partial and fleeting apparitions of the lover peculiar to these poems; they are fragmentary images made all the more potent by their symbolic condensation.

Set in a narrative mode with the season of the Qingming festival as its background, this poem, written to the longest *ci* pattern *Ying ti xu*, is an engrossing *tour de force* in its recollection of and lament for a bygone love:

1 The lingering chill afflicts one sick with wine—
   I close ornamented doors of aloewood.
   Swallows come late, flying over the western city wall,
   As if announcing the lingering end of springtime.
5 Painted boats have already carried away the Qingming
       festival;
   In clearing mist tender are the Wu Palace trees.
   I muse on how the traveler's moods drift on,
   Changing into light catkins in the wind.

   Ten years ago at West Lake,
10 I tethered the horse by the willow
   And followed charmed dust in a soft haze.
   Tracing red petals upstream step by step, I was
       summoned to Fairy Creek,
   And Brocade Maid furtively conveyed your deep
       feelings.

---

[52] In fact, not only these lines but the whole poem has received high praise; cf. the various comments on it quoted in *Songci sanbaishou jianzhu*, ed. Tang Guizhang (1931; rpt. Taipei: Xuesheng shuju, 1971), p. 213.

Behind the silver screen spring was indulgent but our
    dream was confined:

15   Soon falling rouged tears soaked your singing fan and
    gold-thread gown.

At dusk the dike was empty.

Lightly we took the sunset

And returned it all to the gulls and egrets.

Orchids quickly age,

20   Pollias grow again,

And I still journey among river villages.

Since parting I've revisited Six Bridges—no news.

Our affair's in the past, flowers have wilted,

Interred jade and buried fragrance

25   Have gone through much wind and rain.

Long waves envied your glance,

Distant hills were shamed by your brows,

Fishing lamps scattered reflections in the spring river
    night—

I recall our small boat at Peach Root Crossing.

30   The green chamber seems a mirage

Where I inscribed poems at parting on walls now
    crumbled,

Tears and ink are dulled by dust and soil.

From a high pavilion I gaze on the horizon—

Color of grass to the world's edge;

35   I sigh at my hair, half turned white.

Secretly I count the parting tears and happy stains

Still coloring your silk handkerchief—

The dangling phoenix lost its way back,

The simurgh on the broken mirror no longer danced.

40   Fervently I want to write down

My eternal sorrow in a letter,

But into blue mist over a distant sea passing wild geese
    sink.

In vain I play my love-yearning into the mournful
    zither's strings.

Grieving over a thousand *li* south of the river,

111

45   With rueful song I summon you again,
        But is your severed soul still there?

(QSC 4/2907–08)

殘寒正欺病酒，
掩沈香繡戶。
燕來晚、飛入西城，
似說春事遲暮。
畫船載、清明過卻，
晴煙冉冉吳宮樹。
念羈情遊蕩，
隨風化爲輕絮。

十載西湖，
傍柳繫馬，
趁嬌塵軟霧。
遡紅漸、招入仙溪，
錦兒偷寄幽素。
倚銀屏、春寬夢窄，
斷紅溼、歌紈金縷。
暝隄空，
輕把斜陽，
總還鷗鷺。

幽蘭旋老，
杜若還生，
水鄉尚寄旅。
別後訪、六橋無信，
事往花委，
瘞玉埋香，
幾番風雨。
長波妒盼，
遙山羞黛，
漁燈分影春江宿，
記當時、短楫桃根渡。
青樓彷彿，
臨分敗壁題詩，
淚墨慘澹塵土。

危亭望極，
草色天涯，

欺鬢侵半苧。
暗點檢、離痕歡唾，
尚染鮫綃，
亸鳳迷歸，
破鸞慵舞。
殷勤待寫，
書中長恨，
藍霞遼海沈過雁，
漫相思、彈入哀箏柱。
傷心千里江南，
怨曲重招，
斷魂在否。

Notes

1.6 "Wu Palace trees" stand for trees in Hangzhou. Hangzhou was the capital of the Wu-Yue kingdom during the Five Dynasties period. It was of course the Southern Song capital during Wu's lifetime. Depending on the context, "Wu" or "Wu Palace" can also refer to Suzhou.

1.12 This alludes to the story about Liu Chen and Ruan Zhao, who met two fairy maidens on Mount Tiantai by a stream lined with peach trees. See *You ming lu (Linlang mishi congshu* ed.), 15b–16b.

1.13 Brocade Maid: a name which stands for a maidservant who acts as a secret go-between for her mistress, delivering messages to her lover.

1.22 Six Bridges: a scenic spot at West Lake in Hangzhou.

1.29 Peach Root Crossing is not a real place name but is reconstituted from the Jin poet Wang Xianzhi's two poems about his mistress Peach Leaf. See *Yutai xinyong, j.*10. The name is used for the sake of its romantic connotations, specifically the parting of lovers.

The narrative mode in this poem effects an uncommon sequential flow in the presentation, one structured along the division of the tune pattern into four stanzas. After the delineation in the opening stanza of the season (late spring), place (Hangzhou), and mood of the persona (solitary and retrospective)—familiar signifiers of a love poem of remembrance in Wu's system of representation—the past unfolds as the recollection begins in the second stanza. With typical stylistic compression, Wu depicts telescopically in this stanza the contour of the romance and its accompanying emotional process, from the excitement of the meeting and the subsequent involvement to the joy of the consummation of love, and finally to the sorrow of separation, all in a few masterful strokes. In telling his story, Wu alludes to a tale of romance about two men who met two fairy maidens on Mount Tiantai by a stream lined with blossoming peach trees. By casting his own romantic encounter in this fairy tale mode, he gives it an elusive and dreamlike quality appropriate to the description of a beautiful love affair that has vanished.

The last three lines of the stanza sum up symbolically the careless letting go of an enchanted love: "At dusk the dike was empty. / Lightly we took the sunset / And returned it all to the gulls and egrets." The interpretation of these somewhat enigmatic lines hinges on the word "empty": to the persona the dike at West Lake, the scene of the romantic past, is now empty, deprived of the love he had thoughtlessly forgone. The sunset, something beautiful but ephemeral, could stand for their love as well as for the pleasures they had enjoyed together, and it had been too easily, too unthinkingly relinquished. The carefree gulls and egrets are as separate from human affairs as the past is severed from the present. The suggestion of regret in these lines follows logically from the imminence of the lovers' separation implied in the preceding two lines: "By the silver screen spring was indulgent but our dream was confined, / Soon falling rouged tears soaked your singing fan and gold-thread gown."

Stanza three continues the narrative after the parting, when the persona returned to Hangzhou after his traveling and discovered that his lover had died some time ago. This tragic discovery triggered more flashbacks of their time together and of their parting. Here also, the image of the dilapidated walls in her chamber where he had inscribed parting poems and of the inscription now covered by dust both give the long passage of time a concrete presence. Time, however, never seems to bring him oblivion nor does it ease his "eternal sorrow." The concluding stanza is an unconsolable lamentation over the lover's death.

Very different in mood and expression but equally moving is a short imagistic poem written to the tune *Huan xi sha*:

1   Behind the gate, dense flowers: I dream of the old
              haunt.
       In a wordless sunset, mournful, the swallows' return.

114

Delicate white hands stir with fragrance a small curtain
hook.

Noiseless falling catkins, tears shed by spring.
5   Behind shadows of moving clouds, a demure moon.
At nightfall the east wind is colder than autumn.

(*QSC* 4/2894)

門隔花深夢舊遊。
夕陽無語燕歸愁。
玉纖香動小簾鉤。

落絮無聲春墮淚，
行雲有影月含羞。
東風臨夜冷於秋。

Nowhere in this lyric does the persona express his emotions
directly. yet in the way the images are constructed, a wistful
mood, sadness, and nostalgia unmistakably permeate the world
expressed in the poem. As the poem begins by depicting a dream
of the "old haunt," it immediately implies a past in the persona's
life, one that he cannot forget and that has remained to obsess
him. The dream motif of the opening line leaves the remaining
two lines of the first stanza ambiguous and elusive, hovering as it
were between dream and memory. This ambiguity in fact asserts
the equivalence between dream and memory, both of whose
contents are impalpable. While the melancholic atmosphere
created by pathetic fallacy in line 2 can be an attribute of the
dream, it can also belong to the dreamlike content of memory. A
dead stillness and inaccessibility surround the past that surfaces
in dream and memory; the persona is separated from the "old
haunt," the scene of past romance, by temporal and spatial
distance, represented by the thick growth of flowers and the gate,
and the longed-for vision of the beloved is characteristically
fleeting and metonymic.

The second stanza continues to deploy images of a spring night
in a dreamlike ambience. But the memory of the beloved subtly
colors the perception of these springtime images. Endowed with
feminine sensitivity, the falling catkins are perceived to be tears
shed by spring and the moon partly obscured by clouds to be shy,

so that the elements of dream or memory remain fused with reality. Throughout the poem, the negation of sound intensifies the visual qualities of the images. Not only is the sunset "wordless" and the falling catkins "noiseless," but nature images often associated with sound—swallows and wind—are apprehended through emotional empathy and thermal sensation, rather than auditory perception.

The style of this poem exemplifies the poetics of indirection at its best. The last line in particular has been cited by the eminent Qing critic Chen Tingzhuo as an exemplary poetic closure subsuming emotion in imagery, ideal in the way it defers closure of emotional response even at the end of the poem.[53] In order to fully appreciate the subtle art and emotion of the closural line, we should take note of the key words "flowers," "spring," and "east wind," whose function as cyclical constants in the realm of nature contrasts with the vicissitudes of the world of man. The poem begins with the persona's dream of a beautiful spring in the past associated with his love, which is contrasted with the lonely loveless spring of the present. This implied contrast produces the poignant irony of the last line in which the persona experiences spring, a season of warmth and growth, as being chillier than autumn.[54]

In the next poem to be examined, written to the tune *Manjiang hong*, the season is summer, the locale Suzhou. The poem's preface provides a reference to the time and place of composition unusually specific in the corpus of love poems: "In the year *Jiachen* (1244), I passed the Double Fifth while lodging outside Pan Gate." Pan Gate remains today as a gateway on the southwestern limit of Suzhou, with both land and water routes to areas to the south. We recall from the biographical chapter that the years 1243–1244 were a period of unrest and transition in Wu Wenying's life. During these two years he traveled several times

---

[53] *Baiyuzhai cihua* (*Cihua congbian* ed., vol. 11), pp. 3807–8.

[54] Chinese critics have quoted lines by earlier poets which play with the idea of the displacement of springtime and autumn to show the precedents for this line. See Yu Pingbo, *Tang Song ci xuanshi* (Beijing: Renmin wenxue chubanshe, 1979), p. 252, n. 5. In the way it subsumes emotion and conveys it entirely through imagery, Wu's line surpasses its models in sophistication.

to Hangzhou, and eventually terminated his period of residence in Suzhou. Indeed 1244 turned out to be a decisively tragic year in his personal life, as he had to part with his Suzhou mistress. All four poems with prefaces dated 1244 were written on festival occasions and, without exception, contain oblique reference to the separation.[55] Chronologically the poem under consideration is the earliest expression of regret and longing after the departure of the Suzhou mistress:

1   With artemisia bound into fairy shapes,
       Demons howling on rafters are still not quelled.
       Outside the desolate city, listless, I look on idly—
       A trace of rustic smoke.
5   Baby plums have not yellowed and I am depressed by
            the night rain,
       The pomegranate flower is not seen worn in autumn-
            snow hair.
       Again—writing fragrant lyrics in scarlet words on
            folded silk—
       The festival of past years.

       Affair behind the curtain,
10   Only the swallows speak about.
       Joined-happiness silk strips,
       A pair of bracelets.
       Since fragrance vanished with her flushed arms,
       Past feelings have all changed.
15   Zizania leaves mourn the Xiang River's departed soul,
       No dream of Yangzhou, half the bronze mirror is
            missing.
       I ask the flute to blow asunder clouds in the night sky,
       To see the new moon!

                                    (*QSC* 4/2877)

結束蕭仙，
嘯梁鬼、依還未滅。
荒城外，無聊閒看，

---

[55] Besides *Manjiang hong*, the other three are *Xi qian ying*, *QSC* 4/2918; *Wei fan*, *QSC* 4/2928; and *Feng qi wu*, *QSC* 4/2937. The last mentioned is discussed further on in this section.

野煙一抹。
梅子未黃愁夜雨，
榴花不見簪秋雪。
又重羅紅字寫香詞，
年時節。

簾底事，
憑燕說。
合歡縷，
雙條脫。
自香消紅臂，
舊情都別。
湘水離魂蘭葉怨，
揚州無夢銅華闕。
倩臥簫、吹裂晚天雲，
看新月。

Note

1.6 What I have translated as "autumn-snow hair" is simply "autumn snow" in the original, a metonym whose referent is not entirely obvious. As object of the verb *zan* "to pin on a cap," it can be interpreted as referring to the poet's white hair.

It is to be expected that in a poem expressly stated to have been written on the Double Fifth, the imagery and allusions would be dominated by the multifarious appurtenances of this important festival.[56] Since Han times, the Double Fifth has become the major summer festival, combining the dual function of commemorating the drowned spirit of Qu Yuan and of ritual prevention of evil influences, diseases, and pestilence brought by the onset of summer heat. The *Jingchu suishiji*, a sixth-century work describing seasonal observances in south-central China, provides a concise account of the customs and ritual practices of the Double Fifth as it had come to be observed since the Han:

> The fifth month is popularly known as the evil month. One should avoid roofing a house.... It is said that one

[56] For an informative study of the Double Fifth and its amalgamation of certain Summer Solstice observances, see chap. 8 in Derk Bodde, *Festivals in Classical China* (Princeton: Princeton University Press, 1975).

should not climb a roof in the fifth month, as one is apt to encounter demons up there.... On the fifth day of the fifth month, people gather artemisia to make man-shaped figures for hanging on doorways. This is done in order to exorcise noxious influences. On this day boat races are held; it is the custom for mourning the death of Qu Yuan who drowned himself in the Miluo.... Five-color silk streamers, called "charms to ward off weapons," are worn on the arm for protection against diseases and epidemics; presents of bracelets and other woven articles are also exchanged [on this occasion]....[57]

This passage shows at a glance how thoroughly Wu Wenying has incorporated Double Fifth material into the text of the poem. In what follows, we shall see how the same imagery and allusions are also used to effect mood and atmosphere and to express personal sentiments.

As indicated by the numerous apotropaic practices, the fifth month was regarded as an ominous time of year, when evil forces are on the ascendent. The first two lines of the poem capture the sinister aspect of the Double Fifth, providing a perfect backdrop to the persona's negative state of mind expressed in the two succeeding strophic units. It is not, however, until line 6 that the reader gets a hint of the reason for the persona's despondency. That the pomegranate flower, in its fifth month a brilliant red color, is missing from the poet's capped white hair underscores the absence of the woman—she was not there to pin it on for him, or, in her absence, he was in too despondent a mood to put on such a symbol of gaiety. Once the note of romantic remembrance is introduced, the poem's imagery shifts correspondingly to the colorful and sensuous aspects of the Double Fifth associated with the presence of the woman in the past. Line 7 alludes to the making of silk amulets to be hung on gates or worn on the chest.[58] Whether or not in the process "fragrant lyrics," love poems, that is, instead of appropriate demon-quelling spells, were written on

[57] Zong Lin, *Jingchu suishi ji* (*Sibu beiyao* ed.), 7b–8b.
[58] Derk Bodde discusses inscribed Double Fifth silk charms with quotes from Han sources in *Festivals in Classical China*, p. 306–7.

the silk becomes immaterial; that it was an activity shared in the past with a lover and mistress endows it with romantic associations. But that was the Double Fifth of former years.

Images in the second stanza reveal the lost romance from different Double Fifth angles. The silk streamers and bracelets, charms that could have been worn on the person of the woman on this occasion, are now left unused. Even grammatically they are left as isolated nouns, put into a strophic unit without verb or context. Yet the mere fact of their existence generates a contiguous vision of her sensual arms where these objects would have belonged. An emphatic twist of a Double Fifth allusion occurs in line 15, in which the personal element threatens to overtake the legendary: in "Zizania leaves mourn the Xiang River's departed soul," the ostensible reference is to Qu Yuan and the custom of commemorating his suicide by throwing ricecakes wrapped in zizania leaves into the river. But the underlying drive of the line is a deep longing for a departed person (the mistress), a reading which is lent support by the allusions in the parallel line (line 16).

Line 16 involves a complex mélange of allusions. Coming at the crucial position of the penultimate strophe as the second half of a parallel couplet, this line bears the strong burden of summing up both the subject matter of the Double Fifth and the theme of lost romance to complement the particular closure technique used in this poem. The dissolution of romantic love is conveyed cleverly enough through alluding to the gay city of Yangzhou, long turned into a poetic symbol of romance and pleasure by Du Mu's poetic record of his dalliance there. Textually Du Mu's famous line: "After ten years at last I wake from my Yangzhou dream" accounts for the first half of the line—"No dream of Yangzhou" signifies the loss of romantic love and gaiety.[59] The second half of the line hints at a story of parted lovers who, when separating, broke a mirror and each kept half as a love token that they would try to match together again.[60] In this poem, that half the mirror is still missing precludes the possibility of reunion.

[59] From the quatrain entitled *Qian huai* ("Written to ease my mind") in *QTS*, 16:5998.

[60] Meng Qi, *Benshi shi* (*Congshu jicheng chubian* ed., vol. 2546), p. 1.

How does all this relate to the Double Fifth? Conscientious craftsman that he is, Wu in his use of allusions seldom strays from the topic. In this case, though, the application of the Yang-zhou allusion and the mirror image to the Double Fifth turns out to be quite superficial and factitious: according to the Tang work *Tang quoshi bu*, a former tribute to the court from Yangzhou used to be a special bronze mirror cast in the middle of the river on the Double Fifth![61] Plainly, the layers of references and cross-references, which try to satisfy two apparently unrelated subjects, detract from each other and weaken the immediate impact of the line when the structural demand requires an emotional climax to offset the effort at self-transcendence expressed in the closure. In contrast to the opaqueness of some of the preceding allusions, the closural expression of transcendence of sorrow—using the symbolic imagery of breaking through the clouds after the rain (delusion) to see the new moon at the beginning of the month (light, truth)—is refreshingly clear and transparent.

Two months later, in the seventh month of the same year (1244), a poem was written with a preface that dates from the night of the Double Seventh festival:

> **To the tune *Feng qi wu***
> Night of the Seventh in the year *Jiachen* (1244)

1   The southern bough having blossomed, flowers fill the
        yard.
    Under a new moon in the west chamber
    We had promised to thread needles together.
    On tall trees cicadas are seeing the evening off with a
        few chirrs
5   When the homecoming dream is shattered at twilight.

    In the night scene the Milky Way is one expanse of
        feeling.
    Stolen joy beneath a light canopy—
    A silver candle grieved beside the silk folding screen.
    Past traces disperse like mist blown by the dawn wind.

[61] Li Zhao, *Tang guoshi bu* (Shanghai: Gudian wenxue chubanshe, 1957), p. 64.

10   The clasp that holds up the curtain gathers cobwebs in
          vain.

(QSC 4/2937)

甲辰七夕

開過南枝花滿院。
新月西樓，
相約同針線。
高樹數聲蟬送晚。
歸家夢向斜陽斷。

夜色銀河情一片。
輕帳偷歡，
銀燭羅屏怨。
陳迹曉風吹霧散。
簾鈎空帶蛛絲捲。

The night of the seventh day of the seventh month celebrates the
annual reunion between the Weaver Girl and Herdboy, two star
(-crossed) lovers (Vega and Aquila) separated by the river of the
Milky Way. Legend has it that magpies form a bridge on this
night to help the Weaver Girl cross the celestial river to meet her
lover. It is quite natural that, given the background, poems
written on this festival occasion would contain overtones of love-
longing. In this poem, the one overt reference to the Double
Seventh (line 3) is the custom for women to thread needles in the
moonlight on this night and pray for skill in sewing.[62] Wu uses
this custom in a personal and novel way by implying that he and
his mistress had arranged for her to return, so that they might
celebrate the occasion by threading needles together, and that
she had failed on some account to keep her promise, thus pro-
longing their separation.

    The loneliness of the present leads to reveries and memories of
the past in the second stanza. In the presentation, the time sense
is foreshortened and past and present are intermingled. The
entire duration of the past romance is symbolically embodied by
one night in the image-bank of his memory: the empathetic

---

[62] See Zong Lin, *Jingchu suishi ji*, 9a.

candle that witnessed the "night" of love felt grief for its brevity. Since the late Tang, with lines such as "The wax candle's heart suffers at our parting: / Its tears drip for us till the light of dawn" by Du Mu,[63] and "The candle-wick turns to ashes before its tears dry" by Li Shangyin,[64] a guttering candle had become a favorite image of love. Through this conceit, love is perceived to be evanescent and self-consuming. The night of passion ("Stolen joy beneath a light canopy") symbolizing the bygone years is presented as if it were the present night. But in the light of morning (reality), all dreams and visions of the past recede into insubstantiality. The desolate state of the present, long severed from the sustenance of the past, is all too apparent in the spectral imagery of the last line.

The happy occasion of the celestial lovers' reunion acts as a sad reminder to the poet's own forlorn state in another poem written on the Double Seventh:

To the tune *Li zhi xiang jin*
Night of the Seventh

1   Dozing lightly I hear from time to time
        The din of evening magpies in the courtyard trees.
        Again they are saying that tonight at the celestial ford
        The joyful reunion will be by the west shore.
5   Cobwebs have imperceptibly locked in the red pavilion
        Where swallows had flitted through the curtains.
        In heaven, love cannot be as bitter as on earth.

        My autumnal hair has changed,
        I envy Sister Moon her eternal charm.
10   Rain passes in the west wind,
        The few leaves on the paulownia by the well dance
            sadly.
        In a dream I reach Indigo Bridge:
        A few scattered stars shine on a vermilion door—
        Teardrops on the sandy shore where I stand and wait.

                                  (*QSC* 4/2890)

[63] In the second of two quatrains entitled "At Parting," in *QTS*, 16:5988.
[64] "Untitled," in *QTS*, 16:6168–69.

七夕

睡輕時聞 ，
晚鵲噪庭樹 。
又說今夕天津 ，
西畔重歡遇 。
蛛絲暗鎖紅樓 ，
燕子穿簾處 。
天上 ，未比人間更情苦 。

秋鬢改 ，
妬月姊 、長眉嫵 。
過雨西風 ，
數葉井梧愁舞 。
夢入藍橋 ，
幾點疏星映朱戶 。
淚溼沙邊凝竚 。

Dream, myth, and reality are all mingled in the images of the poem. The legendary magpies heralding the joyful event in the heavenly realm as they set out to perform their altruistic deed only bring the poet a rude awakening to his earthly plight. The total inaccessibility of a beautiful past is most forcefully conveyed through the image of the red pavilion locked in thick cobwebs. Hence the pain of his own irrevocable separation from his mistress is perceived to be greater than that suffered by the Weaver Girl and Herdboy, who at least have the certainty of being together once a year. In the end he can only try to seek love and deliverance in dream at Indigo Bridge. Indigo Bridge, an allusion often used in love poems, is the place in a Tang wonder tale where a mortal man encountered and wed a fairy maiden.[65] However, the wish for a love-meeting is a dream within a dream that cannot be fulfilled. The poem ends with a dream landscape skillfully constructed with Double Seventh imagery, in which the persona finds himself waiting for his lover by the shores of the Milky Way (ironic twist of fate!). Through the juxtaposition of

[65] The story entitled "Pei Hang" collected in *Taiping guangji* (*Xiaoshuo congshu daguan* ed.), *j*.50/27a–28a.

stars and teardrops, a metaphorical link between the two images is produced, evoking a pervasive sense of sadness.

In a most lyrical expression containing a brief recollection of the past, the allusion to Indigo Bridge figures again as a symbol of an unattainable state of love:

To the tune *Qi tian yue*
Thoughts while drinking white wine alone

1   Dew in the heart of the lotus at midnight,
Lush fragrance rinsed in the spring water of the jade
        well.
I wash the silver cup,
And slowly begin the pale drink.
5   The moon falling into an empty cup has no reflection.
When shadows in the courtyard are not yet dark,
The cicadas make a new song
Whose autumn rhymes merit listening to.
My thin bones seem immersed in ice,
10   I fear they will be startled by the deep night's cold on
        the bamboo mat.

In times past we carried wine on the lake,
Where emerald clouds parted,
A snow white face in a mirror of waves.
Stirred to the depths by this nephrite broth,
15   With a thousand stalks of snowy hair—
Mist locks in the path of flowers by Indigo Bridge.
I linger in the dusky scenery
Just to steal a little solitary joy
And try to heighten the autumn mood.
20   Drunken I lean against the tall bamboos,
The night wind blows, making me half sober.

(QSC 4/2884)

白酒自酌有感

芙蓉心上三更露，
茸香漱泉玉井。
自洗銀舟，

125

徐開素酌，
月落空杯無影。
庭陰未暝。
度一曲新蟬，
韻秋堪聽。
瘦骨侵冰，
怕驚紋簟夜深冷。

當時湖上載酒，
翠雲開處共，
雪面波鏡。
萬感瓊漿，
千莖鬢雪，
煙鎖藍橋花徑。
留連暮景。
但偷覓孤歡，
強寬秋興。
醉倚修篁，
晚風吹半醒。

Note

1.14 "Nephrite broth" has a double meaning: in the context of the poem, it stands for the white wine he is drinking; in the context of the allusion to Indigo Bridge of which it forms a part, it is the name of the love elixir offered by the fairy maid to Pei Hang in the story.

Most of the poem is built on a description of the solitary imbibing of a pale-colored wine in an autumn evening. Consequently many of the images have a limpid and translucent quality, partaking of the water element: dew, spring water of the jade well, ice, snow white face, and so forth; their coolness mirrors the sedate mood of the poet. In this autumnal calm of both scene and emotion, the past surfaces briefly through a slightly intoxicated state of mind in a vivid vision of the beloved's face, only to dissolve quickly again in the sober solitude of the present moment. The failure of the search for love is symbolized by the impenetrability of a mist-locked Indigo Bridge.

Wu Wenying wrote a number of love poems in the *yongwu* mode. Invariably the objects of these poems are species of flowers—real as well as painted—that are associated in his mind with his former mistresses or, on particular occasions, stir up memories of them. *Yongwu* love poems in the former category usually attempt to combine some formal description of the object with reference to the lover, as in the opening strophe of the poem to the tune *Suochuang han* on the magnolia discussed in the previous section. In the latter category, objects (flowers) often function as stimuli to free association. In such cases, references to the object are mainly textual and not descriptive. In other words, object-related textual allusions are there by virtue of *yongwu* conventions, but their descriptive function, being irrelevant to the lyrical core of the poem, is largely ignored.

To the tune *Feng ru song*
Cassia

1   The magnolia boat tosses on rising waves,
I grieve that it is barred by the low bridge.
In evening haze and drizzle, on the way to West
       Garden,
I have missed Lady Autumn, brows lightly touched
       with palace-yellow.
5   Once again I order wine, moored at the posthouse
Where I had seen her off in the twilight.

Cicada-notes drag on in vain on another branch,
Like a melody that does not become the autumn mode.
By a gauze screen she waved her singing fan:
10   I recall opening a window overlooking West Lake.
With wine I seek once more that obscure dream,
Only the scent has already vanished from the faded
       quilt.

                                 (*QSC* 4/2906–07)

桂

蘭舟高蕩漲波涼。
愁被矮橋妨。
暮煙疏雨西園路，
誤秋娘、淺約宮黃。
還泊郵亭喚酒，
舊曾送客斜陽。

蟬聲空曳別枝長。

似曲不成商。

御羅屏底翻歌扇，

憶西湖、臨水開窗。

和醉重尋幽夢，

殘衾已斷熏香。

Notes

1.4 Qiuniang (Lady Autumn), a common term in *ci* that stands for a courtesan or concubine, originates in two Tang poems written about two women with this name: Du Mu's poem on a courtesan named Du Qiuniang and Li Deyu's poem "Dreaming of Jiangnan," which mourns the death of his concubine Xie Qiuniang. It is therefore an apt epithet for Wu's own mistress.

1.6 The line is literally "Where I had seen the guest off in the twilight." In Wu's *ci* the character *ke* ("guest") is often short for *qinke* ("Zither Guest") the name of the Tang poet Liu Hun's singing girl-cum-concubine who was made to remarry.

The obvious element that clearly identifies this as a *yongwu* poem is the stated subtitle "Cassia," an autumn-flowering shrub with fragrant clusters of tiny yellowish blossoms. To an untutored eye, there may seem to be nothing about the cassia in the poem. There are, however, three references to the cassia: in line 1 "magnolia boat" carries an oblique textual reference by alluding to the *Chuci* line: "Cassia oars and magnolia boat-sweeps";[66] in line 4, Lady Autumn with the fashionable yellow brow-makeup stands as a personification of the autumn cassia; and the "scent" in the last line is *xunxiang* in the original—incense burnt in a brazier for perfuming clothes and bedding. In the present context it suggests the kind made from cassia.[67] Once the references are identified, it is all the more obvious that the cassia does not constitute the subject of the poem, although its color and fragrance have worked like the taste of Proust's *petite Madeleine* in arousing memories of the past—of the time of parting and of an idyllic love at West Lake. The poem begins and ends with images

[66] In "Xiang jun" of the "Nine Songs," in *Chuci jizhu*, p. 33.

[67] There are numerous lines in Tang poems which refer to the burning of cassia for fragrance. Cf. Li Shangyin's line, "The brazier is warm with hidden embers of cassia," in his poem "Apricot Blossoms," in *QTS*, 16:6179.

that act as obstacles to the poet's realization of the love remembered and longed for. With the disappearance of the scent, the link to the remote dream of the past is severed.

Love poems in the *ci* genre tend toward the extremes of an objective impersonality or frank eroticism in expression, as exemplified by the respective works of Wen Tingyun and Liu Yong.[68] These traits in part reflect the casual nature of amorous relationships in the pleasure quarters. In hindsight we can say that the erotic and the impersonal assumed the form of generic conventions, for later Song *ci* poems on women and love in the main continued to be characterized by these traits. Wu Wenying's corpus is exceptional in that it is highly personal and revolves around two relationships in his life that he could not forget. The memory of these experiences was given various expression in his poetry. By way of conclusion, it may be interesting to note a Western parallel. The English novelist Thomas Hardy wrote more than one hundred poems covering a period of forty-two years, all centering around the relationship with his wife. Carl Weber, in his preface to *Hardy's Love Poems*, ranks Hardy's poems third in English love poetry, after Shakespeare's and Elizabeth Browning's love sonnets.[69] They certainly present a tempting case for comparison with Wu's corpus. Weber contends that their preeminence lies in "their emotional range and variety: the intensity, the originality, the tenderness, the poignancy, the delicacy, the wistfulness, are all reflected in a paralleling profusion of metres and stanzaic forms."[70] The same can be said for Wu's love poems, except that they go beyond the variety of tune patterns employed to the variety of modes and settings we have examined. If one were to rank Hardy and Wu Wenying, with ready bias perhaps, Wu's expertise in the *ci* genre endows his love poems with an elegance of diction and imagery beside which Hardy's poems do seem to pale.

[68] See James J. Y. Liu's discussion on the world of romantic love in *ci* poetry in his article "Some Literary Qualities of the Lyric," in Cyril Birch, ed., *Studies in Chinese Literary Genres*, pp. 135ff.

[69] Carl J. Weber, ed., *Hardy's Love Poems* (London: Macmillan & Co., 1963), pp. vff.

[70] *Ibid.*, p. viii; the list after the colon is taken from p. vii.

III. Self and Other in Occasional Poetry

The direction in which occasional *ci* poetry developed in the Southern Song can be regarded in many ways as representing the decline of a genre. As dicussed in the section on *yongwu ci*, early literati *ci* were mainly songs for entertainment, written in a diction marked by elegance and modal and emotional imagery, to be performed by singing girls at banquets and parties, and it was not until Su Shi that *ci* began to be used as a common verse form for occasional poetry. This new function to which *ci* was put was reflected in the appearance of information-oriented prefaces, which indicate the situation or event occasioning the composition, and in a corresponding broadening in vocabulary and thematic scope. Even then, there were major mid and late Northern Song poets, such as Qin Guan, He Zhu, and Zhou Bangyan, whose works on the whole did not reflect these changes and who continued to write *ci* along more orthodox lines.

With the political transition to the South in 1127, the situation changed considerably. What was a nascent function in the Northern Song became an entrenched practice. On the basis of the works of many high-ranking bureaucrats in the Southern Song era, it can almost be said that *ci* flourished by virtue of its applicability as a tool for superficial social intercourse. A clear sign of this sad turn is the sudden increase of *shouci*, "*ci* poems celebrating birthdays"—a formal occasion less than stimulating to the creation of good poetry. Yet court officials composed formal *ci* poems celebrating the august birthdays of the imperial family; friends and officials wrote birthday poems to each other; and poets presented them to patrons. Seldom are such poems informed with any dimension of the self of the person writing them, on the level of either thought or feeling; most often they are simply a congeries of hackneyed images, clichés, and platitudes designed to please and flatter the person addressed.[71]

Birthday poems may represent the extreme degeneration of

---

[71] Eminent scholar-officials in the Southern Song such as Wei Liaoweng, Wu Qian, Li Zengbo, and Liu Kezhuang were all prodigious writers of birthday and other social occasional *ci* poems, see the numerous examples in their respective works in *QSC*, vol. 4.

social occasional *ci* poetry. But in the hands of lesser poets and officials with pretensions to poetic ability, other types of occasional poetry fared no better. In the affluent and cultured society of the Southern Song, every conceivable situation and event in life or nature became an occasion to be commemorated in verse. The performance aspect of *ci* no doubt lent it to use as a popular form of social and aesthetic pastime. Thus when social convention rather than individual inspiration dictated the exigency of versification, the products are often artificial and dull.

With the overwhelmingly social nature of occasional *ci* poetry in the Southern Song, the elements of "self" and "other" become obvious criteria by which to distinguish a merely perfunctory social art from genuine poetic expression. The treatment of self and other is of course very often tied to the nature of the occasion. Some occasions decidedly require verse that is completely oriented toward the other, the party for whom one is writing; some obvious instances are found in poems celebrating birthdays, official promotion, or someone taking on a concubine, where the only aspect of self that may be appropriately expressed is one that tries to curry favor or makes a show of envy and admiration. Other occasions provide more freedom, while some are more conducive to self-expression.

Parting poems are good examples of occasional poetry that can be dispatched easily with established conventions and cliché sentiments, or can inspire more individualistic treatment, accompanied by expressions of genuine emotion and thought. On the whole, however, trite examples are the rule. The formality of the situation, the relation between the poet and addressee (for example, that between two officials of similar rank, superior and inferior, poet and patron), and the cause for the departure all might affect the style used and sentiments expressed. Therefore, according to the combination of circumstances, the poem can be mechanically churned out from a readymade store of stock symbols, appropriate allusions, and in a proper level of language. If the person is leaving to assume a new post, it will be suitable to mention the merits and honors he will attain, using masculine, heroic expressions with proper allusions to historical models; similarly, if the person is going to retire from official duty, the poem should be seasoned with allusions exalting the eremitic ideal. Parting poems by Xin Qiji are often exceptions, and bear the stamp of his stylistic temperament; he usually feels and expresses strong emotions toward the person leaving. Often he would find something that he himself shares in common with the departing person, whether it be a view of life, patriotic sentiments, or drinking, and by doing so he makes the other person in some way meaningful and important to himself. The pain of parting is thus given the reality of genuine experience as the poet's emotional self is engaged. Xin can even be truly innovative in writing a parting poem. In his famous poem written to the tune *He xinlang* on the occasion of parting from his cousin, he structures the entire poem around the idea of separation.[72] First he describes the cuckoos' cries as symbolic of the regret they feel for the parting of spring; he then contrasts nature's regret with the greater pain at parting suffered in the human world by alluding to five historical episodes associated with separation, and in doing so intensifies the personal grief he experiences on this particular occasion of parting from his cousin.

Among occasional *ci* poems, those written on visits to historic sites are often most expressive of the poet's thoughts and feelings. However, the extant quantity of such poems is relatively small compared to that of other categories of occasional *ci*. There are several possible explanations for this. Visiting historic sites was not an activity engaged in as frequently as attending the endless Southern Song varieties of banquets and celebrations; nor was it an occasion that required the writing of commemorative verse, as a banquet gathering often was (therefore if one was not moved to compose poetry, there would be no poem). It may also be possible that the small number of *ci* on historic sites is the result of generic discrimination exercised both by poets specializing in *ci* and by poets who wrote both *shi* and *ci*, for the latter might have preferred to use the genre considered serious, in which the contemplation of history was a well established theme with a venerable tradition. Xin Qiji stands again as a striking

---

[72] *He xinlang*: "Parting from my twelfth cousin Maojia," in *QSC* 3/1914–15.

exception. His large *ci* collection contains many excellent pieces written at historic sites.

It should be clear from the preceding, as well as from the biographical chapter that Southern Song upper-class society and its style of life exerted a great measure of influence on the kind of occasional *ci* produced under their aegis. Wu Wenying, having lived much of his life as a guest-poet on the staff of prominent patrons, was in this sense very much a poet of his times. He had to satisfy what must have been frequent demands for social occasional poems, as his collected *ci* testifies. According to the information provided in the poem prefaces, nearly half of the entire collection can be designated social occasional poems. Among those poems that might be characterized as relatively superficial so far as personal involvement of the poet is concerned, the collection includes examples that range from the highly ornate and insipid birthday poems for Prince Sirong to a pretty poem dashed off at a gala banquet at the request of three singing girls.[73] In fairness to Wu, Xia Chengtao concludes his biochronology by remarking that among the peregrine poets of the Southern Song, Wu was never a sycophant in his occasional poems written to people of wealth and power.[74] Moral extenuation aside, these are rightly not the poems for which Wu Wenying is remembered.

Parting poems are of course legion among Wu Wenying's occasional verse. They were written to all manner of friends and acquaintances, officials and patrons. Many of these are, of course, purely occasional pieces in the sense that they lack a point of interest of their own beyond the occasion of composition. All the same, in some of them a novel motif can be observed, one that derives from a topos peculiar to *ci*. This is the amorous nuance that Wu often injects into a parting poem, a touch that is not generally characteristic of farewell poems written in *ci* and would surely be a flagrant violation of decorum in *shi*. Woven among common motifs found in a parting poem—scene and time of

---

[73] *QSC* page references for Wu's birthday poems to Prince Sirong and his wife are: 2879/4, 2882/5, 2885/2, 2886/5, 2915/2. The banquet poem referred to is *Shengsheng man*, *QSC* 4/2920.

[74] Xia Chengtao, *Tang Song ciren nianpu*, p. 483.

departure, anticipated journey ahead, imagined life after arrival—
a line or two, or perhaps a strophic unit, may make reference to
the romantic life of the departing party. Wu may intimate the
sadness felt by the lovers and concubines being left behind, or he
may picture the happy reunion ahead if the person is traveling
home. The parting poem to Feng Qufei,[75] an official who was
Wu's one-time friend in Suzhou and on this occasion on a jour-
ney home, closes with the following lines depicting a projected
romantic scene upon Feng's arrival:

> A single skiff crossing reeds on the returning tide:
> Just then by the west window, lamplight blossoms
>   herald the joyous news.
> With willowy Man and cherry-lip Su
> Serving wine, fighting for affection,
> You can't help but be inebriated.

(Zhuying yao hong, QSC 4/2914–15)

> 一棹回潮度葦。
> 正西窗、燈花報喜。
> 柳蠻櫻素，
> 試酒爭憐，
> 不教不醉。

Commenting on a farewell poem written to Yin Huan, Wu's
friend, and possibly, a patron, Chen Xun notes that "the title is
about Wu Wenying seeing off Yin Huan; the lyric concerns grief
at Yin Huan's departure, but the grief is that of someone else. Wu
assumes the stance of a sympathetic observer."[76] The first two
stanzas of this poem portray the emotional state of Yin Huan's
lover:

To the tune *Ruilong yin*
    Sending off Meijin (Yin Huan)

1   Soul-searing the parting!
     Broken-hearted, the duckweed borne away on water,
     The halted boat moored to a willow.
     Pretty moon and graceful flowers of Wu Palace—

---

[75] Feng's biography is in *Song shi*, 36:12677.
[76] Chen Xun, *Haixiao shuoci* (*Cihua congbian* ed., vol. 12), pp. 4425–26.

5   To his drunken verse her sorrows incline,
    Young Cardamon of the southern river.

    Dashing off spring-embroidered lines.
    From his brush, how many lovely sentiments
    For her sparkling eyes and crescent brows.
10   New garden locked tight in gloomy shadows,
    Dewy chrysanthemums wilt in neglect,
    Half an acre of cold fragrance.

                 (QSC 4/2891)

送梅津

黯分袖。
斷腸去水流萍，
住船繫柳。
吳宮嬌月嬈花，
醉題恨倚，
蠻江豆蔻。

吐春繡。
筆底灑情多少，
眼波眉岫。
新園鎖卻愁陰，
露黃漫委，
寒香半畝。

Note
  1.9 "Crescent brows" translate *meixiu*, brows arched like the contour
of hills.

The language of the poem is extremely figurative: Yin Huan's
departure appears in the image of duckweed drifting away, his
romantic lyrics are likened to vernal embroidery (literally
"spewing forth spring embroidery"), his lover appears in the
kenning "cardamon," which, as we have seen, is used to stand for
a pubescent beauty,[77] her loneliness is reflected in the image of
the deserted garden, and her despondency during his absence to
chrysanthemums fading away, uncared for. Both the metaphoric
imagery and the elliptical shifts in time perspective—from the

[77] See the analysis of *Xinghua tian* in sec. 1 of this chapter.

present (lines 1–3), to past (lines 4–9), and to future (lines 10–12)—are reminiscent of Wu's own love poems.

By incorporating romantic elements into parting poems Wu is on the one hand breaking conventions that have evolved around this subgenre. On the other, however, insofar as the expression and exploration of various aspects of love belong in the generic tradition of *ci*, such liberties do not seem entirely out of place. That Wu did have a tendency to do this indicates perhaps that he was on intimate terms with certain friends and patrons, and was well acquainted with their private lives and feelings, at least to the extent that he felt comfortable enough to make poetic reference to them. This tendency may be at the same time a displaced, subliminal expression of his own personal concerns, a possibility well suggested by the preponderance of love poems in his work.

Wu would sometimes reveal his own thoughts and attitudes in parting poems written to poet-friends who belonged to more or less the same station in life as he did himself, that is to say, the class of poets dependent on patronage. These poems communicate aspects of the self that do not surface in the more formal, public kind of parting poems. A parting poem he wrote to Weng Mengyin furnishes an excellent example, one that also invites extraliterary speculation:

To the tune *Mulanhua man*
Seeing Weng Wufeng off to his travels in Jiangling

1   Seeing the autumn cloud off to thousands of miles,
    It rolls and unrolls, does it have a heart of care?
    I sigh at the path winding and turning
    Where men build dwellings, swallows nests;
5   Frosts cover the wanderer's hatpin,
    Assailed by sorrow.
    Sleeves covered with thick dust,
    Though enfeoffed, what is there to envy the Marquis
        of Huaiyin?
    Just be drunk with fine cress and delicate perch,
10   Not having the heart to let pine and chrysanthemum
        grow old untended.

Parting music:
I hear again the west wind—
The tree by the gold well begins its autumn recital.
My vision stops at the river at dusk,
15   Far far away flies the wild goose,
In sky so solemn and dark.
Tears dampen my lapels
At the nocturnal notes of the pipa,
Ask Yang Qiong, events of the past come to the cold
        fulling block.
20   How can it compare to the year's end amidst lakes and
        hills,
Or sharing a cup under the fragrance of serene plum
        trees?

                      (QSC 4/2917)

送翁五峯遊江陵

送秋雲萬里，
算舒捲總何心。
歎路轉羊腸，
人營燕壘，
霜滿蓬簪。
愁侵。
庾塵滿袖，
便封侯、那羨漢淮陰。
一醉尊絲膾玉，
忍教菊老松深。

離音。
又聽西風，
金井樹、動秋吟。
向暮江目斷，
鴻飛渺渺
天色沈沈。
沾襟。
四絃夜語，
問楊瓊、往事到寒砧。
爭似湖山歲晚，
靜梅香底同斟。

137

Notes

1.9 Cress translates *chun*, an edible water plant. *Chun* soup and sliced perch (here in the euphemistic "sliced jade") were the regional delicacies of the southeast, where the Jin official Zhang Han came from. Zhang gave up his office in the north to return to the countryside for these rustic enjoyments. *Jin shu, j.*92, vol.8, 2384.

1.19 The meaning of the line is ambiguous. Presumably, Yang Qiong, identified by Yang Tiefu (*Mengchuang ci quanji jianshi*, p. 241) as a lover of music in ancient times, would understand why Wu is moved by the sound of the pipa. The fulling block usually refers to women fulling cloth to prepare clothes for their departing husbands; it may hint at a woman in Weng's life in the past.

The poem states unequivocally Wu's negative attitude toward patronage seeking, as opposed to a life of reclusion. I shall deal in detail with the expression of this attitude in the poem later; first, however, the preface calls for some expansion. Reference has been made to Weng Mengyin in the biographical chapter. Weng is chiefly known as a peregrine poet who was a periodic "guest" on the staff of Jia Sidao. The frequency of his travels, often associated with seeking out patrons, can be surmised from the three poems—all written at parting—addressed to him in Wu's collection. It is unfortunate that the poem under consideration cannot be dated, for it contains sentiments that form a perplexing antithesis to the poem *Qinyuan chun* (*QSC* 4/2906), dated to 1259 and referred to in the biographical chapter, which is full of positive sentiments regarding Weng Mengyin's journey to join Jia Sidao's retinue in Hubei.

It is unlikely that this poem was written after 1259, since Wu Wenying himself became a guest-poet at the residence of Prince Sirong around that time. It would then have been highly improper and hypocritical for him to espouse such antipatronage views. Whatever the date of composition or the external circumstances surrounding Weng's trip, it is apparent from the poem that Weng had not been faring too well at the time: he was growing old and still roaming around in search of support. Wu advises him not to get involved in the life of officialdom and politics and sings the praise of a life of retirement. All these thoughts are conveyed through a consummate blending of metaphors sui generis, historical allusions, and conventional symbols.

Weng Mengyin's wandering is compared to the drifting of autumn clouds; autumn because this was the season of Weng's departure. The autumn motif recurs again in lines 9 and 10 and in the beginning of the second stanza. Not having "a heart of care" is an apt enough epithet for scudding clouds, but applied to Weng in the extended metaphor, it implies a contrary reality beneath deceptive appearances: Weng was in truth quite careworn. Weng's frazzled state is made explicit in the second strophe in which life is seen as a long and uncertain road on which man and beast try to build up comfort and security, efforts that ultimately do not alleviate the assaults of old age and sorrow. The historical allusion to Han Xin, the Marquis of Huaiyin, is a most potent warning of the dangers of involvement in political life. The successful career of Han Xin, a man of humble origins, in the end only earned him decapitation and the extermination of his clan.[78] Though Weng Mengyin was not seeking public office himself, to be a literary retainer on the staff of a public figure could entail rise and fall with the political fortunes of one's patron, which were beyond one's control.[79] In contrast to such potential hazards (perhaps quite real—we do not know the concrete situation surrounding Weng's trip), Wu posits the peace and integrity to be found in a life of retirement, represented by the familiar eremitic symbols of cress and perch, pine and chrysanthemum. Most of the second stanza is taken up with expressing the sadness that Wu felt at the scene of parting, and the poem closes with a reiteration of the rustic loftiness of the reclusive life. The message is strong and clear: "Don't go!" Weng Mengyin must have been in desperate circumstances if he left after receiving such an ill-omened poem.

Subjective attitudes are rarely expressed so overtly in Wu Wenying's occasional poetry. But personal reflections not infrequently appear in his poems written on visits to historic sites. These poems, though very few in number, comprise some of the

[78] See Han Xin's biography in *Han shu* (Beijing: Zhonghua shuju, 1962), 7:1861–78.

[79] The *ci* poet Shi Dazu had his face tattooed as a punishment after his patron, the chief councillor Han Tuozhou, fell from power. See Ye Shaoweng, *Sichao jianwen lu* (*Congshu jicheng chubian* ed., vol. 2763), p. 151.

finest and most frequently anthologized pieces—and justifiably so—among his work. The emotional depth in these poems arises from the concerns of the self, but these go beyond the personal scope of the love poems and extend to the broader, more universal levels of man, nation, and history, in short, life itself in the traditional Confucian Weltanschauung. Yet, surely, emotional amplitude alone does not suffice to make good poetry, no matter how proper the subject of emotion is; indeed, second-rate poets of the heroic style have been criticized precisely for the emotional excess that mars their works. Wu's greatness lies in his superb poetic art, which fuses profound thought and emotion with brilliant imagery, thereby giving them tangible and affective form. At the same time, it is true that this image-oriented practice produces a fragmentary and disjointed effect in his lesser poems, a weakness that has incurred criticism. Wu's masterpiece, written on a visit to Mount Lingyan near Suzhou, is cited by Shuen-fu Lin as exemplary of the sensory impact found in Southern Song *ci*:

> **To the tune *Basheng Ganzhou***
> An Outing on Mount Lingyan with colleagues from
> the Grain Transport

1   An endless void, mist to the four distances.
     What year was it
     The meteor fell from the clear sky?
     Illusory green crags and cloud trees,
5   Celebrated beauty's Golden Chamber,
     Failed Leader's palace walls.
     On Arrow Creek a sour wind impales the eyes,
     Creamy water stains the flower's stench.
     At times tripping lovebirds echo:
10   An autumn sound in corridor leaves.

     In the palace the King of Wu is dead drunk,
     Leaving the weary traveler of Five Lakes
     To angle alone, cold sober.
     Ask the blue waves: they don't talk.
15   How can grey hairs cope with the mountain's green?

The water envelops the void;
From the balcony's height
I follow random crows and slanting sun dropping
              behind Fisherman's Isle.
Again and again I call for wine
20   And go to climb Lute Tower:
Autumn level with the clouds.[80]

                                            (QSC 4/2926)

陪庚幕諸公遊靈巖

渺空煙四遠，
是何年、青天墜長星。
幻蒼厓雲樹，
名娃金屋，
殘霸宮城。
箭徑酸風射眼，
膩水染花腥。
時靸雙鴛響，
廊葉秋聲。

宮裏吳王沈醉，
倩五湖倦客，
獨釣醒醒。
問蒼波無語，
華髮奈山青。
水涵空、闌干高處，
送亂鴉、斜日落漁汀。
連呼酒，
上琴臺去，
秋與雲平。

Lin comments that "even his allusions impress us more for their sensory content than for their historical references."[81] Though

---

[80] Trans. James R. Hightower in Chia-ying Yeh Chao, "Wu Wen-ying's Tz'u," pp. 167–68; quoted by Shuen-fu Lin, *The Transformation of the Chinese Lyrical Tradition*, p. 184. In her article, Prof. Chao provides penetrating and exhaustive exegeses for this poem and another written about a visit with Feng Qufei to the grave of Yu (*Qi tian yue, QSC* 4/2883). These two poems will not be dealt with in detail here.

[81] Shuen-fu Lin, *The Transformation of the Chinese Lyrical Tradition*, p. 185.

this observation only points to one side of the picture, Wu's art of creating a surface brilliance is undeniable. As I shall try to demonstrate in the following analyses, the sustaining power of this brilliant superstructure is very much based upon a vital conceptual core.

Wu Wenying's long sojourn in the ancient and cultured milieu of Suzhou left its mark in his occasional poetry. Mention has been made in the biography of the many social occasional pieces he wrote there that belong to the category of "other." But the antiquity of the area, particularly the historical figures and sites associated with the ancient state of Wu, seems to have had a great deal of affective power on him, which he translated into masterful poems in contemplation of the past. Witness, in the *Basheng Qanzhou* quoted above, the dramatic recreation of a ghostly past associated with King Fucha on Mount Lingyan and his own profound response to that history. Tiger Hill, located just outside the northwestern part of Suzhou, is another historical site associated with the state of Wu. It is recorded that King Helu, the father of Fucha, was buried there with three thousand swords under a pond, which came to be known as the Sword Pond.[82] This historic hill occasioned two poems by Wu, one of which is the following:

To the tune *Mulanhua man*

An excursion to Tiger Hill with colleagues from the Grain Transport. At this time Wei Yizhai has already been selected for transfer, and Chen Fenku and Li Fang'an will soon finish their terms.

1 Black-maned bays neighing on frozen grass,
 Dawn clouds veil the frowning peaks.
 Now snow has just vanished from the orchid blades,
 On the pine's waist the jade is thin,
5 Like a worn and weary Zhen Zhen.
 With light canes we thread our way along steep stone
   steps,
 Treading on wild moss we still can discern traces of the
   buried flowers.

[82] *Yue jue shu* (*Sibu congkan* ed.), *j*.2.

Perennial grief for a thousand ages' rise and decline,
On mid-hill, fading sunset and a solitary cloud.

10 Opening winejugs
We mourn again the ghost of Wu.
The emerald chill of the mountain mist clears our light
        intoxication.
How many times lodging here at night
Have I risen in the moonlight to watch—
15 Patterns of stars on the sword-entombing pond.
Though we climb here to gaze, we will inevitably
        depart,
But still for the fragile blossoms, there will be early
        seekers of their fragrance.
Looking back—blue waves, ancient park,
20 At dusk in misty rain and falling plum blossoms.

                            (*QSC* 4/2916)

虎丘陪倉幕遊。時魏益齋已被親擢，
陳芬窟、李方庵皆將滿秩

紫騮嘶凍草，
曉雲鎖、山眉顰。
正蕙雪初銷，
松腰玉瘦，
憔悴真真。
輕黎漸穿險磴，
步荒苔、猶認瘞花痕。
千古興亡舊恨，
半丘殘日孤雲。

開尊。
重弔吳魂。
嵐翠冷、洗微醺。
問幾曾夜宿，
月明起看，
劍水星紋。
登臨總成去客，
更軟紅、先有探芳人。
回首滄波故苑，
落梅煙雨黃昏。

143

Notes

1.17 Wu often uses the term "soft red" (*ruanhong*), translated as "fragile blossoms," to refer to the worldly splendors associated with the capital. As Suzhou used to be the capital of Wu, *ruanhong* carries that implication as well as being the more obvious metonym for flowers.

1.18 "Blue waves" makes reference to the ancient topography of the area around Tiger Hill. Tiger Hill was originally called Sea-surging Mountain in the Spring and Autumn period, as it was surrounded by lakes and marshes. See *Wujun tujing xuji* (*Xuejin taoyuan* ed.), *j.*2/18b.

The poem is a complex working in *ci* of the *huaigu* subgenre, which involves meditation occasioned by the visit to an ancient historical site. Reflections on time—on the changes wrought by time, on permanence versus impermanence—constitute the central theme, which is introduced in a seemingly offhanded manner in the preface: Wu casually mentions three names of people whom he has worked with and befriended in the Grain Transport Office; however, it should be noted that this is done in the context of their imminent departure. The excursion was thus undertaken as an affirmation of friendship before friends were separated by life's current. From this perspective, the occasion must have been dominated by a mood of pensiveness, and this is reflected in the poem itself.

In recording the thought and experience of an occasion, this poem presents probably the most clearly structured temporal and spatial progression to be found in Wu's otherwise elliptical style. It refers in natural sequence to the matinal scene of departure, the scenery upon arrival, the ascent, the overnight stay and the return, neatly framed by seasonal indicators. Worked into this straightforward narrative progress of the event is a complexity of temporal dimensions: of time past and time future, and of timeless eternity, and a concomitant meditation on man's lot in the scheme of time and history. This complexity is achieved mainly through two historical allusions, one woven into the semantically tiered description of the scenery in the first stanza, the other coordinated with the topical associations of *denglin*, "to ascend to a high place and contemplate (the past)."

The first allusion is introduced through the description of the scenery at the destination of the excursion (lines 3–5). Zhen Niang, "Lady Zhen" (changed to Zhen Zhen due to the requirement of rhyme), was a famous courtesan of the Wu region whose grave was also situated at Tiger Hill. It was said that visitors, moved by her legendary beauty, competed to celebrate it by inscribing poems on the tree by her grave.[83] With this background, the line "on the pine's waist the jade is thin" takes on different levels of meaning. On the literal level, it is descriptive of the actual scenery of early spring at Tiger Hill, jade being used as a metonym for snow, forming a parallel to the melting snow on the orchid grass in the previous line. On a figurative level, "thin jade," generated by the metonym "waist" used for the pine trunk, acquires nuances of femininity, thus bringing in the tree's association with Zhen Niang's grave. On this level, the line's reading approximates: "the pine is delicate and slim like a woman's waist." This meaning is made explicit by the juxtaposition with "a worn and weary Zhen Zhen" of the next line. The juxtaposition not only evokes a sense of desolation in the scenery around the tomb, but it also evokes the presence of the famous courtesan whose physical beauty has not survived the passage of time. The past remains to haunt the imagination of sensitive minds in the form of a grave and a legend.

The tiered description continues in the next two lines as the party of friends proceeds up the boulder-paved path of Tiger Hill: "With light canes we thread our way along steep stone steps, / Treading on wild moss we still can discern traces of the buried flowers." While the image of wild moss on the boulders intensifies the sense of bleakness already introduced, it also signifies the timeworn antiquity of the site. In this thought-provoking landscape, fallen flowers, a conventional symbol of transience, are described as "buried" with remnants still visible; they are not simply perceived as signs of nature's ephemeral beauty but hark back to the relics of the beautiful courtesan. Thus far the poem has refrained from any direct expression of thought or emotion; the theme of mutability seen from the aspect of beauty is completely submerged in the descriptive imagery, which pertains to both the natural and the human world. As though no longer able to bear the strain of suppressed emotion, the last strophe of the

[83] Fan Shu, *Yunxi youyi* (*Congshu jicheng chubian* ed., vol. 2832), 35.

t stanza erupts on mid-hill into a lament for the ceaseless cles of change in history and signals the transition to the nysical as well as the contemplative goal of the climb.

The "ghost of Wu" is of course King Helu, the mighty ruler of Wu during the Spring and Autumn period. The group of friends commemorated his past glories with libations when they reached his underwater tomb on top of Tiger Hill. The somber occasion calls for more contemplation: on a moonlit night, on the summit of this burial mound, an individual existence confronts momentarily the intersection between the images of nature, history, and eternity as the poet watches the stars reflected in the pond water engulfing Helu's swords. Wu clearly excels in capturing the profundity of the moment in its beauty, and its beauty in the profundity.

The rest of the poem is devoted to an elaboration of the *denglin* topos and the departure. For a Chinese poet, to ascend to an elevation and look into the distance means to contemplate yet again the sobering theme of human transience in the face of nature's perpetuity. In Meng Haoran's poem "On ascending Mount Xian with some friends," this idea is explicitly stated:

> Human affairs rise and decline in succession,
> Coming and going, they make up past and present.
> Mountains and rivers leave their beauty,
> We again climb up to have a look. . . .[84]

> 人事有代謝，
> 往來成古今。
> 江山留勝迹，
> 我輩復登臨。

Wu Wenying sees the act of *denglin* as an integral part of the constant flux in human life, being itself a marker of the inevitability of change and movement: "Though we climb here to gaze, we will inevitably depart." In the same breath, Wu also affirms

---

[84] *QTS*, vol. 5, 1643. Cf. discussions of this poem by Hans H. Frankel, "The Contemplation of the Past in T'ang Poetry," in *Perspectives on the T'ang*, ed. Arthur F. Wright and Denis Twitchett (New Haven: Yale University Press, 1973), pp. 345–47.

this act and the evanescent splendors of this world in their sure recurrence—not only this time, this group, but in future times, in all times, other people have done and will do the same again. The final vision, the looking back, bridges the time gap by fusing the rain-shrouded hill of the present with the hill surrounded by lakes of Helu's time.

Visiting a Suzhou garden with a more recent history brings topical allusions into the only poem in which Wu comments directly on the state of affairs in the late Song:[85]

> **To the tune _Jinlü ge_**
> Viewing plum blossoms at Canglang Garden in the
> company of Mr. Lüzhai

1   Clouds and vapors rise from lofty trees
     Where we search for relics of the hero of the
             Restoration,
     And secretly ponder past events.
     Scant help did the war ships get from the east wind:
5   His dream was shattered in the old kingdom.
     Soon after, he built a little dwelling in the idle grounds
             of Wu Palace.
     To the pillar in moonlight the crane returns at night,
     Sighing over the flowers and bamboos of old now come
             to this.
     Dew on the branches, spilling clear tears.

10   The governor's little spring-outing troop,
     Treading on green moss, seeking secluded spots by the
             detached wall,
     To ask the plum whether it has flowered.
     Again we sing new tunes by the plum trees
     To hasten the sprouting of frozen buds on cold twigs:
15   Hearts with the same desire as the spring god.

---

[85] With the possible exception of the undated poem _Shuilong yin_: "Sending off Wan Xinzhou" (_QSC_ 4/2880). As suggested by Zheng Qian, the opening lines: "How often have we discussed over and again current events, / At the banquet we both regret the setting sun's decline," may be a comment on the current, more advanced deterioration in Southern Song politics, in comparison to its initial years; _Cixuan_, p. 134.

The future will not compare to the present, the present
      to the past.
Both wordless, facing each other by the waters of the
      Canglang.
Harboring this grief,
We seek solace in a last drink.

(QSC 4/2939–40)

陪履齋先生滄浪看梅

喬木生雲氣。
訪中興、英雄陳迹，
暗追前事。
戰艦東風慳借便，
夢斷神州故里。
旋小築、吳宮閒地。
華表月明歸夜鶴，
歎當時、花竹今如此。
枝上露，
濺清淚。

遨頭小簇行春隊。
步蒼苔、尋幽別隖，
問梅開未。
重唱梅邊新度曲，
催發寒梢凍蕊。
此心與、東君同意。
後不如今今非昔，
兩無言、相對滄浪水。
懷此恨，
寄殘醉。

Notes

Preface: Lüzhai is Wu Qian's sobriquet. This poem is dated to 1238,
when Wu Qian was Administrator of Suzhou. (See chap.1, p. 24).

l.7 The night crane alludes to the story of a man by the name of Ding
Lingwei in the *Sou shen ji*. Ding left home to study to become an
immortal. When he returned in the form of an immortal crane to the
pillar by his village cemetery, he found that the faces of people in the
village were all new and unfamiliar.

The Canglang Garden, whose site dates back to the Five Dy-
nasties period, is often associated with its early Northern Song

owner, the scholar-poet Su Shunqin, who gave it its name. But even more so, and especially during Wu's time, it is known for having been the residence of the great Southern Song general Han Shizhong (1089–1151) during the Shaoxing period (1131–1162).[86] In fact Wu Qian, whom Wu Wenying accompanied on this visit, refers to it as "Han's Canglang Garden" in the preface to his poem written on this occasion to match Wu Wenying's rhymes.[87]

The first stanza makes topical reference to the career of the famous general, aptly styled here as the "hero of the Restoration." In the early years of Gaozong's reign (1127–1161), during the 1130s, Han Shizhong and two other patriotic generals, Yue Fei and Zhang Jun, were scoring a series of brilliant victories against the Jurchens in an effort ot recover the north.[88] After Gaozong eventually decided in favor of an appeasement policy toward the Jurchens, the generals were ordered to return to court from the front in 1141. Yue Fei was subsequently imprisoned on trumped-up charges and murdered. At odds with the court's pacifist policies, Han Shizhong retired from politics with his hopes for recovery of the North prematurely crushed. Wu uses two details from Han's life with poetic license to emphasize the sense of futility and frustration a man of Han's temperament must have felt under the circumstances. Line 4 alludes to the only battle recorded in Han's career in which his fleet suffered heavy casualties due to the lack of a favorable wind, and the enemy was able to escape back north.[89]

This defeat took place in 1130 and was not by any means the end of Han's ambition to recapture the north, as it is portrayed in the poem, for Han went on to greater battles and victories in the next ten years. The real cause that eventually shattered Han's revanchist dream is carefully displaced, it being the humiliating peace treaties by which the Southern Song bought its existence from the Jurchens. According to his biography in the *Song shi*, Han retired to Hangzhou and not Suzhou, though it is quite

---

[86] Gong Mingzhi, *Zhongwu jiwen* (*Congshu jicheng chubian* ed., vol. 3155), p. 21.
[87] *QSC* 4/2730.
[88] See their biographies in *Song shi*, vol. 36, 11355ff; 11375ff; and 11297ff.
[89] A detailed description of this battle is found in Li Xinchuan, *Jianyan yilai xinian yaolu* (Beijing: Zhonghua shuju, 1956), 1:634–35.

possible that he spent time at the Canglang Garden during the ten years of retirement until his death in 1151. The point is that these disparate historical elements function effectively within the logic and structure of the poem to evoke the pathos embodied in the frustrated career of Han Shizhong. This pathos is intensified by the allusion in the next line (line 7). The allusion to the returned crane by the pillar generally suggests the vicissitudes and transitoriness of human life. Wu's application of it here makes a qualitative judgment of these changes; he is in effect saying that were Han Shizhong's spirit to return like the immortal crane, he would only see that the times have changed for the worse. The crane's sigh and the tearful dewdrops on the branches also become symbols of the poet's own lament at the deterioration from the past to the present. The chain of deterioration is seen even to go beyond the present into the future, impervious to man's ardent hopes and desires to the contrary. Wu spells his pessimism out quite plainly in the second stanza. Such a despairing view of things has not earned him praise from later critics, but it may in part explain his eschewal of politics both in life and in poetry.

The occasion of passing by the grave of an ancient historical figure brought to Wu's mind a lesson to be learned from history, and the poem that records this experience also reflects a basic distrust of the world of politics:

To the tune *Gaoyang tai*
Passing Zhong Mountain—the grave of Wen Zhong of Yue

1   Sails drop with the incoming tide
      As I return to the ancient kingdom;
      With heavy heart I roam again this mountain top.
      The bow was snapped in the frosty chill,
5   By a scheming mind the seagull was felled.
      Before the lamp a precious sword—the light breeze
            stopped,
      Just then there on Five Lakes, a rainhat of bamboo on a
            tiny boat.
      Most unfeeling

150

These wild flowers on the crag,
10   Infusing spring's sorrow with their sanguinary odor.

At that time, from the path of white rocks and green
             pines
He turned back his reins to the imperial carriage—
Mists hide the mountain's shame.
The woodcutters' song has come to an end.
15   Youth a dream on the desolate hills.
Year after year the west wind comes to the ancient park,
And wild geese cry in grief amidst autumnal reeds in
             green waters.
Don't climb up to gaze—
Only a few trees in fading haze
20   From the tall tower in the northwest.

                                    (*QSC* 4/2923)

過種山，即越文種墓

帆落迴潮，
人歸故國，
山椒感慨重遊。
弓折霜寒，
機心已墮沙鷗。
燈前寶劍清風斷，
正五湖、雨笠扁舟。
最無情，
巖上閒花，
腥染春愁。

當時白石蒼松路，
解勒回玉鞚，
霧掩山羞。
木客歌闌，
青春一夢荒丘。
年年古苑西風到，
雁怨啼、綠水葓秋。
莫登臨，
幾樹殘煙，
西北高樓。

151

Notes

    Preface: Zhong Mountain was so called because Wen Zhong, minister of the state of Yue, was buried there. It is located in Shaoxing, Zhejiang province. In Song times it had come to be an old name for Wolong Mountain. See *Shaoxing fuzhi*, comp. Li Hengte (1792; rpt. Taipei: Chengwen chubanshe, 1975), vol. 1, 77.

In order to decode the montage of images in this poem, one needs to know the historical tragedy that informs it. One can assume that in the case of traditional Chinese readers, this knowledge is taken for granted; Wen Zhong was a key figure in the intrigues between the states of Wu and Yue in the Spring and Autumn period. One of the two able ministers who assisted King Goujian of Yue to stage his final defeat of Wu, Wen Zhong stayed on in the service of Goujian after the victory, while Fan Li, the other minister, wandered off as a recluse. In the *Shiji* account of the aftermath, Fan Li is reported to have relayed a message to Wen Zhong, warning him of Goujian's distrustful and ruthless character, and advised him to leave. Since Goujian had fulfilled his ambition to conquer Wu, Wen Zhong's ability as a strategist would be regarded as a liability. Wen, however, did not heed Fan Li's advice and met his end as Fan Li had predicted when Goujian, suspicious of seditious plots, ordered him to commit suicide by sword.[90]

    Finding himself at the burial site of this self-immolated victim, Wu felt profoundly affected by Wen Zhong's death, which he saw as the result of a mistaken choice between two lifestyles. The grid of symbolic images and allusions both conducts the emotional current and accentuates the contrast between a violent death and delitescent freedom. Wen Zhong's gory fate is first symbolized by the shooting of an unsuspecting gull by a hunter's (Goujian) design; the act of his suicide is represented by the sword; and his death, the ceasing of the wind. After this rapid succession of death symbols, the sudden appearance of the rain-capped figure, the wandering recluse Fan Li drifting carefree on a boat over the misty lakes, evokes by powerful contrast the pathetic irony of Wen Zhong's choice. The first stanza ends with a perceptual expression of Wu's deep sympathy for Wen Zhong:

[90] *Shi ji, j*.41 (Beijing: Zhonghua shuju, 1959), 5:1746–47.

"Most unfeeling, / These wild flowers on the crag / Infusing spring's sorrow with their sanguinary odor." The flowers that still bloom at the site are seen as "unfeeling," insensitive. Wu's own acute sensitivity to the disjunction between nature's insentient continuity and the violent and bloody vicissitudes of human history translates into a perceptual language that compounds these opposing qualities into expressive imagery. Here, the sweet fragrance of the flowers is perceived as a sanguinary stench instead, as having been contaminated by Wen Zhong's spilled blood and thus carrying its scent. In the *Basheng Ganzhou* quoted above, which was written on Mount Lingyan, the site of King Fucha's ancient palace grounds, the line "Creamy water stains the flower's stench" carries a similar connotation: nature continues its seemingly oblivious existence, but the poet sees it branded with the signs of human folly.

Before further elaboration of the *huaigu* theme in conjunction with the *denglin* topos, both integral to a poem written at a historical tomb on a mountain, the second stanza begins with a reiteration of Wen Zhong's fatal mistake in not choosing the eremite's life of freedom. This is repeated both for emphasis and to provide a thematic link to the first stanza. "The Proclamation on North Mountain," an essay in parallel prose by Kong Zhigui (447–501), established the convention of employing the pathetic fallacy to underscore the abhorrence at a hermit who abandons his purity by taking up office.[91] Nature, the hermit's abode, is portrayed in this essay as reacting to his apostasy in a full range of human emotions: clouds are angered, streams disappointed, mountains and valleys express their contempt, cranes and apes are grieved, woods humiliated, and so on. In later poetry, these become conventionalized motifs to be used whenever an occasion presents the potential for antithetical play between office and retirement. For example, in a parting poem to an official who is being transferred from one post to another, it is not unusual for mention to be made of a grieved crane waiting for him in the mountain. The second stanza of this poem begins with Wen Zhong's turning away from the "path of white rocks and

[91] In *Wenxuan*, 2:957–60. Trans. James R. Hightower in "Some Characteristics of Parallel Prose," pp. 118–22.

pines"—the life of retirement—thus the mountain is described as being shamed by his desertion. It should have been horrified. The pathos of this passage lies in the reader's knowledge of the destiny that awaited Wen Zhong.

The rest of the poem rises above the life and death of an individual to the rise and fall of a state. The shift in perspective is even more disheartening, for in hindsight history seems to be an inexorable decline. Yue's victory did not last forever; Yue was in turn wiped out by Chu a century and a half later. The rise and fall of the state is depicted in one stroke through the allusion to the woodcutters (line 14), who were men Goujian sent into the mountains to obtain lumber to present to King Fucha of Wu, to encourage him in his extravagance in building palaces. This was part of the long-term strategy of revenge designed for Goujian by Wen Zhong.[92] The allusion therefore stands for the pre-victory days of Goujian, and by extension, to the Yue state in its ascendent period. But their song has "come to an end," all that is left of the victorious Yue are ruins seen from a gloomy hill.

If contemplation from a hill already brings one to an emotional nadir, to ascend to a higher vantage point would surely plunge one into the abyss. The closure, therefore, issues a direct warning: "Don't climb up to gaze from the tall tower!" The emotional devastation is subsumed in the imagined view of desolation from the tower. By making reference to another plane of contemplation—both physical and psychological—without developing it, the closure is almost too obvious as a technique to extend the emotional scope of the poem. In the context of poetic convention, the emotional implications created by the closural arrest would be clearly understood, as "climbing a tower" constitutes a well-established subgenre of poems exhibiting a strong contemplative bent.

As early as the Han, Wang Can wrote his celebrated "Fu on climbing a tower" in which he expressed his homesickness as an exile,[93] and many Tang poets left memorable works written at various traditional architectural colossi. The subgeneric conventions associated with "ascending a tower" evolved with the result

---

[92] *Yue jue shu*, *j*.9.
[93] *Wenxuan*, 1:221–23.

that a poem on such an occasion became a medium for introspective verse; poems on the theme require some reflective comments, whether personal, historical, political or philosophical. Within the tradition, it is understood and expected that the sheer physical elevation should provoke such a response. One often finds the immensity of the view from the tower depicted in some descriptive lines; indeed, this approach is perhaps more common than dwelling on the historical significance of the particular tower. We may recall Tu Fu's well-known "Ascending Yueyang Tower," one of his many "ascending a tower" poems, and Li Shangyin's "The Tower on the city wall of Anding."[94] Both poems begin by establishing the vantage point, followed by a brief description of the vista, then move on for the greater part to self-introspective thought. Li Shangyin's poem in heptasyllabic regulated form is the more extreme, in that only the first couplet refers to the actual tower and the view; the remaining three couplets all express his personal feelings and ambitions in a series of allusions:

> The city wall stretches far; the tower stands a hundred feet.
> Beyond the green willow branches, I see nothing but banks and islets.
> Master Chia in his youth in vain shed tears;
> Wang Ts'an in spring once more went on a distant journey.
> Forever remembering the rivers and lakes to which I would return, white-haired,
> I yet wish to turn around heaven and earth before entering a tiny boat.
> Not knowing the rotten rat was considered tasty,
> The phoenix unwittingly aroused endless suspicions![95]

迢遞高城百尺樓，
綠楊枝外盡汀洲。
賈生年少虛垂涕，

---

[94] QTS, 7:2566 and 16:6191–92 respectively.
[95] Trans. James J. Y. Liu with notes and commentary, in *The Poetry of Li Shang-yin* (Chicago: University of Chicago Press, 1969), pp. 129–30.

王粲春來更遠游。
永憶江湖歸白髮，
欲回天地入扁舟。
不知腐鼠成滋味，
猜意鵷雛竟未休。

Wu Wenying's oeuvre contains only a few "tower" poems. Some of these deserve mention, if not for their exploration of the subgenre in *ci*, then at least for their sheer verbal art. For in Wu's case, the elevated field of vision seems to have excited his imagination as much as inducing introspection, at times perhaps more, Inasmuch as these tower-buildings were ones located in Hangzhou, Suzhou, and Shaoxing, they had served as popular places where the Southern Song upper classes gathered for banquets, drinking parties and other social occasions. Some of Wu Wenying's poems written at these locations are clearly occasional, as indicated by either the preface or content. There are three occasional poems he wrote at the Abundant Happiness Pavilion in Hangzhou. According to a contemporary work, the *Meng liang lu*, this tower-pavilion was situated on the bank of West Lake just outside Fengyu Gate, the western city gate. The *Meng liang lu* further records that it was torn down and rebuilt by the official Zhao Yuchou during the Chunyou period (1241–1252); upon completion, its height "reached up to the clouds," commanding a majestic view of the lake and surrounding scenery. Scholars and officials had frequent gatherings there.[96] In fact, Wu Wenying's preface to one of the three poems reads, "Abundant Happiness Pavilion—newly built by Jiezhai (Zhao Yuchou)" (*QSC* 4/2907). The poem is written to the four-stanza tune pattern *Ying ti xu*, and Wu reportedly inscribed it on the wall of the pavilion to "advertise" himself.[97] Aside from the ostentatious description exaggerating the fantastic height of the building in the first stanza, which was obviously written to dazzle the eye, the poem is an uninspiring piece of occasional verse written for Zhao Yuchou (at the opening banquet?): it eulogizes the peaceful

---

[96] Wu Zimu, *Meng liang lu*; rpt. in *Dongjing menghua lu waisizhong* (Shanghai: Gudian wenxue chubanshe, 1956), p. 230.
[97] See Xia Chengtao, *Tang Song ciren nianpu*, pp. 476–77.

156

times they live in, Zhao's work on the building, and his life as an official. I have selected instead another poem written at the Abundant Happiness Pavilion. Even though, to judge from the preface, this poem also seems as occasional as occasional can be, the poem itself has an emotional content that is personal and a language that does display the positive aspects of Wu's style:

To the tune *Gaoyang tai*
At Abundant Happiness Pavilion, I obtained the character *ru* when rhyme words were distributed.

1   Tall bamboos in glossy dress
And willows hanging down entice riders to stop:
By the railing a few light strokes become a painting.
Who will place an inscription on this mountain
        landscape?
5   Before the pavilion wild geese write a slanting line.
The spring wind hastens the setting sun's departure,
Reviving winter's chill as I grow sober from the
        evening's wine.
Alone and deeply moved:
How many more years have I with these flowers?
10   For suddenly Xiangru grows old.

It is not on a tall pavilion that I lament for spring,
But propped on a pillow by the lamp,
Beside the clothes-censer while it rains outside.
I hesitate to moor my pleasure boat—
15   Looking into the stream I cannot bear my thinness.
If falling petals reach the bottom of West Lake,
Nothing but sorrowful fish would churn up emerald
        waves.
Don't come back!
After the fragrant catkins have all been blown away,
20   Tears will fill the grassy plain.

                              (*QSC* 4/2922)

豐樂樓分韻得如字

修竹凝妝，
垂楊駐馬，

憑闌淺畫成圖。
山色誰題，
樓前有雁斜書。
東風緊送斜陽下，
弄舊寒、晚酒醒餘。
自銷凝，
能幾花前，
頓老相如。

傷春不在高樓上，
在燈前敲枕，
雨外重鑪。
怕艤遊船，
臨流可奈清臞。
飛紅若到西湖底，
攪翠瀾、總是愁魚。
莫重來，
吹盡香絲，
淚滿平蕪。

Note
1.10 The Han poet Sima Xiangru is used as a persona of the poet.

As is wont, the poem opens with a depiction of the view seen
from the height of the pavilion. What is novel is the description
of this landscape as details in a painting, with the line formation
of wild geese in flight across the sky imagined to be the inscrip-
tion on this painting. The transition from description to contem-
plation is effected in the poignant imagery of line 6, in which the
sunset is compared to a guest being seen off by the spring wind. A
moment of beauty quickly disappears, and the poet is reminded
of youth and life slipping away from him. His thoughts leave
the pavilion altogether in the second stanza as he delves into the
theme of lament for the passing of spring, an obvious symbol of
youth and beauty. The unusual affect of an otherwise common-
place theme comes from the reversal of the emotional vantage
point. The poet refutes the conventional association of height
with heightened emotion: "It is not on a tall pavilion that I
lament for spring," he declares, but down in his room, while
listening to the rain at night. The rain implies that the flowers in

bloom are being damaged, and therein lies his regret for the destruction of youth and beauty, which is also mirrored by his own emaciated form. Moving along this inverted vertical scale of sorrow, the poet's imagination dives into the bottom of West Lake with the rain-scattered petals, to impute this pervasive sadness even to the fish playing in the depths. The closure reverts back to the proper emotional scale associated with the elevated view from the pavilion. However, it does so only to assert the utter inescapability of life's transitoriness and the analogous totality of man's sorrow.

Not all of Wu Wenying's finer works are so lugubrious and grave in tone as the above poems may suggest. To end this chapter on a positive note, I have selected a poem he probably wrote in the sunnier period of his manhood, before his vision was clouded by life's shadows:

To the tune *Qi tian yue*
Level-with-Cloud Tower

1   At the break of dawn, a shadow from Yang Terrace
       Flew from the firmament and stayed here.
       Its pillars are level with Orion,
       And curtains hook onto the Dipper's curve:
5   How high this tower on the northwest wall,
       Celestial sounds resemble voices.
       Lightly I push open the gates of the empyrean palace
       And smoothly ascend the rainbow river,
       Wondering through how much rain and shine
10   It has lorded over the plains of Wu, defying time.

       Hills to the west, like darkened brows, are seen in their
           emerald hues,
       But even sharp eyes cannot reach
       The misty horizon where egrets vanish.
       The plaintive chant of the bamboo flute
15   Suddenly rends the layered fog—
       A cold moon spreads its hazy light across many miles.
       I dance intoxicated in the Void,
       Dreaming of a marble white balustrade
       Changing into flying mist.

159

20 Red and green are cleansed
When a sudden rain sweeps across the azure sea.

(QSC 4/2884)

齊雲樓

淩朝一片陽臺影，
飛來太空不去，
棟與參橫，
簾鉤斗曲，
西北城高幾許。
天聲似語。
便闤闠輕排，
虹河平遡。
問幾陰晴，
霸吳平地漫古今。

西山橫黛瞰碧，
眼明應不到，
煙際沈鷺。
臥笛長吟，
層霄乍裂，
寒月溟濛千里。
憑虛醉舞。
夢凝白闌干，
化為飛霧。
淨洗青紅，
驟飛滄海雨。

Notes

Preface: The name of the tower alludes to its height. It is derived from the fifth of the "Nineteen Old Poems," the first couplet of which reads: "In the northwest there is a tall tower, / Its top soars, level with clouds." *Wenxuan*, vol. 1, 632. Line 5 also alludes to this couplet.

1.1 Yang Terrace was the dwelling of the goddess in Song Yu's "Gaotang fu." She had described herself as the "dawn cloud." The line alludes to the character "cloud" in the name of the tower. The oblique allusion to this mythical tale in the "Gaotang fu" introduces a mysterious and fantastic dimension to the height of the tower.

1.20 "Red and green" are often employed in Wu's poems as metonym for an edifice, as they are common in the color scheme of traditional Chinese architecture.

In this poem Wu dispenses with, or subverts, subgeneric conventions and gives free rein to his imaginative power. What comes forth is sheer verbal magic. Through his wonderful imagination and magnificent description, the reader derives vicarious enjoyment of the exhilaration of being in the celestial realms on the top of the tower and finally experiences the same sense of purification at the close of the poem.

4. CRITICAL VIEWS

Critical opinion regarding Wu Wenying's *ci* became divided shortly after his lifetime, with Zhang Yan's famous critique in the *Ciyuan*. While Wu had been lauded by his contemporaries Yin Huan and Shen Yifu as the equal of the Northern Song *ci* master Zhou Bangyan, Zhang Yan emphatically faulted him for the obscurity and fragmentation of his poetry. Zhang Yan was himself an important late Song poet and critic; his critical views therefore bore weight and influence among his successors. Zhang's critical statement on Wu Wenying's *ci* had two notable consequences: first, it drew attention to verbal density and surface elegance as the salient characteristics of Wu's *ci* and, second, it emphasized a negative evaluation of these characteristics. Later critical views on Wu often echo Zhang Yan's view, either in agreement and easy dismissal of Wu's *ci* or in disagreement and counter elaboration in Wu's defense. However, articulation of these opposing critical tendencies did not begin to surface until several centuries after the death of both poet and critic.

With the post-Song decline of the *ci* as a poetic genre, it fell outside the mainstream of creative productivity and critical interest. The subsequent Yuan and Ming periods represent more than three barren centuries both in the writing of *ci* and in *ci* criticism. The handful of works on *ci* written during this period contain no critical insight of note, and Wu Wenying's name hardly figures in them at all.[1] Post-Song *ci* poetic criticism is properly seen as a legacy of the Qing period revival of the genre.

[1] Only four works by Ming authors are included in the *Cihua congbian*, see vols. 1 and 2.

Renewed interest in *ci* poetry began in the late Ming and early Qing, when poets again took up the writing of *ci*. The Ming loyalist Chen Zilong (1608–1647), and many early Qing literary talents such as Wu Weiye (1609–1672), Zhu Yizun (1629–1709), and Chen Weisong (1625–1682), to name but a few, all left behind reputable collections of *ci* poetry.

Critical interest in the genre also revived at this time, as indicated by the appearance of contemporaneous writings devoted to the discussion of *ci* poetry. Some of these writings contain the earliest Qing comments on Wu Wenying. His name is generally mentioned in the context of discussions of Southern Song *ci*, often in comparison to *ci* of the Northern Song period. In the eyes of early Qing critics, Northern Song *ci* were characterized by a quality of "naturalness," while that of the Southern Song exhibited stylistic subtlety and sophistication. Although the two "styles" seem to have been valued, each for its own merits, some of the comments show a marked appreciation for the "art" in the Southern Song style, with which Wu Wenying is at once associated. This favorable disposition toward Southern Song *ci* is especially evident in the writings of the eminent *shi* poet and theorist Wang Shizhen (1634–1711) and his friends Zou Zhimo (fl. 1666) and Peng Sunyu (1631–1700). In the *Huacao mengshi* Wang noted that:

> Since the Song moved south, with poets such as Meixi (Shi Dazu), Baishi (Jiang Kui), Zhuwu (Gao Guanguo), and Mengchuang (Wu Wenying), *ci* reached its ultimate in elegance and beauty. Even Qin [Guan] and Li [Qingzhao] cannot be their match in some ways. Although their *ci* may have less resonance and naturalness, one is made to sigh with admiration at their unsurpassed excellence.[2]

To Wang Shizhen, the only weakness in the Southern Song style was a diminution of the resonant and natural quality found in Northern Song *ci*, and this does not seem to deter his estimation of its artistry. Wang's view is echoed by Zou Zhimo in his discussions of *manci*:

---

[2] *Huacao mengshi* (*Cihua congbian* ed., vol. 2), p. 675.

Long tunes were the last development in *ci*. The out-
standing works among Southern Song poets all excel in
this form. In the works of Meixi (Shi Dazu), Baishi (Jiang
Kui), Zhuwu (Gao Guanguo), and Mengchuang, lovely
sentiments and beautiful diction reached the highest ex-
pression. Moreover, their embellishment and polish have
a marvel of movement like the subtle traces left by snakes
and earthworms linked in a continuous flow.[3]

Zou made this statement in support of his view that the *manci*
form was handled perfectly only by Southern Song *ci* poets. He
even criticized Zhou Bangyan's *manci* for their crude fluency.[4]
But the stylistic ornamentation, which Zou notes with such
admiration, is to him as much or even more of an achievement
than structural organization. Poetic diction is an engaging char-
acteristic of Southern Song *ci* for these critics. In Wu Wenying's
case, Peng Sunyu perceives it to be excessive and thus to
overshadow the expression of emotion. He notes with regret that
"although Mengchuang's *ci* is full of ornamentation, it is some-
what lacking in emotional appeal."[5]

The comments made by Wang Shizhen's group are illuminat-
ing in that they show the style of Southern Song *ci* to have had a
strong appeal during the early stages of the Qing revival and Wu
Wenying's work to have been representative of that appeal. The
group, however, did not formulate any consistent theories, nor
did it advocate any models for emulation, and Wang Shizhen
himself gave up the study and writing of *ci* very early on in his
career. Consequently, their writings did not have significant
influence on later developments. It is with a contemporary of
Wang Shizhen, the early Qing poet Zhu Yizun, that definite
trends were set in the world of *ci*.

Zhu Yizun was a prolific *ci* poet with a commanding reputation
among his contemporaries and a scholar of versatile talent, but he
did not leave behind any work on *ci* criticism. Yet, through him,
Southern Song *ci* was placed on the pedestal of perfection. This

---

[3] *Yuanzhizhai cizhong* (*Cihua congbian* ed., vol. 2), p. 647.
[4] *Ibid.*
[5] *Jinsu cihua* (*Cihua congbian* ed., vol. 2), p. 707.

was the result both of the models Zhu professed to emulate in his practice of writing *ci* and of the influential anthology of *ci* poetry he compiled. The *Cizong*, completed in 1678, the first *ci* anthology to appear in the Qing, was timely in its appearance, as interest in *ci* was burgeoning. In it the major late Song poets are favored with the greatest number of selections. We have already quoted Zhu Yizun's famous pronouncement in the explanatory foreword to the *Cizong* in which he claimed that "only in the Southern Song did the *ci* attain its perfection, and only at the end of the Song did it exhaust its transformations." This is immediately followed by the statement that "Jiang Yaozhang (Jiang Kui) is the most outstanding [*ci* poet in the late Song.]"[6] In prefaces Zhu wrote to *ci* collections by his contemporaries and in his own poems, he states in no uncertain terms his preference for Jiang Kui among Southern Song *ci* poets.[7] He depicts Jiang Kui's poetry as the matrix of the late Song style from which ten other poets, among them Wu Wenying and Zhang Yan, represent offshoots.[8] In practice, he advocates Jiang Kui and Zhang Yan as models for imitation.[9] Since Zhu Yizun is completely at one with Zhang Yan's ideal of *ci* poetry, one wonders where Wu Wenying stands in his scheme; in point of fact, mostly in the shade by default. For Zhu did not follow Zhang Yan's lead in using Wu as a foil to his poetic ideal, and left no specific comment regarding Wu Wenying's poetry.[10]

Wu Wenying, along with most other *ci* poets of the past, remained a subordinate name for a century or so after Zhu Yizun's time. During this period when poets interested in the genre were engaged in the writing of *ci*, stylistic models became

[6] In *Cizong*, (1691; rpt. Shanghai: Shanghai guji chubanshe, 1978), 1:10.

[7] See the third poem under the tune *Shui diao ge tou*, in *Pushuting ci*, pp. 36–37, in *Qing mingjia ci*, ed. Chen Naiqian, vol. 3, (Hong Kong: Taiping shuju, 1963).

[8] See Zhu's preface to Shen Anding's *ci* collection, *Heidiezhai ci*, p. 1, in *Qing mingjia ci*, vol. 4. Zhu does not elaborate on how the poetry of these ten poets represent different aspects of Jiang Kui's style. The sentence is repeated by Wang Sen, the co-compiler of the *Cizong*, in the preface he wrote to the anthology; see *Cizong*, 1:1.

[9] See Zhu's preface to Cao Rong's *ci* collection, the *Jingtitang ci*, p. 1, in *Qing mingjia ci*, vol. 1.

[10] Zhu did include a good number of Wu Wenying's *ci* (45) in the *Cizong*, see j.19.

165

the catchword for many. The most prominent models were of course Jiang Kui and Zhang Yan, representing the late Song style of elegance and refinement, which had its rival in the *haofang* ("heroic") style modelled after Su Shi and Xin Qiji.[11] By the late-eighteenth century, objections were raised to the practice of Qing epigones, who were thought to have succeeded only in developing the worst traits of each style.

The criticism hailed from a group of *ci* poets and critics in Changzhou (Jiangsu) with the classical scholar Zhang Huiyan (1761–1802) as its founding authority; the group subsequnetly became known as the Changzhou School of *ci* criticism.[12] To rectify the faults to which Qing *ci* writers had degenerated, and to elevate the *ci* genre to a proper status in the literary tradition, Zhang Huiyan compiled an anthology of *ci* poetry, the *Cixuan* (printed in 1797), in which he advanced the method of allegorical interpretation and applied it to *ci* poetry after the manner of *Shijing* and *Chuci* exegetes to reveal the poems' hidden moral and political tenor.[13] However forced Zhang Huiyan's methodological application may have appeared to later critics, the undertaking belonged to a venerable tradition and was not questioned by his immediate followers.

With respect to the development of *ci* criticism, Zhang Huiyan's epoch-making critical approach profoundly affected the course of Qing studies on the genre. It significantly redirected attention toward meaning and content and away from the sole preoccupation with style prevalent in his day. Zhang's

[11] Zhu Yizun and his followers who took Jiang Kui and Zhang Yan as models represent the Zhexi School. Poets who wrote in the *haofang* style were collectively known as the Yangxian School. Each school was named after the region to which most of its members belonged. Chen Weisong was the leading poet writing in the *haofang* style.

[12] For a detailed study of the critical theory and practice of the Changzhou school, see Chia-ying Yeh Chao, "The Ch'ang-chou School of *Tz'u* Criticism" *HJAS*, 35 (1975):101–32. A revised version of this article appears in *Chinese Approaches to Literature from Confucius to Liang Ch'i-ch'ao*, ed. Adele A. Rickett (Princeton: Princeton University Press, 1978) pp. 151–88. See also Wu Hongyi, *Changzhou pai cixue yanjiu* (Taipei: Jiaxin shuini gongsi wenhua jijinhui, 1970).

[13] It is commonly noted that Zhang Huiyan's training as a classicist influenced his approach to *ci*. Zhang provides allegorical interpretation for 40 of the 116 *ci* in the *Cixuan*.

theoretical emphasis, however, entailed strong partiality. His selections show a predilection for *ci* poems with indefinite and ambiguous reference, leaving them open to allegorical treatment, and for *ci* in which there are discernible signs of an allegorical dimension. The former tend to be short lyrics by poets from the late Tang to the Northern Song, the latter, *ci* poems by Southern Song poets such as Xin Qiji and Wang Yisun.[14] Zhang Huiyan excluded Wu Wenying from his anthology with one pithy comment in the preface: "Scattered parts that do not form a whole."[15] This is just Zhang Yan's critique put in a capsule.

It is evident from this brief historical outline that there had been no real critical interest in Wu Wenying for well over a century into the renaissance of *ci*. Zhang Huiyan would even dismiss him summarily. Ironically, the turning point for Wu Wenying came with Zhou Ji (1781–1839), Zhang's most important successor in the Changzhou School. A few decades after the publication of the *Cixuan*, Zhou Ji elaborated on and refined Zhang Huiyan's critical approach. In Zhou Ji's works, Wu Wenying is raised from neglect into a position of prominence. Zhou Ji left behind two anthologies of *ci* poetry, the *Cibian* [*Ci* differentiations] and the *Song sijia cixuan* [*Ci* by the Four Masters of the Song], and a short work of critical comments, *Jiecunzhai lunci zazhu* [Miscellaneous Notes on *Ci* from Jiecun Studio]. Zhou Ji's critical discussions are contained in the *Jiecunzhai lunci zazhu* and the prefaces to the two anthologies. Zhou was not a prolific critic, but what he did write is incisive and reflects a solid connoisseurship that can only have been the result of dedicated study combined with a native sensitivity to the subject of his interest.

In view of Zhou Ji's stature as a *ci* critic and his importance in the history of Wu Wenying criticism, it is worthwhile to take a brief look at the evolution of Zhou's involvement with *ci*. He provides a most candid account in the preface (dated 1812) to his earliest work, the *Cibian*. Zhou tells us that he began writing *ci* at the age of sixteen (in the same year Zhang Huiyan's *Cixuan* was

---

[14] On Wang Yisun's *yongwu ci*, see Chia-ying Yeh Chao, "On Wang I-sun and His *Yung-wu Tz'u*," *HJAS*, 40, no. 1 (1980):55–91.

[15] Zhang Huiyan, *Cixuan* (1797; rpt. Beijing: Zhonghua shuju, 1958), p. 8.

printed). In 1804, while still a young man of twenty-three (and a year before he obtained his *jinshi* degree), he came into contact with Zhang's theories through meeting Zhang's nephew Dong Shixi (fl. 1811). According to Zhou, Dong Shixi, who was his junior, was already a more accomplished *ci* poet. During the next two years the two friends discussed and argued over their differing opinions regarding the *ci* poets of the Song. In the course of their exchanges, the most significant points were when Zhou convinced Dong of Zhang Yan's inferiority as a *ci* poet—"his ideas end with his words"—and when, through Dong's coaching, Zhou acquired a deep appreciation of Zhou Bangyan's *ci*, which he had at first disliked. Later (sometime before 1812, when this preface was written), while Zhou Ji was in Wusong (Jiangsu) tutoring a student surnamed Tian in *ci* composition, he compiled a ten *juan* anthology of *ci* poetry, which he entitled *Cibian*, meant to illustrate various features in *ci*, both positive and negative, with examples drawn from the past.[16] The original manuscript of the *Cibian*, as Zhou records later in the postface to *Jiecunzhai lunci zazhu*, was given to his student Tian, who was traveling north by boat, and accidentally fell into the river. Zhou subsequently managed to reassemble only the first two *juan* from memory.[17]

Zhou Ji is noted for developing Zhang Huiyan's simplistic method of locating allegorical meaning into a sophisticated concept of allegory that allows for a kind of reader-induced plurisignation: there is no one fixed meaning to a poem, and each reader arrives at his interpretation, his own "truth," from interaction with the metaphorical structure of the poem.[18] This idea was introduced in the preface to the *Cibian*. In Zhou's later elaborations on allegory (*jituo*) from the poet's point of view, he distinguishes between "intentional" and "unintentional" allegory. In these discussions, however, Zhou remains circumscribed by Zhang Huiyan's allegorical models. He sees an unin-

---

[16] See Zhou Ji's preface to the *Cibian* in *Tanping Cibian Song sijia cixuan* (Taipei: Guangwen shuju, 1962).

[17] *Jiecunzhai lunci zazhu* (*Cihua congbian* ed., vol. 5), p. 1629.

[18] Cf. Chia-ying Yeh Chao's discussion in "The Ch'ang-chou School," pp. 126–32.

tentional allegorical dimension in some late Tang and Northern Song *ci* poetry, while the allegorical content in Southern Song *ci* is seen to be intentional. Moreover, the former type of poetry is judged to be superior, an ideal that one should aim for in writing *ci*.[19]

In the context of critical views on Wu Wenying, the Changzhou School's focus on content rather than style in *ci* poetry must have indirectly contributed to Zhou Ji's insight into the "substance" of Wu Wenying's poetry. In the *Jiecunzhai lunci zazhu*, Zhou Ji has this to say about Wu Wenying:

> Yin Huan knew what he was saying when he compared Mengchuang to Qingzhen (Zhou Bangyan). In Mengchuang's *ci* there are often leaps and turns in the void; it can only be achieved if one has great mental power. It is true that there are difficult and obscure pieces in his work, but they are far better than any empty and facile poem. What's more, his best poems have the feel of celestial radiance and cloud reflections undulating in green waves; one can never tire of enjoying them and seeking after their elusiveness. Junte (Wu Wenying) has deep thoughts about the times. But the manner in which he expresses his emotion is not tightly structured, and this makes it difficult to infer its presence.[20]

For the first time a critic penetrates what had seemed to be a blinding brilliance of style, takes cognizance of the substratum of thought and emotion in Wu Wenying's poetry, and explains, however briefly, why it is not easy to get at its meaning. In another passage, Zhou Ji also accounts for the general failure to perceive what is subtle and profound in *ci* poetry, and Zhang Yan is found to be the culprit:

> Shuxia (Zhang Yan) was a latecomer to the critics' scene. He was a contemporary of Bishan (Wang Yisun) and moreover differed from Mengchuang in style. Therefore

[19] See *Jiecunzhai lunci zazhu* (*Cihua congbian* ed., vol. 5), p. 1624; and the "Preface to *Song sijia cixuan*" (*Cihua congbian* ed., vol. 5), p. 1630.

[20] *Jiecunzhai lunci zazhu* (*Cihua congbian* ed., vol. 5), p. 1626.

he overestimated Baishi (Jiang Kui) and advocated the poetics of transparency to the exclusion of everything else. In later ages, his views led to an inability to carefully examine complexity and depth in *ci* poetry.[21]

Zhou Ji's criticism was primarily directed at the detrimental effect the overwhelming popularity of Jiang Kui and Zhang Yan's styles had had on critical perspective. The reference to Wu Wenying alludes to the opposition between the poetics of transparency and density postulated by Zhang Yan, which had put Wu in an unfavorable light. The widespread inability to appreciate depth, then, encompasses an inadequate understanding of Wu Wenying's poetry.

Although Zhou Ji's ruminations on allegory have their source in the general context of Changzhou theories, his remarks on specific poets often impress one as highly original and perceptive. Certainly the impartial recognition he gives Wu Wenying in the *Jiecunzhai lunci zazhu* is without precedent in the Qing. But the comments in the *Jiecunzhai lunci zazhu* only mark the beginning of Zhou Ji's growing esteem for this somewhat controversial poetic figure. In 1832, almost thirty years after he first came into contact with the critical canons of the Changzhou School, Zhou Ji came out with his own anthology of Song *ci* poetry, the *Song sijia cixuan*. The work represents Zhou Ji's definitive evaluation of *ci* poets of the Song. Alongside Zhou Bangyan, Xin Qiji, and Wang Yisun, Wu Wenying is designated one of the four exemplars of Song *ci*, under whose leading styles other major Song *ci* poets are arranged. Zhou Ji begins the preface to the anthology with a brief characterization of these four principal styles:

> Qingzhen (Zhou Bangyan) is the great synthesizer of styles. Jiaxuan (Xin Qiji) puts in check his heroic ambitions and finds an outlet in lofty tunes; he transforms the delicate mode into an expression of tragic sorrow. Bishan's (Wang Yisun) burdened heart keeps to the principle of speaking about one thing and referring to another;

[21] *Ibid.*, p. 1623.

the tone and expression in his poetry can all be traced. Mengchuang's poetry has extraordinary thought and intense beauty; it soars to the heights and plumbs the depths; it turns away from the shallow clarity of the Southern Song and returns to the full richness of the Northern Song.[22]

These comments capture the essence of what is superlative in Wu Wenying's poetry. If we examine the configuration of the four poets, it still posits the Northern Song style as the ideal of ci poetry and, furthermore, recognizes Wu Wenying as the one poet whose style approaches the "richness" of Northern Song ci. The latter point may seem both vague and untenable. But the clue to its logic lies in the choice of Zhou Bangyan as the orthodox model, the supreme master of all times. Zhou Bangyan's stylistic sophistication and refinement embraced much of the mainstream developments in the Northern Song and became the model of inspiration behind much of the Southern Song's concern with elegance and artistry. The gap between Zhou Bangyan and Wu Wenying is thus not so difficult to bridge. In fact, their names had been linked together in the Southern Song, first by Yin Huan (whose remark is judged to be apposite by Zhou Ji), and then by Shen Yifu, who believed that Wu Wenying "had truly obtained the secret" of Zhou Bangyan.[23] Zhou Ji's scheme, while upholding the Northern Song style as ideal, actually comes close to a total affirmation of much Southern Song ci in critical appreciation. In the program he proposes for the aspiring ci poet, Wu Wenying represents an important stage to be reached: "Seek the way of Bishan (Wang Yisun), then go through Jiaxuan (Xin Qiji) and Mengchuang to return to the wholeness of Qingzhen (Zhou Bangyan)."[24] If the dictum is considered in conjunction with Zhou Ji's exposition of the four styles, it can be paraphrased as follows: "Begin with imitable good technique, express respectable emotion, fuse the two in an original way, and then you can approach perfection."

[22] "Preface to *Song sijia cixuan*" (*Cihua congbian* ed., vol. 5), p. 1630.
[23] *Yuefu zhimi* (*Cihua congbian* ed., vol. 1), p. 230.
[24] Preface to *Song sijia cixuan* (*Cihua congbian* ed., vol. 5), p. 1630.

Zhou Ji's elevation of Wu Wenying is nothing less than a flat contradiction of Zhang Huiyan's denigration. As a follower of Changzhou tenets, Zhou Ji offers an explanation for the discrepancy: "Gaowen (Zhang Huiyan) dismissed Mengchuang because his vision was circumscribed by the path of Bishan (Wang Yisun);" and elaborates on his own approbation of Wu Wenying: "Mengchuang expresses elevated thought with far-reaching implications. The rest cannot equal him in this respect."[25] Presumably, Zhang Huiyan could discern allegorical elements in Wang Yisun's *ci*, but with Wu Wenying's *ci*, he could not even put the pieces together, much less see anything beyond. Zhou Ji, however, is not wholly uncritical in his attitude toward Wu Wenying, as the reference in the *Jiecunzhai lunci zazhu* to the difficulty and obscurity in some of Wu's *ci* already indicates. The present passage also goes on to point out another fault: "But he delights too much in ornamentation, and has thus been criticized for it. Yet, among his works, those that achieve balance between the abstract and the concrete cannot be surpassed even by Qingzhen (Zhou Bangyan)."[26] Wu Wenying has always been praised and condemned on the same ground of his figurative density. It took a man of Zhou Ji's critical acumen and poetic sensitivity to elucidate the real strength of Wu Wenying as a poet—his ability to express what really moves him in superb language.

Credit should also be given Ge Zai (fl. 1821), a contemporary of Zhou Ji, who seems to have independently arrived at a similar view regarding Wu Wenying's *ci*.[27] Ge Zai's special interest in *ci* is prosody. His anthology of *ci*, the *Song qijia cixuan* [*Ci* by Seven Masters of the Song], which came out in 1837, was compiled to illustrate the elegant sound of *ci*. The seven poets he selected are, with the exception of Zhou Bangyan, all the noted Southern Song "technical experts." Ge Zai's criteria for inclusion of particular poems are "perfection in structure and meaning and finesse in meter and rhyme."[28] Because of the nature of his interest, Ge

---

[25] *Ibid.*, p. 1633.

[26] *Ibid.*

[27] Ge Zai moved in a different circle and there is no indication of interaction with the Changzhou group. See He Guangzhong, *Lun Qing ci*, in *Lidai shishi changbian*, ed. Yang Jialuo (Taipei: Dingwen shuju, 1971), 23:20–21.

[28] "Song qijia cixuan tici," 1a, in *Song qijia cixuan* (Hong Kong: Wenchang shuju, n.d.)

Zai offers very few literary-critical comments. But he does defend Wu Wenying against Zhang Yan's charge:

> Mengchuang's *ci* excels in the subtle and beautiful. The ideas he conveys are profound and his technique in diction and structure is unfathomable and vastly different from the others. On the surface his poems may seem glutted with figurative embellishment, but they are actually animated by an inner force. If one reads and recites them carefully, one will find that their flavor is more exquisite than [Fang] Hui's (He Zhu) *ci*, and be led into a state of enchantment. They can be faulted neither for obscurity nor for artificial ornateness.[29]

Ge Zai's wholesale rebuttal of Zhang Yan's critique arises in part from his own inordinate fondness for Wu Wenying's *ci*. He confesses that he has not succeeded in his attempt to model his own *ci* after Wu Wenying and, since he "loves Wu's *ci* to the extreme," he has included more selections by him.[30]

Wu Wenying's position in the hierarchy of *ci* criticism became firmly established in the mid Qing with the pioneer championship of Zhou Ji and Ge Zai. By illuminating its essential merits, their discerning remarks indicate to the reader what to look for in Wu Wenying's *ci* poetry, and thus suggest a way to its appreciation. Most subsequent critics followed suit with comments that are generally variations on a theme. Wu is discussed on the same level as Zhou Bangyan and Jiang Kui, as a major representative of the subtle and delicate mode in *ci*. Vagaries in taste still produced differences in grading the relative superiority of the three, and there is a lingering note of circumspection with regard to the potentially negative elements in Wu's style for a learner; but on the whole, Wu is viewed from an extremely positive angle. Major late Qing critics such as Feng Xu (1843–1927), Chen Tingzhuo (1853–1892), and Kuang Zhouyi (1859–1926) all made favorable observations about Wu's poetry. Among them, Kuang Zhouyi is an avowed admirer of Wu Wenying's greatness as a poet. One of his remarks is an apt and readily understood meta-

---

[29] *Ibid.,* j.4/38ab.
[30] *Ibid.*

phoric description of Wu's poetry: "In the dense texture of his poems, Mengchuang can animate countless beautiful words into a lively dance, like the profusion of flowers that create spring."[31]

Criticism, as we have already noted, is but one side of the Qing interest in the *ci*. Most *ci* critics were *ci* poets as well, and the pursuit of an effective model remained an absorbing concern. Many critical remarks written in the late Qing on Wu and other poets were in fact delivered from the perspective of writing *ci*. With the critical scale tipped so much in favor of Wu Wenying, it is inevitable that his style would be sought after as a desirable model; Ge Zai had already heralded the trend. At the height of its popularity in the late Qing, Wu Wenying's style became the hegemon among models to be imitated. In other words, exit Zhang Yan. Even Jiang Kui at times did not escape from the association with Zhang Yan. In 1876, the critic Tan Xian (1832–1901) recorded in his diary that "recent talks are all centered on the *ci* poets of the Southern Tang and Northern Song, and on Qingzhen (Zhou Bangyan), Mengchuang and Zhongxian (Wang Yisun); Yutian (Zhang Yan) and Shizhou (Jiang Kui) are regarded as old straw dogs," that is, worthless models to be discarded.[32] In 1937, Wu Mei (1884–1939), another latter-day lover of Wu Wenying's poetry, summarized the extent of Wu's influence, albeit rather hyperbolically: "In our age, people who imitate Mengchuang number almost half the world."[33]

Wu Mei's statement, at the time it was made, already belonged to another world in another age. Hu Shi's anthology of *ci*, the *Cixuan*, had already been published in 1928, and with it, *ci* ventured into the domain of modern, post–May–Fourth non-*ci* specialists, whose values and critical standards necessarily represent a break with the past. Hu Shi emphasizes the "historical" perspective, and is typically vocal in his critical judgments. He

---

[31] *Huifeng cihua* (Hong Kong: Commercial Press, 1961), p. 47.

[32] *Futang cihua* (*Cihua congbian* ed., vol. 11), p. 4025. Until this century, "Shizhou" was taken to be one of Jiang Kui's style names. The cause for this mistaken identity comes from a number of poems in Wu Wenying's collection addressed to a person by the name of Jiang Shizhou. Xia Chengtao has proven that Jiang Kui and Jiang Shizhou were in fact two different people; see *Jiang Baishi ci biannian jianjiao* (Shanghai: Zhonghua shuju, 1958), pp. 283–86.

[33] In his preface to Cai Songyun's *Yuefu zhimi jianshi*, in Xia Chengtao and Cai Songyun, *Ciyuan zhu Yuefu zhimi jianshi*, p. 92.

endorses the popular origin and vernacular aspect of ci and views the generic evolution solely as a degeneration from an "alive" literature of the common people to a "dead" plaything of the literati. Southern Song ci—the "ci of craftsmen"—stands at the bottom of his scale of values.[34] With some help from Zhang Yan, Hu Shi categorically denounces Wu Wenying's ci as an incoherent heap of clichés and allusions devoid of any meaning or emotional appeal. He further notes that many recent ci poets have been "poisoned" by it.[35] In modified and more moderate fashion, Wu Wenying's ci has been criticized along the same lines by the "moderns."[36]

Since 1949, the Marxist perspective has emphasized the social dimension of literature in criticism. Ci poets who stand up best under ideological scrutiny are the "progressive" patriotic heroes of the Southern Song, with Xin Qiji in the lead. The lack of proper ideological content and the dominance of aesthetic formalism in Southern Song ci have earned it the epithet of "decadent." In anthologies and histories of Chinese literature, Wu Wenying's poetry appears as one of the worst examples of ci in its decline; it shows a decided absence of "content," that is to say, concern with social and political realities.[37]

Research and critical studies on ci came to a complete halt with the onset of the Cultural Revolution (1966–1976). For nearly a decade, not a word was published on the subject. Only in the mid seventies did some ci poets reappear in articles dressed up in legalist and patriotic garb.[38] Interest in Wu Wenying began in the early years of the present decade, largely stimulated by the

[34] Hu Shi, *Cixuan* (Shanghai: Commercial Press, 1928), pp. 5–11.

[35] *Ibid.*, p. 343.

[36] See for example, Hu Yunyi, *Songci yanjiu* (Shanghai: Commercial Press, 1926), pp. 176–79; and Zheng Zhenduo, *Chatuben Zhongguo wenxueshi* (1932; rpt. Hong Kong: Commercial Press, 1961), 3:589.

[37] See Hu Yunyi, more than thirty years later, in *Songci xuan* (Shanghai: Zhonghua shuju, 1962), pp. 361–62. The emphasis on "content" is clearly stated in the introduction. We have already referred to Liu Dajie's view in his *Zhongguo wenxue fada shi* in chap. 2.

[38] Xin Qiji is the all-time patriot. Chen Liang (1143–1194) is not noted for his ci; but the utilitarian bent in his prose writings made him into a "legalist" whose ci was worth discussing. See articles listed in *Cixue yanjiu lunwenji: 1949–1979*, ed. Huadong Shifan Daxue Gudianwenxue Yanjiu shi (Shanghai: Shanghai guji chubanshe, 1982), pp. 535–36.

1980 mainland publication of Yeh Chia-ying's collection of essays on *ci*, the *Jialing lunci conggao*, which contains a critical reevaluation of Wu Wenying's *ci*.[39] But even in the latest article (1984) on Wu Wenying, the mainland author still feels a need to defend him on the question of "content."[40]

My own study has aimed to show precisely the literary qualities of Wu Wenying's poetry in the context of Southern Song *ci*; that his poetry is characterized by an extremely metonymic diction, syntactic density, an associative and implied rather than explicit logic in structure, and a unique handling of imagery. In his best works, these diverse elements of his "art" are unified into superb poetic structures that are informed with significant themes. Today in the West, we can perhaps read and enjoy Wu Wenying's poetry with fresh eyes without ignoring the tradition to which it belongs, and at the same time acknowledge its part in the affirmation of the artistic integrity of literature.

[39] It contains the original Chinese version of Chia-ying Yeh Chao, "Wu Wenying's *Tz'u*."

[40] Chen Bangyan, "Du Mengchuang ci qianyi," *Wenxue yichan*, no. 1 (1984): 84–92.

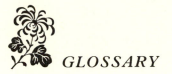

GLOSSARY

(See also bibliography for Chinese names and book titles.)

Bai xingyue man 拜星月慢
Basheng Ganzhou 八聲甘州
bisu yu 鄙俗語
Cao Xun 曹勛
Cao Zhi 曹植
caoyun 漕運
changdiao 長調
Chen Fenku 陳芬窟
Chen Qi 陳起
Chen Weisong 陳維崧
Chen Zilong 陳子龍
Chuci 楚辭
chun 尊
Ci yun Yang Gongji fengyi meihua
　次韻楊公濟奉議梅花
ci 詞
cishe 詞社
Dai Fugu 戴復古
daizi 代字
dan 但
denglin 登臨
Ding fengbo 定風波
Ding Lingwei 丁令威
Ding xiang jie 丁香結
Ding Yu 丁宥
Director of the Bureau of Music
　提舉大晟府
Dong Shixi 董士錫

Dong xian ge 洞仙歌
Du Fan 杜範
duotai huangu 奪胎換骨
Duzong 度宗
er 而
Fan Chengda 范成大
Fang Hui 方回
Fang Wanli (Huiyan) 方萬里
　(蕙巖)
Fansu 樊素
Faqu xianxian yin 法曲獻仙音
Feng gi wu 鳳棲梧
Feng Qufei 馮去飛
Feng ru song 風入松
Feng Xu 馮煦
Fengchi yin 鳳池吟
fu 賦
Ganyu 感遇
Gao Jiuwan 高九萬
Gaoyang tai 高陽臺
ge 隔
geng 更
gengnengxiao 更能消
gong 公
Goujian 句踐
Gu xiang man 古香慢
guai 怪
guimao 癸卯

177

guirenjia 貴人家

Guo Xidao 郭希道

Han Shizhong 韓世忠

Han Tuozhou 韓侂冑

Han Xin 韓信

hao 號

haofang 豪放

He Sun 何遜

He xinlang 賀新郎

He Zhu 賀鑄

Helu 闔閭

Houleyuan 後樂園

Hua fan 花犯

huaigu 懷古

huairen ci 懷人詞

Huan jing le 還京樂

Huan xi sha 浣溪沙

huanyou 還又

ji 及

Jia Sidao 賈似道

Jia Yi 賈宜

jiachen 甲辰

Jiang Kui 姜夔

Jiangdu chun 絳都春

Jiangnan chun 江南春

Jiangshenzi 江神子

jiaofang zhi xi 教坊之習

Jiaxiang shouci 賈相壽詞

jie 嗟

Jin shu 晉書

jing 景

Jinghunanbei 荊湖南北

jingzi 靜字

Jinlü ge 金縷歌

jinshi 進士

jituo 寄託

juan 卷

jun 君

Kang Yuzhi 康與之

Kong Zhigui 孔稚珪

kongtou zi 空頭字

kuang 况

lan 蘭

Li Boyu 李伯玉

Li Deyu 李德裕

Li Fang'an 李方庵

Li Qingzhao 李清照

Li Shangyin 李商隱

Li Yu 李煜

Li Zengbo 李曾伯

Li zhi xiang jin 荔枝香近

Liang Xiaowang 梁孝王

liao 料

lingju zi 領句字

lingzi 領字

Liu Chen 劉晨

Liu Chenweng 劉辰翁

Liu chou 六醜

Liu Hun 柳渾

Liu Kezhuang 劉克莊

Liu Yong 柳永

Liushao qing 柳梢青

Lizong 理宗

lu 露

Lu Xiangshan (Jiuyuan) 陸象山 (九淵)

Lu You 陸游

Luo Binwang 駱賓王

man 慢

manci 慢詞

Manjiang hong 滿江紅

Mao Hetang 毛荷塘

Meijin ji 梅津集

Meng Haoran 孟浩然

Meng liang lu 夢梁錄

Moqi Shaozhi 万俟紹之

Moqi Xue 万俟咼

Moqi Yong 万俟詠

moshi 莫是

Mulanhua man 木蘭花慢

nai 奈

nakan 那堪

GLOSSARY

Ningzong　寧宗
Ouyang Xiu　歐陽修
patriotic poets　愛國詞人
Pei Hang　裴航
Pingjiang　平江
Qi tian yue　齊天樂
Qian huai　遺懷
Qin fu　琴賦
Qin Guan　秦觀
Qin Gui　秦檜
qing　情
qingkong　清空
Qingyuan prefecture　慶元府
Qinke　琴客
Qinyuan chun　沁園春
ran　然
ran ze fei yu　然則非歟
ren　任
Ruan Zhao　阮肇
Ruihe xian　瑞鶴仙
Ruilong yin　瑞龍吟
San shu mei　三姝媚
Sanbu yue　三部樂
Sao hua you　掃花遊
Shangshu　尚書
Shaoxing fu　紹興府
shen　甚
Shengsheng man　聲聲慢
shi　詩
Shi Dazu　史達祖
Shi jing　詩經
Shi Miyuan　史彌遠
Shi Songzhi　史嵩之
shi yan zhi　詩言志
Shi Yue　施岳
Shi Zhaizhi　史宅之
Shidao pitai　詩道否泰
Shiji　史記
shijing yu　市井語
Shizhou　石帚
shizi　實字

shouci　壽詞
Shuang ye fei　霜葉飛
Shuanghua yu　霜花腴
Shuilong yin　水龍吟
shuixiang　睡香
Shupin　書品
Shuying　疏影
Si jiake　思佳客
Sima Xiangru　司馬相如
Siming　四明
Sirong Wang (Prince Sirong)
　嗣榮王
Sou shen ji　搜神記
Su Shi　蘇軾
Su Shunqin　蘇舜欽
Su wu man　蘇武慢
Sun Weixin (Jifan)　孫惟信
　（季蕃）
Sun Wuhuai　孫無懷
Suochuang han　瑣窗寒
Ta suo xing　踏莎行
tan　歎
Tan fangxin　探芳新
tianci (filling in words)　填詞
wang　望
Wang Can　王粲
Wang Xianzhi　王獻之
Wang Yisun　王沂孫
Wazi xiang　瓦子巷
Wei fan　尾犯
Wei Jun　魏峻
Wei Liaoweng　魏了翁
Wei Yizhai　魏益齋
Wen Tianxiang　文天祥
Wen Tingyun　溫庭筠
weng　翁
Weng Fenglong (Jike, Shigui)
　翁逢龍（季可，石龜）
Weng Mengyin　翁孟寅
Weng Yuanlong (Shike, Chujing)
　翁元龍（時可，處靜）

wo 我

Wolong Mountain 臥龍山

wu 吾

Wu Qian (Lüzhai) 吳潛 (履齋)

Wu Weiye 吳偉業

Wu Wenying (Junte, Meng-
chuang) 吳文英 (君特，夢窗)

Xi ping yue man 西平樂慢

Xi qian ying 喜遷鶯

Xi qiuhua 惜秋華

Xiang zhong yuan jie 湘中怨解

xiang 想

xiansheng 先生

Xiao Gang (Emperor Jianwen of
the Liang) 蕭綱 (梁簡文帝)

Xiao Man 小蠻

xiaoling 小令

Xie Tiao 謝朓

Xin Qiji 辛棄疾

xinci (new lyrics) 新詞

Xinghua tian 杏花天

xuzi 虛字

ya 雅

yaci 雅詞

Yan qingdu 宴清都

Yan Shu 晏殊

yayue 雅樂

ye 耶

ye 也

yi 伊

yi 矣

Yin County 鄞縣

Yin Huan 尹煥

Ying ti xu 鶯啼序

yong yi wu 詠一物

Yong yu le 永遇樂

yongwu 詠物

yongwu ci 詠物詞

yongwu fu 詠物賦

yongwu shi 詠物詩

you 又

youqueshi 又卻是

yu 歟

yu 玉

Yu zhu xin 玉燭新

Yue Fei 岳飛

Yulou chi 玉漏遲

zai 哉

Zhang Han 張翰

Zhang Jun 張浚

Zhao Rumei 趙汝楳

Zhao Yuchou 趙與篤

Zhedong circuit 浙東路

Zhen Niang 眞娘

zheng 正

Zheng Wenzhuo 鄭文焯

zhengsheng 正聲

Zhexi circuit 浙西路

zhishi 質實

zhongdiao 中調

Zhou Bangyan 周邦彥

Zhu Dunru 朱敦儒

Zhuying yao hong 燭影搖紅

zi 字

Zui luopo 醉落魄

zuiwuduan 最無端

BIBLIOGRAPHY

Ban Gu 班固. *Han shu* 漢書. Beijing: Zhonghua shuju, 1962.

———. *Han Wu gushi* 漢武故事. In *Xu tan zhu* 續談助. *Congshu jicheng chubian* ed., vol. 272.

Baxter, Glen W. *Index to the Imperial Register of Tz'u Prosody.* Cambridge: Harvard-Yenching Institute, 1956.

———. "Metrical Origins of the *Tz'u*." In *Studies in Chinese Literature,* edited by John L. Bishop, pp. 186–225. Cambridge: Harvard University Press, 1966.

Birch, Cyril, ed. *Studies in Chinese Literary Genres.* Berkeley: University of California Press, 1974.

Bishop, John L., ed. *Studies in Chinese Literature.* Cambridge: Harvard University Press, 1966.

Birrell, Anne. *New Songs from a Jade Terrace.* London: George Allen & Unwin, 1982.

Bodde, Derk. *Festivals in Classical China: New Year and Other Annual Observances during the Han Dynasty.* Princeton: Princeton University Press, 1975.

Chang, Kang-i Sun. *The Evolution of Chinese Tz'u Poetry: From Late T'ang to Northern Sung.* Princeton: Princeton University Press, 1980.

Chang, Kang-i Sun. *Six Dynasties Poetry: From T'ao Ch'ien to Yü Hsin.* Princeton: Princeton University Press, 1986.

———. "Symbolic and Allegorical Meanings in the *Yueh-fu pu-t'i* Poem-Series." Paper presented at the Workshop on Issues in Sung Literati Culture, 17–18 May 1985, at Harvard University.

Chao, Chia-ying Yeh (Yeh Chia-ying). "The Ch'ang-chou School of *Tz'u* Criticism." *HJAS,* 35 (1975): 101–32.

———. "On Wang I-sun and His *Yung-wu Tz'u.*" *HJAS,* 40:1 (1980): 55–91.

———. "Wu Wen-ying's *Tz'u*: A Modern View." In *Studies in Chinese Literary Genres,* edited by Cyril Birch, pp. 154–91. Berkeley: University of California Press, 1974.

Chen Bangyan 陳邦炎. "Du Mengchuang ci qianyi" 讀夢窗詞淺議. *Wenxue yichan*, no. 1 (1984), pp. 84–92.

———. "Wu Mengchuang shengzu nian guanjian" 吳夢窗生卒年管見. *Wenxue yichan*, no. 1 (1983), pp. 64–67.

Chen Lianzhen 陳廉貞. "Du Wu Mengchuang ci" 讀吳夢窗詞. *Guangming Daily*, 1957; rpt. in *Tang Song ci yanjiu lunwenji*, pp. 186–94. Beijing: n.p., 1969.

Chen Naiqian 陳乃乾, ed. *Qing mingjia ci* 清名家詞. 10 vols. Hong Kong: Taiping shuju, 1963.

Chen Tingzhuo 陳廷焯. *Baiyuzhai cihua* 白雨齋詞話. *Cihua congbian* ed. Vol. 11, 3791–4011.

Chen Xun 陳洵. *Haixiao shuoci* 海綃說詞. *Cihua congbian* ed. Vol. 12, 4401–43.

Cihua congbian (See Tang Guizhang).

Ci pu 詞譜. 8 vols. 1715; rpt. Beijing: Zhongguo shudian, 1979.

Cixue yanjiu lunwenji 詞學研究論文集. Ed. Huadong Shifan Daxue Gudianwenxue Yanjiushi. Shanghai: Shanghai guji chubanshe, 1982.

Dai Fugu 戴復古. *Shiping shiji* 石屏詩集. *Sibu congkan xubian* ed.

Du Fan 杜範. *Du Qingxian ji* 杜清獻集. *Siku quanshu zhenben erji* ed. Taipei: Commerical Press, 1971.

Fan Shu 范攄. *Yunxi youyi* 雲溪友議. *Congshu jicheng chubian* ed. Vol. 2832.

Fang Hui 方回. *Yingkui lüsui* 瀛奎律髓. *Siku quanshu zhenben baji* ed. Taipei: Commercial Press, 1978.

Fang Xuanling 房玄齡 et al. *Jin shu* 晉書. Beijing: Zhonghua shuju, 1974.

Franke, Herbert. "Chia Ssu-tao (1213–1275): A 'Bad Last Minister'?" In *Confucian Personalities*, edited by Arthur Wright, pp. 215–34. Stanford: Stanford University Press, 1962.

Frankel, Hans H. "The Contemplation of the Past in T'ang Poetry." In *Perspectives on the T'ang*. Ed. Arthur F. Wright and Denis Twitchett. New Haven: Yale University Press, 1973.

Ge Zai 戈載. *Song qijia cixuan* 宋七家詞選. 1837; rpt. Hong Kong: Wenchang shuju, n.d.

Gong Mingzhi 龔明之. *Zhongwu jiwen* 中吳紀聞. *Congshu jicheng chubian* ed. Vol. 3155.

Goodrich, L. C. *The Literary Inquisition of Ch'ien-lung*. Baltimore: Waverly Press, 1935.

Graham, William T., Jr. "Mi Heng's 'Rhapsody on a Parrot.'" *HJAS*, 30:1 (1979): 39–54.

Hawkes, David. *Ch'u Tz'u: Songs of the South*. Oxford: Oxford University Press, 1959.

He Guangzhong 賀光中. *Lun Qing ci* 論清詞. In *Lidai shishi changbian*, Vol. 23. Taipei: Dingwen shuju, 1971.

Hervouet, Yves, ed. *A Sung Bibliography*. Hong Kong: The Chinese University Press, 1978.

Hightower, James R. "Some Characteristics of Parallel Prose." In *Studies in Chinese Literature*, edited by John L. Bishop, pp. 108–39. Cambridge: Harvard University Press, 1966.

———. "The Songs of Chou Bang-yen." *HJAS*, 37 (1977): 233–72.

———. "The *Wen Hsuan* and Genre Theory." *HJAS*, 20 (1957): 512–33.

Ho Ping-ti. *The Ladder of Success in Imperial China*. New York: Science Editions, 1964.

Hu Shi 胡適. *Cixuan* 詞選. Shanghai: Commerical Press, 1928.

Hu Yunyi 胡雲翼. *Songci xuan* 宋詞選. Shanghai: Zhonghua shuju, 1962.

———. *Songci yanjiu* 宋詞研究. Shanghai: Commercial Press, 1926.

Hu Zi 胡仔. *Tiaoxi yuyin conghua* 苕溪漁隱叢話. 2 vols. Rpt. Beijing: Renmin wenxue chubanshe, 1981.

Huang Qingshi 黃清士. "Tan yongwu ci" 談咏物詞. *Yilin conglu*, 5 (1964): 84–91.

Huang Shaofu 黃少甫. *Mengchuang ci jian* 夢窗詞箋. Taipei: Jiaxin shuini gongsi wenhua jijinhui, 1969.

Huang Sheng 黃昇. *Hua'an cixuan* 花庵詞選. Preface 1249; rpt. Hong Kong: Zhonghua shuju, 1962.

Huang Zhaoxian 黃兆顯. *Yuefu buti yanjiu ji jianzhu* 樂府補題研究及箋注. Hong Kong: Xuewen chubanshe, 1975.

Ji Yougong 計有功. *Tangshi jishi* 唐詩紀事. 1224; rpt. Beijing: Zhonghua shuju, 1965.

Jiang Runxun 江潤勳. *Cixue pinglunshi gao* 詞學評論史稿. Hong Kong: Longmen shudian, 1966.

Kracke, E. A., Jr. "Region, Family, and Individual in the Examination System." In *Chinese Thought and Institutions*, edited by John K. Fairbank, pp. 251–68. Chicago: University of Chicago Press, 1957.

———. *Translations of Sung Civil Service Titles*. Paris: Mouton & Co., 1957.

Kuang Zhouyi 況周頤. *Huifeng cibua* 蕙風詞話. Rpt. Hong Kong: Commercial Press, 1961.

Leung, Winnie Lai-fong. "Liu Yung and His *Tz'u*." Master's thesis, University of British Columbia, 1976.

Li E 厲鶚. *Dongcheng zaji* 東城雜記. *Congshu jicheng chubian* ed. Vol. 3174.

———. *Songshi jishi* 宋詩紀事. Rpt. Shanghai: Commercial Press, 1937.

Li Fang 李昉, comp. *Taiping guang ji* 太平廣記. 978; *Xiaoshuo congshu daguan* ed.

Li Hengte 李亨特, comp. *Shaoxing fuzhi* 紹興府志. 7 vols. 1792; rpt. Taipei: Chengwen chubanshe, 1975.

Li Xinchuan 李心傳. *Jianyan yilai xinian yaolu* 建炎以來繫年要錄. Rpt. Beijing: Zhonghua shuju, 1956.

Li Zhao 李肇. *Tang guoshi bu* 唐國史補. Rpt. Shanghai: Gudian wenxue chubanshe, 1957.

Lin, Shuen-fu. *The Transformation of the Chinese Lyrical Tradition: Chiang K'uei and Southern Sung Tz'u Poetry*. Princeton: Princeton University Press, 1978.

Lin Wen-yueh 林文月. "Nanchao gongtishi yanjiu" 南朝宮體詩研究. In *Wen shi zhe xuebao*, 15 (1966): 407–58.

Liu Dajie 劉大杰. *Zhongguo wenxue fada shi* 中國文學發達史. Rpt. Taipei: Zhonghua shuju, 1962.

Liu, James J. Y. *Major Lyricists of the Northern Sung*. Princeton: Princeton University Press, 1974.

————. *The Poetry of Li Shang-yin*. Chicago: University of Chicago Press, 1969.

————. "Some Literary Qualities of the Lyric (*Tz'u*)." In *Studies in Chinese Literary Genres*. Edited by Cyril Birch, pp. 133–53. Berkeley: University of California Press, 1974.

Liu Su 劉肅. *Da Tang xingyu* 大唐新語. *Congshu jicheng chubian* ed. Vols. 2741–42.

Liu Wenying 柳文英. "Xi Shi di xialuo wenti" 西施的下落問題. *Yilin conglu*, 5 (1964): 315–20.

Liu Xie 劉勰. *Wenxin diaolong zhu* 文心雕龍註. 2 vols. Beijing: Renmin wenxue chubanshe, 1958.

Lo, Irving Y. *Hsin Ch'i-chi*. New York: Twayne Publishers, 1971.

Long Yusheng 龍榆生. *Ci qu gailun* 詞曲概論. Shanghai: Shanghai guji chubanshe, 1980.

————. "Songci fazhan di jige jieduan" 宋詞發展的幾個階段. In *Xin jianshe*, no. 8 (1957), pp. 44–50.

————. *Tang Song ci gelü* 唐宋詞格律. Shanghai: Shanghai guji chubanshe, 1978.

Lu Kanru 陸侃如 and Feng Yuanjun 馮沅君. *Zhongguo shishi* 中國詩史. Beijing: Zuojia chubanshe, 1956.

Lu Xiong 盧熊. *Shzhou fuzhi* 蘇州府志. 1379; Seikadō Bunko ed.

Luo Genze 羅根澤. *Zhongguo wenxue pipingshi* 中國文學批評史. Shanghai: Gudian wenxue chubanshe, 1957.

Luo Jun 羅濬 and Fang Wanli 方萬里. *Baoqing Siming zhi* 寶慶四明志.

Song Yuan difangzhi congshu ed. Vol. 8. Taipei: Zhongguo dizhi yanjiuhui, 1978.

Ma Jianzhong 馬建忠. *Mashi wentong jiaozhu* 馬氏文通校注. 2 vols. Beijing: Zhonghua shuju, 1961.

Marney, John. *Liang Chien-wen ti.* Twayne's World Author Series. Boston: G.K. Hall & Co., 1976.

Meng Qi 孟棨. *Benshi shi* 本事詩. *Congshu jicheng chubian* ed. Vol. 2546.

Miao Yueh 繆鉞. *Shi ci sanlun* 詩詞散論. 1948; rpt. Shanghai: Shanghai guji chubanshe, 1982.

Owen, Stephen. *Poetry of the Early T'ang.* New Haven: Yale University Press, 1977.

Peng Sunyu 彭孫遹. *Jinsu cihua* 金粟詞話. *Cihua congbian* ed. Vol. 2, 707–11.

Pian, Rulan Chao. *Sonq Dynasty Musical Sources and Their Interpretation.* Cambridge: Harvard University Press, 1967.

Quan Tang shi 全唐詩. 25 vols. Rpt. Beijing: Zhonghua shuju, 1979.

Rickett, Adele A., ed. *Chinese Approaches to Literature from Confucius to Liang Ch'i-ch'ao.* Princeton: Princeton University Press, 1978.

———. "Method and Intuition: The Poetic Theories of Huang T'ing-chien." In *Chinese Approaches to Literature from Confucius to Liang Ch'i-ch'ao,* edited by Adele A. Rickett, pp. 97–119. Princeton: Princeton University Press, 1978.

Shen Yazhi 沈亞之. *Shen Xiaxian ji* 沈下賢集. *Sibu congkan chubian* ed.

Shen Yifu 沈義父. *Yuefu zhimi* 樂府指迷. *Cihua congbian* ed. Vol. 1, 229–47.

Shen Yiji 沈翼機 et al., comp. *Zhejiang tongzhi* 浙江通志. 1736; rpt. Shanghai: Commercial Press, 1934.

Siku quanshu zongmu tiyao 四庫全書總目提要. Shanghai: Commercial Press, 1933.

Sima Qian 司馬遷. *Shi ji* 史記. Beijing: Zhonghua shuju, 1959.

Song Yuan difangzhi congshu 宋元地方志叢書. 12 vols. Taipei: Zhongguo dizhi yanjiu hui, 1978.

Tan Xian 譚獻. *Futang cihua* 復堂詞話. *Cihua congbian* ed. Vol. 11, 4013–44.

Tang Guizhang 唐圭璋, ed. *Cihua congbian* 詞話叢編. 12 vols. 1934; rpt. Taipei: Guangwen shuju, 1967.

———. *Quan Song ci* 全宋詞. 5 vols. Beijing: Zhonghua shuju, 1965.

———. *Songci sanbaishou jianzhu* 宋詞三百首箋注. 1931; rpt. Taipei: Xuesheng shuju, 1971.

Tang Song ci yanjiu lunwenji 唐宋詞研究論文集. Ed. Zhongguo yuwen xueshe. Beijing: n.p., 1969.

BIBLIOGRAPHY

Tao Erfu 陶爾夫. "Shuo Mengchuang ci *Ying ti xu*" 説夢窗詞鶯啼序. *Wenxue yichan*, no. 3 (1982), pp. 110–19.

Tuo Tuo 托托 et al. *Song shi* 宋史. Beijing: Zhonghua shuju, 1977.

Twitchett, Denis, and John K. Fairbank, eds. *Sui and Tang China*. Vol. 3:1 of *The Cambridge History of China*. [Eng.]; New York: Cambridge University Press, 1979.

Wagner, Marsha L. *The Lotus Boat: the Origins of Chinese Tz'u Poetry in T'ang Popular Culture*. New York: Columbia University Press, 1984.

Wang Li 王力. *Hanyu shilü xue* 漢語詩律學. Shanghai: Shanghai jiaoyu chubanshe, 1963.

Wang Guowei 王國維. *Renjian cihua* 人間詞話. *Cihua congbian* ed. Vol. 12, 4243–70.

Wang Shizhen 王士禎. *Huacao mengshi* 花草蒙拾. *Cihua congbian* ed. Vol. 2, 667–80.

Wang Wen'gao 王文誥. *Su shi bianzhu jicheng* 蘇詩編注集成. 24 vols. 1888 ed.

Wang Xiangzhi 王象之. *Yudi jisheng* 輿地紀勝. Preface 1221; rpt. Taipei: Wenhai chubanshe, 1962.

Wang Zhuo 王灼. *Biji manzhi* 碧雞漫志. *Cihua congbian* ed. Vol. 1, 17–82.

Weber, Carl J., ed. *Hardy's Love Poems*. London: Macmillan & Co., 1963.

Wei Qingzhi 魏慶之. *Shiren yuxie* 詩人玉屑. Preface 1244; Rpt. Shanghai: Gudia wenxue chubanshe, 1958.

Wellek, Rene, and Austin Warren. *Theory of Literature*. 3d ed. New York: Harcourt, Brace & World, 1962.

Wright, Arthur, ed. *Confucian Personalities*. Stanford: Stanford University Press, 1962.

———. *The Sui Dynasty*. New Haven: Yale University Press, 1978.

Wu Hongyi 吳宏一. *Changzhou pai cixue yanjiu* 常州派詞學研究. Taipei: Jiaxin shuini gongsi wenhua jijinhui, 1970.

Wu Mei 吳梅. *Cixue tonglun* 詞學通論. 1932; rpt. Hong Kong: Taiping shuju, 1964.

Wu Xiuzhi 吳秀之 et al., comp. *Wuxian zhi* 吳縣志. Rpt. Taipei: Chengwen chubanshe, 1970.

Wu Zeng 吳曾. *Nenggaizhai manlu* 能改齋漫錄. *Cihua congbian* ed. Vol. 1, 83–126.

Wu Zimu 吳自牧. *Meng liang lu* 夢梁錄. Preface 1274; rpt. in *Dongjing menghua lu waisizhong*. Shanghai: Gudian wenxue chubanshe, 1956.

186

BIBLIOGRAPHY

Xi Kang 嵇康. *Xi Kang ji jiaozhu* 嵇康集校注. Beijing: Renmin wenxue chubanshe, 1962.

Xia Chengtao 夏承燾. *Jiang Baishi ci biannian jianjiao* 姜白石詞編年箋校. Shanghai: Zhonghua shuju, 1958.

―――. *Tang Song ci luncong* 唐宋詞論叢. Shanghai: Gudian wenxue chubanse, 1956.

―――. *Tang Song ciren nianpu* 唐宋詞人年譜. 1961; rpt. Shanghai: Shanghai guji chubanshe, 1979.

Xia Chengtao and Cai Songyun 蔡嵩雲, annotators. *Ciyuan zhu Yuefu zhimi jianshi* 詞源註樂府指迷箋釋. Beijing: Renmin wenxue chubanshe, 1981.

Xia Chengtao and Wu Xionghe 吳熊和. *Duci changshi* 讀詞常識. Beijing: Zhonghua shuju, 1962.

Xianchun Lin'an zhi 咸淳臨安志. *Song Yuan difangzhi congshu* ed. Vol. 7.

Xiao Tong 蕭統. *Wenxuan* 文選. 2 vols. Rpt. Hong Kong: Commercial Press, 1978.

Xu Ling 徐陵, comp. *Yutai Xinyong* 玉臺新詠. Shanghai: Shijie shuju, 1935.

Xu Yongduan 徐永端. "Xuan ren yanmu de jingjie" 炫人眼目的境界. *Cixue*, no. 1 (1981), pp. 176–79.

Xue Liruo 薛礪若. *Songci tonglun* 宋詞通論. Taipei: Kaiming shudian, 1958.

Yang Tiefu 楊鐵夫. *Mengchuang ci quanji jianshi* 夢窗詞全集箋釋. 1936; rpt. Taipei: Haixue chubanshe, 1974.

Ye Shaoweng 葉紹翁. *Sichao jianwen lu* 四朝見聞錄. *Congshu jicheng chubian* ed. Vols. 2763–65.

Yeh Chia-ying (Chia-ying Yeh Chao) 葉嘉瑩. *Jialing lunci conggao* 迦陵論詞叢稿. Shanghai: Shanghai guji chubanshe, 1980.

―――. *Jialing tanci* 迦陵談詞. Taipei: Chunwenxue congshu, 1970.

Yoshikawa Kōjirō. *An Introduction to Sung Poetry*. Trans. Burton Watson. Cambridge: Harvard University Press, 1967.

Yu Pingbo 俞平伯. *Tang Song ci xuanshi* 唐宋詞選釋. Beijing: Renmin wenxue chubanshe, 1979.

Yuan Zhai 遠齋. "Shizi xuzi yu yongdian" 實字虛字與用典. In *Yilin conglu*, 4 (1964); 52–55.

Zhang Huiyan 張惠言. *Cixuan* 詞選. 1797; rpt. Beijing: Zhonghua shuju, 1958.

Zhang Shouyong 張壽鏞, ed. *Siming congshu* 四明叢書. 1936; rpt. Taipei: Guofang yanjiuyuan, 1966.

Zhang Yan 張炎. *Ciyuan* 詞源. *Cihua congbian* ed. Vol. 1, 177–227.

Zhao Wanli 趙萬里, ed. *Jiaoji Song Jin Yuan ren ci* 校輯宋元金人詞. 1931; rpt. Taipei: Tailian guofeng chubanshe, 1971.

Zhao Wenli 趙聞禮, comp. *Yangchun baixue* 陽春白雪. Ca. 1244, *Yueyatang congshu* ed.

Zheng Dian 鄭奠 and Mai Meiqiao 麥梅翹, comp. *Guhanyu yufaxue ziliao huibian* 古漢語語法學資料彙編. Beijing: Zhonghua shuju, 1964.

Zheng Qian 鄭騫. *Cixuan* 詞選. 1952; rpt. Taipei: Huagang chubanshe, 1972.

Zheng Zhenduo 鄭振鐸. *Chatuben Zhongguo wenxueshi* 插圖本中國文學史. 4 vols. 1932; rpt. Hong Kong: Commercial Press, 1961.

Zhou Fagao 周法高. *Zhongguo gudai yufa: zaoju bian* 中國古代語法：造句編. Vol. 1. Taipei: Academia Sinica, 1961.

Zhou Ji 周濟. *Jiecunzhai lunci zazhu* 介存齋論詞雜著. *Cihua congbian* ed. Vol. 5, 1623–29.

———. *Tanping Cibian Song sijia cixuan* 譚評詞辨宋四家詞選. Taipei: Guangwen shuju, 1962.

Zhou Mi 周密. *Haoranzhai yatan* 浩然齋雅談. *Cihua congbian* ed. Vol. 1, 163–76.

———. *Juemiaohao cijian* 絕妙好詞箋. (Published with *Huajian ji* 花間集). Shanghai: Shijie shuju, 1935.

———. *Qidong yeyu* 齊東野語. *Xuejin taoyuan* ed.

Zhu Cunli 朱存理. *Tiewang shanhu* 鐵網珊瑚. 3 vols. Rpt. Taipei: Guoli zhongyang tushuguan, 1970.

Zhu Dongrun 朱東潤. *Zhongguo wenxue pipingshi dagang* 中國文學批評史大綱. N.p.: Kaiming shudian, 1944.

Zhu Xi 朱熹. *Chuci jizhu* 楚辭集注. Shanghai: Shanghai guji chubanshe, 1979.

Zhu Yizun 朱彝尊 and Wang Sen 汪森, comp. *Cizong* 詞綜. 2 vols. 1691; rpt. Shanghai: Shanghai guji chubanshe, 1978.

Zong Lin 宗懍. *Jingchu suishi ji* 荊楚歲時記. *Sibu beiyao* ed.

Zou Zhimo 鄒祇謨. *Yuanzhizhai cizhong* 遠志齋詞衷. *Cihua congbian* ed. Vol. 2, 637–66.

INDEX

189

INDEX

Wen Tianxiang, 40
Wen Tingyun, 50, 85, 129
Wen Zhong, 150–54
Weng Fenglong, 4–5, 12–14, 18, 26
Weng Mengyin, 28–29, 136–39
Weng Yuanlong, 5–6, 26, 45
Wenxuan, 78
Wenyuan as poetic persona, 95, 97. *See also* Sima Xiangru
West Lake, 22, 110, 113–14, 127–28, 156–59
Woman Adrift, 99–100
Wu Mei, 174
Wu Qian, 14–15, 147–49; in relation to Wu Wenying and Jia Sidao, 12–13, 24–26, 28–31
Wu Weiye, 163

Xi qiuhua, 74–76
Xi Shi, 100
Xia Chengtao, 3n, 4n, 14n, 19–22, 60, 107, 133
Xin Qiji, 40, 73, 102n, 132, 167, 170–71, 175; and *haofang* style, 36–39, 52, 166
Xinghua tian, 95–97
Xu Ling, 84
Xue Yishu, 5
xuzi, 40, 55–56. *See also* empty words

ya, see elegance
Yan Shu, 85
Yangzhou, 28, 117, 120–21
Yanyi Tower, 5
Yeh Chia-ying, 25, 71n, 106n, 141n, 176
Yin County, 3–4
Yin Huan, 15, 134–35, 162, 169, 171; as patron, 12–13, 23–24; preface to Wu Wenying's *ci* by, 14
Yingti xu, 22, 110–14
yongwu subgenre, 43–44; evolution in *ci*, 85–91; in *fu* and *shi*, 78–84; love

poems in, 126–29; in metaphoric mode, 99–102, 106; as occasional verse, 78–81, 86–87, 91–94. *See also* poems on objects
Yongyu le, 36–39
Yuan Zhai, 57–59
Yue Fei, 149
Yuefu zhimi, 13, 34, 44, 55, 63; on elegance, 48–51; on lead-segments, 66–67; on the poetics of indirection, 52–54; on Wu Wenying's poetic canons, 45, 48. *See also* Shen Yifu
Yutai xinyong, 80–81, 84

Zhang Huiyan, 166–68, 172
Zhang Jun, 149
Zhang Yan, 13n, 44, 28, 90, 95–96, 102–103, 162, 167–70, 173–75; on elegance, 50–52; on lead-segments, 63–66, 74; as model for imitation, 165–66; and the poetics of transparency, 54–56, 70. See also *Ciyuan*
Zhao Yuchou, 14–15, 156–57
Zhedong circuit, 3–4
Zhen Niang, 144–45
Zheng Wenzhuo, 16
Zhexi circuit, 7, 10
zhishi, 55–56. *See also* density: poetics of
Zhou Bangyan, 14, 50–55, 73, 88–90, 130, 164, 168, 174; compared with Wu Wenying, 14, 162, 169, 172–73; importance of, in Southern Song style, 35, 46–47; as orthodox model, 170–71
Zhou Ji, 167–173
Zhou Mi, 6, 13n, 28, 30, 90, 99, 102
Zhu Dunru, 25, 35
Zhu Yizun, 33, 163–65
Zhuying yao hong, 134
Zou Zhimo, 163

Library of Congress Cataloging-in-Publication Data

Fong, Grace S., 1948–
Wu Wenying and the art of Southern Song ci poetry.

Bibliography: p.
Includes index.
1. Wu, Wen-ying—Criticism and interpretation. 2. Tz' u—History and criticism.
3. Chinese poetry—Sung dynasty, 960–1279—History and criticism. I. Title.

PL2687.W83Z64 1987   895.1′14   86-25292
ISBN 0-691-06703-1 (alk. paper)

3